49908

THE MAKING OF
CIVILIZATION

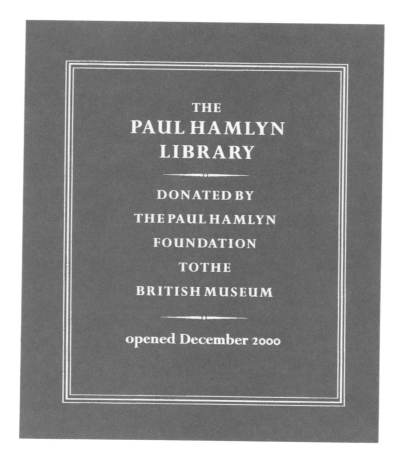

THE MAKING OF CIVILIZATION

HISTORY DISCOVERED THROUGH ARCHAEOLOGY

Ruth Whitehouse and John Wilkins

COLLINS
8 Grafton Street, London W1
1986

First published in Great Britain by
William Collins Sons & Co Ltd
London Glasgow Sydney Auckland
Toronto Johannesburg

The book was created and produced
by Roxby Archaeology Limited
a division of Roxby Press Limited
98 Clapham Common North Side
London SW4 9SG

Editor: Deborah Blake
Design: Eric Drewery and Bob Vickers
Picture Research: Caroline Lucas
Typesetting: Tradespools Limited
Printing and Binding: Tonsa, San Sebastian, Spain

British Library Cataloguing in Publication Data
Whitehouse, Ruth
    The making of civilization : history
    discovered through archaeology.
    1. Civilization—History
    I. Title   II. Wilkins, John
    930   CB69

ISBN 0-00-217417-0

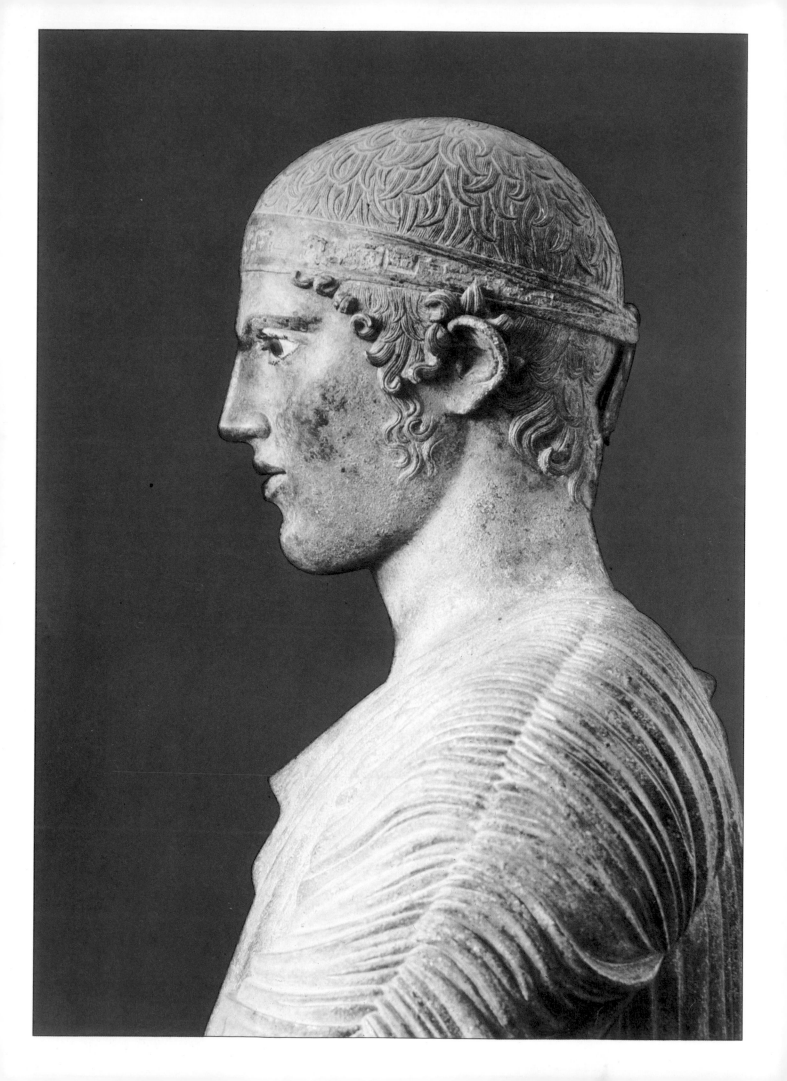

Contents

1　Early Civilizations

Modern warfare, we are told, could now 'destroy civilization as we know it'. Some of us may feel at an intuitive level that we 'know' what civilization is. We may even like to think of ourselves as 'civilized'. But what *is* civilization?

Civilization is something with which we have all grown up. It is something within which we all exist, and to which we owe our social and personal identity. Yet, notoriously, we tend not to see the familiar. It is precisely when we come to analyze the ideas behind such words as 'civilization', 'civilized', 'culture' and the like, that our difficulties begin. We need the willingness and the ability to make an imaginative leap – to stand outside ourselves and cast a dispassionate glance over our own society.

This book studies the early development of civilization. We try to establish when, where and how it started. Did it perhaps just grow, like something organic, once favourable conditions were present? Are there different types of civilization? Has civilization evolved, or have its essential components remained unchanged since antiquity? Is there a direct line of continuity between the ancient civilizations and our own, and what, if anything, can earlier civilizations tell us about our own society?

Definitions

Civilization, then, is the label we give to a phenomenon that we see all around us – the nature and structure of our own type of society. A search for a watertight definition would be unrewarding, but we need to explore some suggestions before we proceed.

One way to investigate our preconceptions about any topic is to look at the implications that lie behind our use of words. The word 'civilization', for example, like 'civil' and 'civilized', derives ultimately from the Latin *civis*: citizen. Other words which we use in much the same connection, such as 'urban', 'urbane' and 'urbanization', can be traced to the Latin *urbs*: city. Terms which we apply to some of the official practices of civilized society, such as 'politics', 'political', 'policy' and even 'police', are derived from the Greek *polis*, which also means city. Certainly as far as such words go, historically we seem to have viewed civilization essentially as city-life.

We can also look at some working definitions that have been put forward by archaeologists and anthropologists. These definitions aim to be free from value judgements about the worth of civilized societies as compared with non-civilized ones. They stress instead the organizational aspects of society. Broadly we may distinguish three approaches. The first approach, adopted by scholars such as A. L. Kroeber and Colin Renfrew, concentrates upon complexity of organization. This interpretation sees civilization as differing from other forms of human

Opposite: Monumental architecture and sculpture are characteristic of civilization. This fine stone head comes from the Maya site of Uxmal.

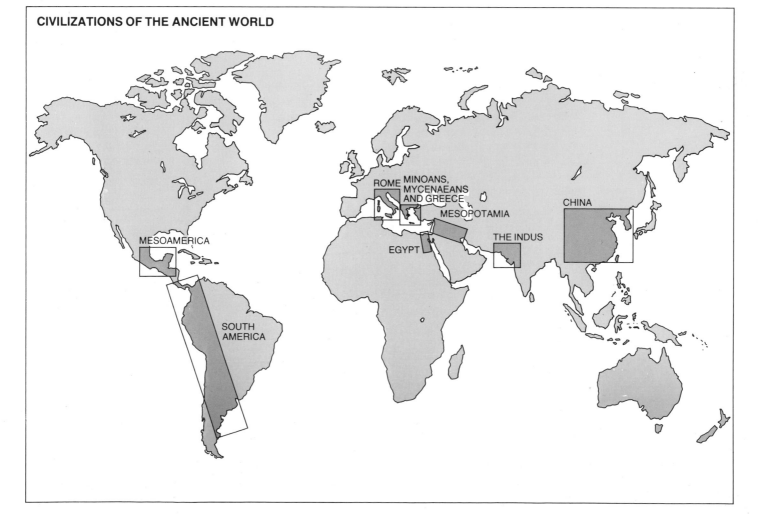

CIVILIZATIONS OF THE ANCIENT WORLD

ROME

MINOANS, MYCENAEANS AND GREECE

MESOPOTAMIA

CHINA

EGYPT

THE INDUS

MESOAMERICA

SOUTH AMERICA

society not in kind, but solely in degree of internal complexity. Such definitions can be criticized for failing to highlight any critical point of development at which civilization may be distinguished from simpler forms of society.

The second approach is also concerned with organization, but this emphasizes the *type* of internal social organization as decisive. This school of analysis is based on the work of evolutionary anthropologists of the nineteenth century – the founding fathers of anthropology – notably on the work of the American scholar, Lewis Morgan. Morgan elaborated a three-part evolutionary classification for society:

> savagery (or band society)
> barbarism (or tribal society)
> civilization (or state society)

Most important and influential has been the concept of *state society*. State society typically shows a highly stratified class structure, a strong centralized government and a professional ruling class. Order and control are maintained by a true legal system and state-run systems of enforcement. The dominant organizational principle is no longer kinship, as it is in simpler societies. Other principles operate, such as class membership, occupational specialization and differential residential patterns.

A third approach seeks rather to isolate a 'clutch' of inter-related defining characteristics for society. The simplest formula is that put forward by the American anthropologist Clyde Kluckhohn, who proposed that civilized societies should possess at least two of the following three features:

> 1. towns of more than 5,000 people
> 2. writing
> 3. monumental ceremonial centres

This suggestion works well as a rule-of-thumb, but excludes many important features.

A much more illuminating variant of this third approach was offered by the prehistorian Gordon Childe, who identified a set of ten characteristics. This analysis is particularly useful in the reformulation proposed by the American archaeologist Charles Redman. Redman re-ordered Childe's ten features and subdivided them into primary and secondary characteristics:

Primary	*Secondary*
1. settlement in cities	6. monumental public works
2. full-time specialization of labour	7. long-distance trade
3. concentration of surpluses	8. standardized monumental artwork
4. class structure	9. writing
5. state organization	10. arithmetic, geometry and astronomy

The primary characteristics are aspects of organization. The secondary characteristics are features of *material culture*, are recognizable in material archaeological remains, and imply the existence of some or all of the primary characteristics.

For instance, monumental public buildings usually indicate a powerful centralized government, and thus represent one piece of evidence for the presence of state society.

This last approach is a useful compromise between the very general definitions of Kroeber and Renfrew, and Kluckhohn's rather basic utilitarian gauge. At the same time it offers a broader and better articulated definition than the second approach, which is based upon the criterion of social organization alone.

A man-made environment

Whichever approach we finally settle for, one consideration must not be neglected. Unless we invoke supernatural intervention in human affairs, civilization is man's own invention. It is man's supreme artefact, an artificial environment rather like a house, which he has contrived for his own benefit. Civilization may thus be regarded as mediating between man and his physical world.

It is also an environment that has been constructed in a very short period of time. The five millennia since the appearance of the first cities span a period of minuscule length, either in proportion to man's own evolutionary development (perhaps five million years); or in relation to the geological age of the planet (some 4,500 million years).

Lastly, it is a fragile environment. We can only wonder how durable man's artifically-contrived world will prove to be.

Opposite: The strictly regular layout of the Roman city of Timgad (ancient Thamugadi) in Numidia, demonstrates the main features of a city. It would have housed a population of thousands centred around the main public buildings including temple, baths, theatre, library and market place.

Below: Writing made an important contribution to the development of civilization. This papyrus of the fourteenth century BC records a prayer to the sun god Re, written in the Egyptian hieroglyphic script.

Mesopotamia

The world's first civilization flourished in the land that we, after the Greeks, call Mesopotamia: 'the land between the rivers' (the Tigris and the Euphrates) in what is now southern Iraq. Today much of this land is desert or semi-desert, the climate is hot and arid, and human population is sparse. Although some of this bleakness may be the result of past over-exploitation, the environment can never have been easy for human settlement. The ancient climate would have been as hot as today's; the land itself, though potentially rich in fertile soil, would initially have offered contrasting watery swamp and arid steppe. Moreover, it was an area remarkably poor in raw materials, with no minerals, stone or metal; even timber for building would have been in short supply. And yet, from the fourth millennium BC this apparently unpromising land supported a civilization characterized by cities housing tens of thousands of people, monumental architecture and a complex administrative system which relied on the invention of writing in order to function. In the course of its history it also saw the development of creative literature, mathematics and

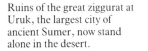

Right: Bronze bust found at Nineveh, thought by some to represent king Sargon of Akkad, who established the first Mesopotamian 'empire' in the later third millennium BC.

Ruins of the great ziggurat at Uruk, the largest city of ancient Sumer, now stand alone in the desert.

science and the elaboration of a legal system and law codes. The growth of this civilization was made possible by the taming of the landscape – the draining of marshes and the transport of water over the arid steppes in irrigation channels – to allow the cultivation of high-yielding cereal crops on the fertile soils. This first civilization – like many of the others we shall be describing in this book – did not emerge without trouble in a naturally favourable environment; rather it was constructed, no doubt laboriously, by its creators: not a Garden of Eden, but a man-made garden wrested from the wilderness through man's own endeavours.

What do we know about this civilization? Some bare facts first. It emerged in the fourth millennium BC, perhaps early in that millennium. The original heartland was in the extreme south of Mesopotamia, in the region of the ancient cities of Ur, Eridu and Uruk; indeed Uruk has a good claim to be the world's first city. We call the civilization Sumerian, after inscriptions which refer to kings of 'Sumer and Akkad', though the Sumerians referred to themselves as 'the black-headed people'. The Sumerian civilization flourished till the late third millennium BC and was followed by two successor civilizations, the Babylonians in the south and the Assyrians in the north. They in their turn survived into the mid-first millennium BC, when the 3,000-year-old Mesopotamian civilization finally succumbed to the forces of the expanding Persian Empire.

What was it like, this earliest civilization? It is perhaps easiest to characterize its physical form. In the first place it was based on cities: from the earliest phases there were at least a dozen large population centres, ranging in size from *c.* 40–50 hectares to the colossal 450 hectares occupied by Uruk in the early third millennium BC. They were surrounded by often massive city walls, enclosing heavily built-up areas of streets and houses and large centrally placed public buildings, usually in their own separate enclosures. The normal building material was sun-dried mud-brick, made from the clay that was the only readily available building material on the alluvial plain, but by the late third millennium BC true fired bricks were often used too. In the northern zone, especially in the later periods, stone was also employed, particularly for monumental buildings.

The public buildings of Mesopotamia fall into two main categories, temples and palaces, which represent two major institutions. The buildings were truly monumental and, not surprisingly, have occupied much of the attention of archaeologists. Temples were the first monumental buildings of Sumer; indeed the temple was the earlier institution of the two. The temples varied in form, but generally shared a number of features. They were usually set in an enclosure, they were often elaborately decorated in a variety of techniques, and frequently they were built on an elevated platform. By the later third millennium BC the temple on its platform had developed into the true *ziggurat* or staged temple tower, for which Mesopotamia is famous.

The temple was not simply the religious centre of the city, it was the economic and administrative centre. Through the information derived from written documents, we know a good deal about how this organization worked. The temple was run as a household, with the god or goddess at its head; every citizen belonged to a temple and was regarded as one of the people of the god or goddess. The temple community comprised food-producers, officials, priests, merchants, craftsmen and people involved in running the temple establishment itself (bakers, brewers, gardeners, etc., and a considerable number of slaves). The temple was itself a major landowner, and it served as a centre for the accumulation and redistribution of most of the food produce of the land. It was also a centre for the concentration and redistribution of raw materials from foreign trade. Equally important, it was a centre for the concentration and organization of labour, which made possible large-scale works beyond the scope of small communities, such as the building of the temples themselves and the construction and maintenance of irrigation canals.

This centralized organization required complex book-keeping, and it was in this context that the first writing seems to have developed. The earliest clay tablets are found in the temples, and are without exception book-keeping documents. Of these, we find two slightly different categories. First, there are the records themselves: labels, lists, accounts and receipts, and calculations of rations or supplies. Secondly, we also have what seem to be 'school exercises' for training new clerks. Writing was to be in use for almost a millennium before it was used for anything other than book-keeping or related narrowly educational purposes.

In the course of the third millennium BC the palace grew to rival and ultimately to supersede the temple as the city's economic and administrative centre. The palace was, like the temple, run as a household, but it had at its head not a deity, but a living king. Perhaps for this reason, the palaces have yielded far more evidence of great wealth than have the temples: the kings and queens of Mesopotamia, and the associated nobility, lived and died surrounded by the symbols and concomitants of their status. The Royal Tombs of Ur have yielded the most famous products of Sumerian craftsmen's skill and provide eloquent testimony to the wealth of their owners: a remarkable range of vehicles, furniture, weapons, jewellery, musical instruments, games and other items. These were made in many

materials, often rare and precious, such as gold, silver, electrum, copper and lapis lazuli, and manufactured with outstanding skill and artistry. (Many of these materials originated from areas outside Mesopotamia, and there is evidence of far-ranging trade with places as far away as Afghanistan.) In the later civilizations of the Babylonians and Assyrians, royal power was dominant, while the temple became a secondary and probably no longer independent institution.

Mesopotamian civilization, although apparently man's first attempt at this social form, proved remarkably resilient and long-lived. It also has to its credit very many achievements: many 'firsts' in the development of technology and other fields. Arguably the most important of all was the invention of writing: the cuneiform writing system (wedge-shaped signs impressed on clay tablets) was used for 3,000 years and adapted for many different languages throughout Western Asia. And though devised for administrative purposes by the early Sumerians, it was developed by their successors for, among other things, religious writings, literary works, mathematics and science. In these and many other fields Sumerian and Babylonian achievement was built upon by the later civilizations of Western Asia and Europe.

Votive statuettes, like these from Tell Asmar, have been found in many Mesopotamian temples. They may provide valuable information about clothing and hairstyles of Sumerian men and women.

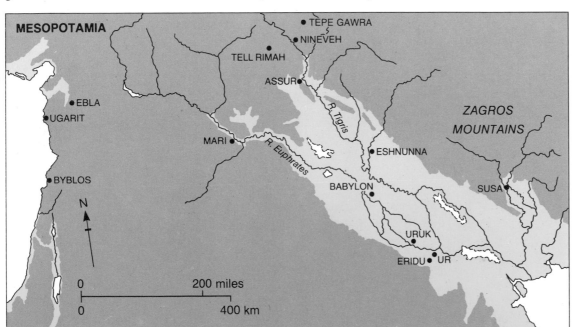

MESOPOTAMIA

- TEPE GAWRA
- NINEVEH
- TELL RIMAH
- ASSUR
- EBLA
- UGARIT
- MARI
- BYBLOS
- ESHNUNNA
- BABYLON
- SUSA
- URUK
- ERIDU • UR

R. Tigris

R. Euphrates

ZAGROS MOUNTAINS

N

| 0 | 200 miles |
| 0 | 400 km |

Egypt

Ancient Egypt is above all the civilization of the Nile Valley. After a tentative start late in the fourth millennium BC, Egyptian civilization soon developed the distinctive qualities that it was to maintain for nearly 3,000 years, until it was essentially absorbed by the classical world in the fourth century BC.

Like the Indus and Mesopotamia, Egypt depended for its genesis and survival upon a major river, crossing a large desert area. Each summer the Nile would flood, bringing down vast quantities of water and rich alluvial deposits from its distant sources in the Ethiopian highlands and the central African lakes. The floodwaters conveniently receded in the autumn, enabling seed to be sown and to germinate in the warm but temperate months of winter and early spring. Extensive shallows and pools would also form, encouraging colonization by freshwater fowl and fish. Marshy areas on the fringe and in the delta at the river's Mediterranean mouth gave support to marginal grasses and weeds.

The profile provided by the sinuous course of the Nile is that of a very long but narrow strip of usable terrain, running from south to north over a distance of some 1,200 km. The moist dark look of this narrow fertile tract contrasted with the bleached and parched face of the surrounding desert so vividly that the early Egyptians called their country 'the Dark' (Kemet), and the desert 'the Red' (Deshret).

The river Nile brought water and fertile alluvial mud to Egyptian fields to produce rich harvests of wheat and barley.

The desert, especially the western desert, spelt death, both literally and symbolically, for the Egyptian, his crops and his livestock. What had in earlier prehistoric times perhaps been the parklands and grasslands of North Africa, had already become an arid waste – partly following climatic trends towards lower rainfall in the postglacial period, and partly as a result of over-exploitation by man.

The agricultural economy that owed its existence to the Nile embraced a range of crops and animals. Characteristic crops were wheat, barley and flax. Barley was popular for the preparation of beer, while flax was used to make linen. Domesticated animals were bred for both utilitarian and ritual purposes. Utilitarian examples are the goat, pig and donkey, but sheep in particular, and to some extent oxen, seem to have been bred more for the sacrifices and meat-offerings that so typified Egyptian religious life.

Apart from the requirements of the sacrifice, however, something further may be seen of the significance of birds and animals for the ancient Egyptian from the central emphasis given to certain of them in state religion. Gods and goddesses frequently took both the names, and in some cases the bodily shapes of animal, bird or insect: for example Horus, the falcon, originally god of the sky and usually identified with the king during his lifetime; Anubis, the jackal, god of the cemetery and patron-deity of mummification; and Khepri, the scarab-beetle, identified with the sun-god Re as creator, and portrayed as a beetle within the sun's circle. The direct appeal and intimacy of some of these images may offer some clue as to how the people of ancient Egypt viewed their daily lives, since there is evidence to connect some of these zoomorphic deities with popular usage.

The evidence that we do have for ancient Egyptian life centres almost exclusively around the all-important figure of the king, and the royal family – the house of pharaoh. The history of ancient Egypt is traditionally divided into three Kingdoms (the Old, the Middle and the New) and into some thirty dynasties, following the analysis of the ancient historian, Manetho, who served in the priesthood under the early Ptolemies (Greek kings of Egypt from 332–30 BC). It is the monumental royal tombs of the pharaohs, the great pyramids, that still dot the western bank of the Nile, as at Giza. It is their great temples, sanctuaries and rock-cut tombs that we find

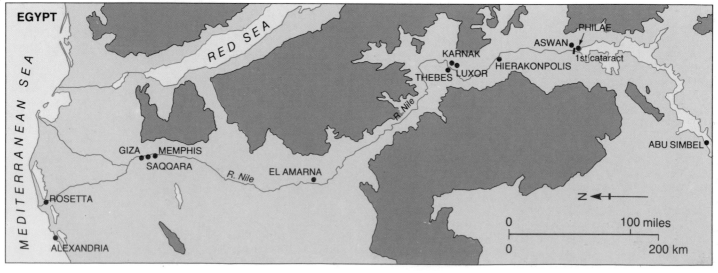

EGYPT

MEDITERRANEAN SEA

RED SEA

PHILAE

ASWAN
1st cataract

KARNAK
HIERAKONPOLIS
THEBES LUXOR

R. Nile

ABU SIMBEL

GIZA MEMPHIS
SAQQARA

R. Nile EL AMARNA

ROSETTA

ALEXANDRIA

N

0   100 miles
0   200 km

further south at such places as Luxor, Karnak and the Valley of the Kings; their rich grave goods that so impress in the tomb of Tutankhamun, whose wealth, though so dazzling, is probably only that of a relatively unimportant king. It is their official state religion that seems to us to show an obsessive preoccupation with eschatological rites and the bizarre ritual of mummification. It was for the eternal service of the immortal king that whole communities of priests came into being, as at Heliopolis. It was further the pharaohs' pressing requirement for a more efficient civil service, notably for the collection of tax revenue, that seems to have stimulated, as in Mesopotamia, the evolution of writing (Egyptian hieroglyphs) and the exploitation of the papyrus plant as a writing material.

Life for the ordinary Egyptian was presumably very different. Even the beneficence of the Nile was not to be enjoyed without effort. The annual flooding certainly did not bring a work-free paradise for the Egyptian farmer. The period immediately following each inundation was a time of intense activity, spent largely in the re-preparation and reorganization of the cultivable areas. Although possibly less use was made of irrigation channels in general than in Mesopotamia, what ditches there were had to be kept cleaned out and constantly maintained. Even if some marginal areas slightly above the general level of the inundation did not need this comprehensive processing, and could be served by the *shaduf* (a mechanism for raising water), the fact remained that intensive labour and extensive co-operation and organization were unavoidable if the seasonal schedules were to be met.

Overall, the dominance of the Nile with its typical narrow land corridor was difficult to escape. This elongated profile influenced Egyptian life and development in many ways, some of them perhaps a little more unexpected. The shape of the country, for example, may well have been unfavourable to the development of large urbanized centres. Its general linear profile suggests a sequence of villages strung out along the Nile, with a smaller number of administrative centres positioned mainly to the north and south, as is the case with Memphis and Thebes.

The flooding of the river had certain advantages that were not exclusively agricultural. Bulky loads could be moved by water with the same ease as light ones, and large blocks for monumental construction could be floated virtually from quarryside to

pyramid at high water levels. However, the almost exclusive use of the river for all transport and communication brought practical difficulties of time and distance, and may well have led to the neglect of available alternatives. The wheel and the horse were virtually unused, and little seems to have been done to develop an efficient road system.

Above all, perhaps, the valley of the Nile is a geographical and climatological special case, isolated in a real physical sense. Moreover, although the impression may arise from the random partiality of the evidence, it is hard to avoid the conclusion that there was also a certain cultural isolation. There is evidence for material links with Mesopotamia, both in the exchange of objects and materials and possibly in the transmission of the new technology of writing. We also know of contact with African tribal cultures to the south, and with the Aegean civilizations to the north. We seem to be left, however, with an image of Egyptian civilization as a closely contained and guardedly national achievement.

Relief carving from the Great Temple of Amun at Karnak showing the kings of Upper and Lower Egypt, the two separate kingdoms that preceded the unification of Egypt before 3000 BC. The king on the left wears the 'white' crown of Upper Egypt, the king on the right the 'red' crown of Lower Egypt.

New Kingdom tomb painting showing a scene of fishing with nets on the Nile, from the tomb of Ipy at Deir el Medineh.

The Indus

The Indus civilization – the third great civilization of the Old World – was discovered only as recently as the 1920s and is one of the least well understood of the ancient civilizations. It too developed around an important river system, the Indus and its tributaries, in what is now Pakistan and north-west India. It occupied a vast area, one million square kilometres in all (much larger than either Mesopotamia or Egypt), and had much wider access to the sea, commanding about 1,200 km of coastline in all. During the second half of the third millennium BC a city-based civilization of considerable complexity flourished in this area. It is less well known than the other ancient Old World civilizations for a number of reasons. One is because the Indus script has not been deciphered, so we have no documentary information; another is because the Indus civilization was relatively short-lived, and there is no continuous tradition into more recent times on which we can draw for evidence.

Like the Nile in Egypt, the Indus brought silt-bearing floods which enabled farmers to cultivate wheat, barley, cotton, fruit and vegetables; rice was also cultivated in a late stage of the civilization. However, the vagaries of the pattern of flooding could bring disaster, and Mohenjo-Daro, one of the two great cities of this civilization, is known to have been flooded repeatedly.

The settlement pattern of the Indus Valley differs from those of the other great valley civilizations. Some 250 Indus settlement sites have been identified, of which two stand out as far larger and more highly organized than the rest: Mohenjo-Daro in the south and Harappa in the north. These cities may have housed populations of 30,000 to 40,000, and were four to ten times larger than any of the other sites. For this reason, and because of the marked cultural uniformity found throughout the entire huge area of Indus civilization, it is often suggested that it was an empire state, with twin capitals at Mohenjo-Daro and Harappa.

The Indus civilization is remarkable for its town planning and building techniques. The capital cities were carefully planned, with a defended citadel mound and a further defensive wall around the whole settlement. The streets followed a grid pattern, and must have been laid out to a planner's design, a striking contrast to the meandering streets of Mesopotamian cities, for example. The highly organized drainage systems of the Indus cities are also remarkable. The streets had covered brick drains with manholes at intervals to enable accumulated waste to be cleared. Almost every house in Mohenjo-Daro had a bathroom, and many had a lavatory, both connected to the street drains by pottery drainpipes and chutes. The public buildings, generally located on the citadel mounds, are impressive in size but often enigmatic in function. One might expect to find both temples and palaces, but none have yet been confidently identified. A great granary has been found at Mohenjo-Daro, along with an outstanding brick-built basin known as the 'Great Bath', which may have been concerned with ritual ablution.

In contrast to their buildings, the material equipment of the Indus population was not particularly impressive: they were competent potters, metal- and stone-workers, but produced few

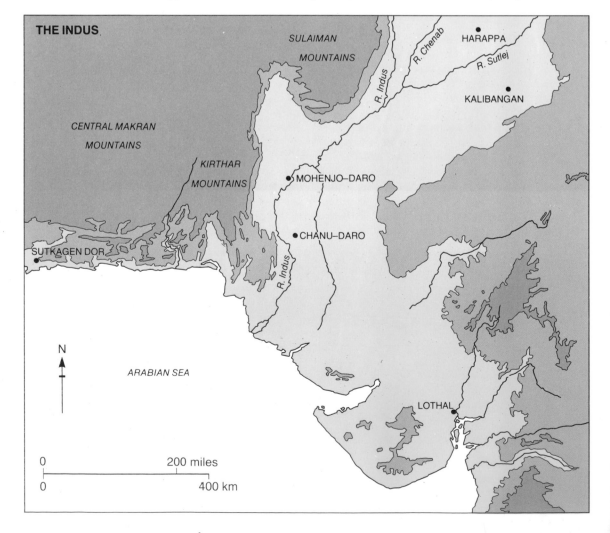

goods comparable to the fine products of Egypt or Mesopotamia. Perhaps their finest artefacts were etched carnelian beads and engraved steatite stamp seals, the source of most of the inscriptions we have in the undeciphered Indus script.

The Indus civilization was not isolated. It is known to have traded extensively overland with what is now Afghanistan and the rest of India, as well as by sea along the Persian Gulf. Indeed the Indus system of weights was being used in Dilmun, another urban civilization based on the island of Bahrein, in the late third millennium BC. An Indus civilization outpost has recently been found at Shortughai in Afghanistan, presumably connected with the trade in lapis lazuli from that area.

It is clear from the degree of uniformity and planning found across the entire culture that it was a highly centralized, presumably hierarchical society, but we have no documentary evidence, no wealthy tombs, nothing that is clearly a palace or a temple. Whatever its basis, the authority of the Indus rulers did not last as long as in Mesopotamia, Egypt or China. Some time after 1900 BC the civilization collapsed. Traditional explanations refer to invasions by Indo-European-speaking Aryans or to environmental disaster (particularly flooding), but it may represent the culmination of internal problems. Whatever the reason, urban life and associated features such as writing disappeared, not to reappear on the Indian subcontinent for several centuries.

Top: View of the excavations at Mohenjo-Daro showing the great accumulation of debris from earlier buildings underlying the main excavated city.

Above right: Aerial photograph of Mohenjo-Daro showing clearly the city's carefully planned grid-iron street system.

Above left: Red sandstone torso from Harappa.

17

China

The fourth great civilization of the world arose in China, far to the east of the Western Asiatic centres and isolated by deserts and mountain chains. Despite the many far-reaching political and economic upheavals that have affected it, present-day Chinese civilization is demonstrably the offspring of the Shang civilization that emerged on the alluvial plain of the Yellow River in northern China in the second millennium BC, making it without doubt the longest-lasting civilization in the world. Perhaps the most impressive evidence of this is the fact that the earliest Chinese writing yet found is a form of the unique 'ideographic' script still used today (see Chapter 7).

Bronze ritual vessel of the Shang period. These vessels, placed in tombs of kings and nobles, held offerings of food and wine for the dead.

Like the civilizations of Mesopotamia, Egypt and the Indus, Shang civilization was centred on the fertile plain of a great river. The Yellow River brings water and enriching mud from the highlands in the west to the dry plain of northern China, and this enabled the early Chinese to grow their staple crops: millet and rice, with wheat and barley being introduced in later Shang times. However, the river carries more silt than any other of the world's great rivers, and has no permanent channel to the sea, with the result that unless confined between dykes it can change its course unpredictably. Moreover, as the river silts up the dykes have to be heightened, a process that continues until in places the river bed is appreciably higher than the surrounding land. If the river breaks free, catastrophic flooding ensues. We do not know how far the Shang controlled the river, nor indeed do we know its exact course in Shang times. It is likely that early sites are still buried beneath silt deposited by the river in flood. Much of our evidence for this first phase of Chinese urbanization comes from the excavation of three cities: Erlitou, Zhengzhou and Anyang, each of which was probably the capital of the Shang at different times between the eighteenth and eleventh centuries BC.

Erlitou, just south of the Yellow River in what is now Henan province, is the oldest Chinese city yet to be discovered, and excavation there has revealed buildings in the *hangtu* (rammed-earth) style typical of early Chinese cities, along with highly developed bronze and jade artefacts. Zhengzhou, east of Erlitou, boasts a massive *hangtu* fortification wall over 7 km long. Only the royal family and elite seem to have lived within these walls, which contain large ceremonial and administrative buildings. The rest of the population lived outside, in semi-subterranean houses grouped in farming villages. Indeed Shang

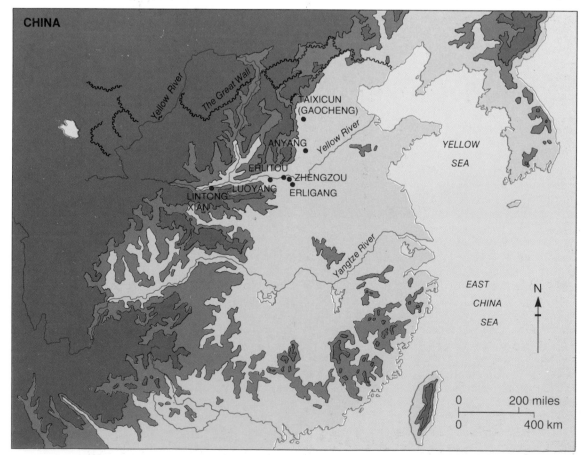

cities seem generally not to have housed large urban populations on the scale of cities in Mesopotamia, for example. Anyang, the most famous Shang site, spread over 24 km² of land, includes a ceremonial complex and a cemetery of very large cross-shaped shaft tombs for royal burials. Rows of satellite human burials are thought to be later sacrifices to the occupants of the tombs.

Large numbers of inscribed oracle bones and tortoise shells have been found at Anyang. They were used for divination and record questions addressed by the king to his ancestors, or the answers to these questions, or the outcome of subjects of divination. Society was strongly hierarchical, with a divine king, an associated aristocracy, commoners and slaves; craftsmen may have belonged to a separate hereditary group. There was considerable craft specialization, craftsmen working in pottery, bronze, bone, lacquer, jade, silk and wool. Shang bronze-working techniques were remarkably advanced, and their highly ornamented ritual vessels, made by a complex casting method unique to China at the time, are the most famous artefacts of early Chinese civilization.

We do not know the exact extent of Shang civilization. The heart of their territory was the lower Yellow River valley, but they traded with other areas and waged war to the north, and possibly even south along the coast towards the Yangtze River.

Some time in the eleventh century BC the Shang were overrun by a pastoral people from the west, who founded the Zhou dynasty, perpetuating many features of Shang culture. Although the Zhou seem impoverished in many ways compared to the Shang, they made an important technological advance: the development of iron-working. Zhou smiths were able both to forge and to cast iron (Europe did not master the latter technique until the Middle Ages),

and on some sites iron-working took place on a massive, truly industrial, scale.

Under the Zhou Chinese civilization expanded throughout northern China and began to absorb the Yangtze River area to the south. Power was delegated by the king to members of the royal family and aristocracy, resulting in a feudal system of government comprising many small states, unified only by their relationship to the king. The nobles controlled the agricultural peasantry, who produced the food and provided unpaid labour for building and other public works. Subsequently centralized authority collapsed and the empire dissolved into a number of independent states. Thus, although the Zhou was the longest-lived dynasty in Chinese history, its later years were marred by conflict.

In the third century BC, after a period of warfare and disintegration, the Qin Empire emerged. The first emperor, Qin Shi Huangdi, standardized the legal code, weights and measures, currency and script throughout the country. He linked up previously existing stretches of rampart to form the Great Wall in the north, in order to exclude barbarian invaders. His huge mausoleum includes an entire buried army of some 7,000 life-size terracotta and bronze figures of soldiers, officers, horses and chariots. He united nearly all the territory that we now know as China, and established an empire that was to last, though not without interruptions, for more than 2,000 years.

Top: View of the Great Wall which runs for more than 2,000 km along China's northern border. As a connected whole it dates from the Qin dynasty (221–206 BC), although parts were built earlier.

Centre: Part of the buried army of life-size terracotta figures found in the tomb of the first emperor of China, Qin Shi Huangdi, in Lintong Xian in northern China.

Left: The earliest writing in China is found on animal scapulae and tortoise shells, like the one shown here. These 'oracle bones' were used for divination and often record questions addressed by the king to his deceased ancestors.

19

Minoans and Mycenaeans

The first civilization to arise on European soil was the short-lived civilization of the Minoans and Mycenaeans. These people were half-remembered in Homer's time but subsequently forgotten, to be rediscovered little more than a century ago by the controversial Homeric scholar Heinrich Schliemann. Unlike Mesopotamia, Egypt, the Indus and China, the Minoan and Mycenaean civilizations were not based on large alluvial valleys, nor were they dependent on high-yielding cereal crops produced with the help of irrigation. Their subsistence base was the 'Mediterranean triad' – cereals, vines and olives – plus the usual domesticated animals. This provided them with a balanced diet and two desirable commodities that could be both stored and traded: wine and olive oil.

The Minoans

The earlier civilization, named after the legendary king Minos, arose on Crete, a long narrow island lying across the southern entrance to the Aegean Sea, well placed for contacts with older civilizations in Egypt and the Levant. Minoan civilization was not imported, however; it was in fact the culmination of a steady development on the island, generally regarded as civilized from *c.* 2000 BC, when the characteristic palace-centred organization was established.

The palaces, at Knossos, Phaistos, Mallia and Zakro, were both the dwellings of the rulers and the economic and administrative centres of their communities. Built on a grand scale, they were two or three storeys high, decorated with fine wall frescoes and equipped with bathrooms, water and drainage systems. The banks of rooms surrounding the central courtyard included public assembly and audience rooms, domestic quarters for the royal families, shrines, workshops, storage magazines and archive rooms. The palaces served as centres for the collection and distribution of food, raw materials and manufactured goods. As in Mesopotamia, the demands of administering this kind of redistributive economy seem to have led to the development of writing – first in hieroglyphs, later in a script known as Linear A. Both are still undeciphered, but comparison with the later Linear B tablets suggests strongly that the earlier scripts were used for the same administrative purposes.

Minoan civilization underwent some changes during its 500- to 600-year history. In about 1750 BC the palaces were all destroyed, perhaps as the result of an earthquake, but all except Zakro were rebuilt. Then, in the middle of the fifteenth century BC, the palaces were again destroyed, either directly by the eruption of the volcanic island of Thera, or in disturbances following that eruption. After *c.* 1450 BC only Knossos was reoccupied on a significant scale and this time, it seems, not by Minoans themselves but by Mycenaeans from the mainland of Greece, who ruled here for a further half-century or so, setting up a new administration and developing the Linear B script.

For 500 years after the first palaces emerged, Minoan civilization dominated the Aegean; but direct control hardly extended beyond the southern part of the sea, with possible colonies on three south Aegean islands. Further afield, trading networks extended to the Greek mainland, Cyprus, Egypt, and the Levant coast of the Mediterranean.

The Mycenaeans

The Mycenaean civilization of the Greek mainland, named after Mycenae, seat of Homer's king Agamemnon, shared many features with that of the Minoans. However, Mycenaean civilization emerged later – not at all before the seventeenth century BC and not in developed form until the fifteenth, when, as we have seen, the Mycenaeans settled Crete and adopted the Minoan palace-based administration and economic organization. One of the main differences between the two civilizations was the markedly more military character of the Mycenaeans. In contrast to the undefended Minoan settlements, most of the Mycenaean towns were surrounded by massive fortification walls; some, like Mycenae and Tiryns, were provided with heavily defended citadels. The

Below left: Wall fresco from a house at Akrotiri on Thera. The quality of the painting illustrates the high standard of living enjoyed by well-off members of Minoan society.

Below right: The Mycenaeans equipped themselves for warfare. This bronze suit of armour was found in a tomb at Dendra.

military aspect is apparent also in grave goods: the richly equipped tombs of the aristocracy contain daggers, swords, helmets and shields. Fighting scenes appear on decorated pottery and military equipment, such as chariots, appears in the inventories recorded on clay tablets.

For the last 250 years of their civilization, after they took over Knossos, the Mycenaeans dominated the Aegean. Their influence spread far further: Mycenaean pottery and other goods were traded to the coast of Asia Minor, Rhodes, Cyprus, Syria, Egypt and to the central Mediterranean in exchange for manufactured goods and raw materials.

Mycenaean palaces, especially Knossos on Crete and Pylos on the mainland, have yielded tablets inscribed in the script known as Linear B. Michael Ventris, who had been a code-breaker during the Second World War, deciphered Linear B in 1952, showing it to record an early form of Greek. It seems likely that when the Mycenaeans overran Crete they adapted the Minoan Linear A script to write their own language: Greek. The tablets are administrative documents recording such data as quotas of foodstuffs and manufactured goods owed to the palace and rations of raw materials and foods issued to craftsmen and palace employees.

From the archaeological and documentary evidence we can build up a picture of Mycenaean society. It was markedly hierarchical, with kings and nobles at the top and slaves (perhaps acquired through war) at the bottom. In between would have been farmers and local community rulers. As in Minoan Crete, craftsmen were dependants of the palace. Merchants are not mentioned in the tablets and there may have been no separate class of traders; we do not know how trade was organized in Mycenaean society.

After *c.* 1200 BC Mycenaean civilization went into abrupt decline, perhaps as a result of attack from outside, or internal tensions, or natural disaster, or the culmination of various long-term difficulties. Whatever the reason, Greece entered a 'Dark Age', which was to last for some 400 years.

Above: View of the strongly fortified citadel at Mycenae. Just inside the wall is Circle A of Shaft Graves, excavated by Heinrich Schliemann.

Left: Mycenaean craftsmen produced goods of very fine quality, like this gold pendant in the form of a pomegranate found at Enkomi in Cyprus.

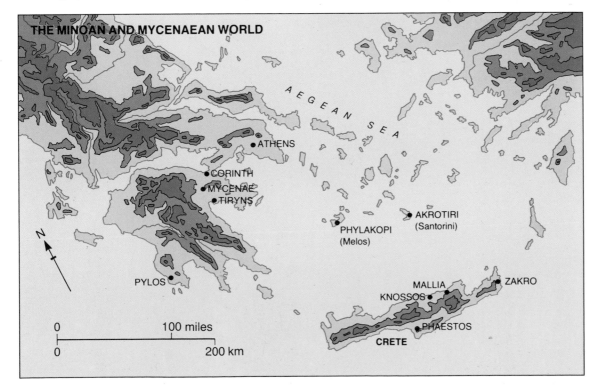

THE MINOAN AND MYCENAEAN WORLD

AEGEAN SEA

- ATHENS
- CORINTH
- MYCENAE
- TIRYNS
- AKROTIRI (Santorini)
- PHYLAKOPI (Melos)
- PYLOS
- MALLIA
- KNOSSOS
- ZAKRO
- PHAESTOS

CRETE

N

0   100 miles
0   200 km

Greece

The evolution of civilization

Civilization has an evolution, and we can make a useful, if old-fashioned distinction between 'primary' civilizations, such as Mesopotamia and Egypt, and 'secondary' ones, such as classical Greece and Rome. Greece and Rome are important precisely because they represent a typically later stage in the evolution of civilization. We need not overstate the case by assigning an enhanced primitivity or originality to the earlier examples, and a wholly derivative status to the latter. Greece and Rome offer documentation for a critical growth point in the progressing pattern of human civilization. They also happen to be the historical link or filter through which ideas, skills and institutional elements from the earlier civilizations have reached us.

Greek or Mediterranean?

Soon after the beginning of the first millennium BC certain formative trends in the development of civilized society began to clarify and consolidate themselves. These developments were not the narrow achievement of one ethnic group, such as the Greeks as opposed to their 'rivals', the Phoenicians or the Etruscans. The notion of a special role for the Greek nation in cultural history – the so-called 'Greek miracle' – is no more acceptable on behalf of the Greeks for cultural achievement than it is for other nations for less praiseworthy accomplishments. Accounts of early Greek history familiar to us from the classical authors and subsequently reflected in our own educational system often show too many signs of anachronistic nationalism for comfort. The point, however, is wider than bias and anachronism. The crucial developmental trends with which we are here concerned are set in the very period when the concept of 'nation', and with it the use of ethnic labels, was still at a pre-formative stage. In several key areas in and around the Mediterranean basin, human social organization at this time may be seen as variously transitional – to be placed somewhere in an evolutionary sequence of tribal, pre-urban and proto-urban stages. The geographical spread was such that we can label these trends 'Mediterranean'. Instead of distributing dubious historical credits, we can then take 'Greek' civilization as one idiomatic case.

Nation and individual

Most striking of these new trends, visible alike in literature, commerce and political institutions, were movements towards a conscious assumption of national identity – nationhood – and towards the self-awareness of the individual citizen. Horizons shifted both for the state and for the individual, as both sought to define their own identity.

The articulation of separate nationhood was a gradual change that had much to do with the spread of the city-state as an organizing unit. This development led to the *nation-state*, and then with the Romans to the *empire-state*. The other side of the coin – the growth of individual awareness in the citizen – was a complementary and related change.

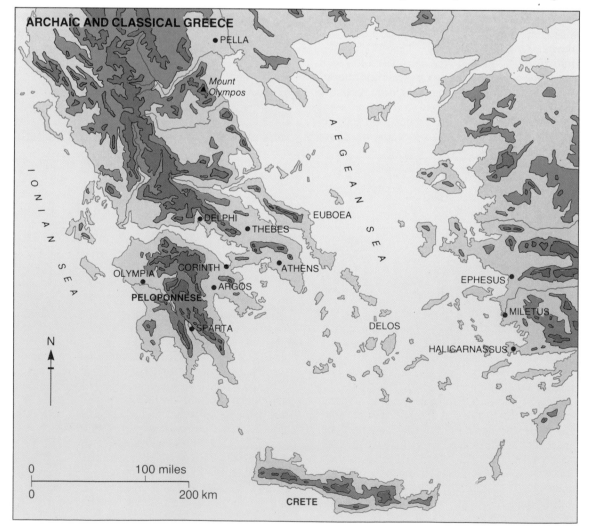

The idea of an analogy between state and individual was an influential concept that found expression in a developing political literature. Personal individualization, however, introduced a fundamental tension that was to have a strong effect upon structures and institutions inside and between states.

Many factors combined together to make up the formative background to these trends. Chief among these are:

the adoption of the alphabet
the switch from redistributive to commercial
economies
the growth of the city-state
changes in systems of land tenure
geographical mobility and the growth of
colonies

The alphabet

An alphabet of 32 letters, based upon a simplified cuneiform, is first found in Ugarit in the middle of the second millennium BC. A slimmed-down version of some 20 to 30 letters was 'exported' by the Phoenicians widely in the Mediterranean basin, and a modified version was taken up by the Greeks by the second half of the eighth century BC. A 'western' version of this Greek alphabet was later adopted by the Etruscans (and thence by the Romans). The increase in efficiency, accessibility and versatility that resulted from this switch to alphabetic script is hard to exaggerate. We might compare it to the invention in Europe in the fifteenth century AD of the printing press or, more recently, to the development of computer databases.

The alphabet represented the latest stage in the development of syllabic script, and it follows that all modern scripts based upon this alphabet trace their parentage to the earlier syllabaries. Even more significant, however, is the degree of conceptual analysis involved in the elaboration of the alphabet. The progression from syllabary to alphabet was not just the introduction of a crafty shorthand, but rather implies a linguistic analysis (see Chapter 7). At some level or other, the abstract categories of something like consonant and vowel were implied for the first time.

However, just as the computer database would be nowhere without the video display and the high-speed printer, so too the 'improved technology' of the new script owes much of its historical impact to the availability of a cheap writing material, such as the papyrus from Egypt. Papyrus and animal hide had already been in use for some time. Both had the advantages over clay, wood or stone of flexibility, portability and easier storage. Both speeded up and simplified the writing process. Papyrus, however, probably had the edge in availability, cheapness and ease of use. Once again, spotting the potential of this material may well have been a Phoenician success. The Phoenician city of Byblos seems to have become an important centre for the distribution of papyrus, and its name was associated by the Greeks with their words for book (*biblos*) and papyrus (*bublos*).

The chief mechanism by which the adoption of the alphabet affected society was in the spread of literacy (see Chapter 7). By this we do not mean large-scale literacy, involving a highish percentage of the population; such a phenomenon is arguably limited to our own century. The pace at which

Above left: Fine mid-fifth-century BC bronze statue of a Greek warrior. This nude figure, more than six feet tall, was found embedded in sand on the eastern shores of Calabria in Italy.

Above right: View of the round temple at Delphi in central Greece. Delphi was the seat of the oracle of Apollo, whose advice was sought by Greek leaders on such subjects as the outcome of wars or the foundation of colonies.

View of the road from Corinth to Lecmaion; in the background is Acrocorinth, the acropolis of the ancient city. Corinth was one of the most important Greek cities and in the Archaic period it dominated trade throughout the Greek world.

literacy spread in the classical world was always at best intermittent and piecemeal. The percentage of the population to benefit was not very high, but began to be significant. Any appreciable growth in literacy, and with it a gradual increase in the creation and dissemination of pamphlets and books (leading eventually to 'institutional' developments such as the establishment of libraries) was bound to create a more literate climate. In this context the interchange of speculative ideas and the practice of critical debate became normal and acceptable.

Briefly, the spread of literacy promoted an acceleration in the development of each of the following:

> literature, both aesthetic and technical
> the use of language as propaganda
> special symbolic 'languages', such as mathematics and geometry
> abstract language for conceptual analysis

Above all, literacy meant that the knowledge and experience of one generation no longer depended purely upon personal and family contact for transmission to the next generation. An accessible writing system is an accumulating device.

Commerce

By the beginning of the first millennium BC the transition from redistributive economies towards commerce was already under way. The final establishment of a market economy was still some way off, however, probably as late as the fourth century BC.

One factor behind the introduction of greater efficiency into writing systems was probably an escalation in the volume of trade, both within the Mediterranean and between the Mediterranean and the East. Trade on any appreciable scale involves keeping records, and an increase in the intensity of trade would have been hampered by the cumbersome and time-consuming methods of recording that were originally developed for limited and localized internal store-keeping. This increase in trade was accelerated both by improvements in shipbuilding technology and the techniques of navigation on the one hand, and by a greater

availability of negotiable surpluses (such as wine and oil) and of 'mass-produced' marketable products (such as fine pottery) on the other.

Critical also was the advent of coinage. Traditionally this development has been credited to the independent country of Lydia on the coast of Asia Minor, although the Greek island of Aegina is now favoured by some. The 'invention' of coinage should be seen not as an overnight inspiration, but rather as the coming together of two traditions, each of which has a long previous history. One was the use of bars, ingots and other objects as primitive currency; the other was the use of personal seals to show ownership, provenance and authority. These very early coins of about the late seventh century BC were made only in precious metals such as gold, silver and electrum and in smallish quantities. They were probably first used by states rather than individuals for their prestige value, and for the safe deposit of wealth. The transition to a widely accepted coinage available to the individual traders was a gradual one, complete by the late Hellenistic period and early Roman Empire.

City-states

The Greeks themselves saw their society as characterized by its cities. Over the first millennium BC in particular, the organization of city-states in and around the Mediterranean showed a changing pattern both externally and internally. It is into this general pattern that the Greek examples fit.

Externally, it is likely that confederations of culturally-related city-states were not new. In such confederations dominance would shift from one particular city to another, although this would not necessarily imply any internal interference in the affairs of member cities. Nor is an aggressive or warlike stance towards other confederations a necessary assumption. On the contrary, these early confederations seem to have been rather self-contained and defensive, challenged perhaps only by outside tribal groups. Internally, they had strongly hierarchical societies, in which the rigidity of class structure and caste differentiation was reinforced by the sanction of an accepted state religion.

During the first millennium BC, however, the external attitude of city-states became more aggressive, acquisitive and warlike, the ultimate trend being, as we have said, towards nation and empire. This trend showed itself first as a would-be imperialism, as exhibited, for example, by the Persians and by Athens itself. Although the Greeks prided themselves on the jealous individuality of their city-states, the swift birth of panhellenism – the sentiment of the ultimate oneness of all Greeks – was an early potent development. Athens, for instance, was quick to appeal to such aspirations as an apology for her would-be imperial dominance.

In effect what we are seeing is a jostling-for-power within an adolescent phase of maturing nationhood. As an illustration, let us take the Athenian propaganda success against rival Euboea, a large island off the east coast of the mainland of Greece. Early transmediterranean contacts and other archaeological evidence indicate that Euboea was in the vanguard of early 'Greek' civilization. This possibility, however, is not exactly stressed in Athenian literature, and modern treatments are still remarkably pro-Athenian.

We could take a similar view of the surviving accounts of the so-called 'synoecism' of Athens. This term describes the process by which, supposedly, the villages of primitive Attica combined to live together in the infant city-state of Athens. As a real historical event this does not make very good sense. The tale has all the hallmarks of the idealist's storybook. Naturally a degree of co-operation is involved in the formation of a city, but crucial to the final appearance of a recognizable city is the reaching of a certain 'trigger' level in the complexity of organization and specialist services required by, and actually available to, a region. This particular 'city-founder' view, which sees the process as both conscious and deliberate, belongs rather with 'foundation' literature: part of a propaganda claim to the greatest possible antiquity and earliest possible urbanization.

Internally, the city-states of the Mediterranean of the first millennium BC also exhibited marked changes. What seems an almost fervent enthusiasm for experimentation, involving intellectual debate and political and social reorganization, is familiar to us from conventional histories of Greece. Tyrants (some good, but mostly bad), oligarchs (nearly all bad), demagogues, democratic assemblies, mobs – all come and go as forms of government in a bewildering succession. Similar switches of power and the transition to a relative openness of debate can be paralleled elsewhere in the Mediterranean, notably in early Rome. An abundant speculative literature, on topics such as the better organization of the state and the basis of social and personal morality, began to erode systems that had previously enjoyed the sanction of the gods or of a lawgiver hallowed by the mists of time.

Land tenure and colonies

Against this changing background, explicit claims to land become characteristic of the period. Some kind of ownership of land had been commonplace for a long time. Land sales are recorded in the Early Dynastic period of Sumer. The change, which again was gradual, was in favour of systems of tenure that for the first time effectively divided the population into the landed and the landless. It was these new systems of tenure, rather than land shortage as such, that exerted pressure. The ownership of land now gave status as well as a livelihood, and became associated with power in the state and, in due course, with voting rights.

Such a change goes some way to explaining the very early moves, for example by the Greeks and the Phoenicians, towards the foundation of so-called colonies. The new systems of tenure put demands upon the supply of land, and introduced an element of competition. Greece was in any case short of arable land for cereal production, the greater part of the country being mountainous and better suited to low-intensity grazing by sheep and goat. A successful strategy was the cultivation of the vine and the olive, which extended cultivable land into the foothills, where even quite steep slopes could be used. With some cereal growth amongst the vines and olives (the so-called 'triad' of Mediterranean polyculture) even greater productivity could be achieved. Furthermore the wine and oil produced could be traded, if necessary, as a cash crop to supply, among other things, any cereal deficiency.

Under the new pressures some groups may well have sought their fortunes by founding alternative settlements in less competitive environments. For the period very early in the millennium, however, the colonial model as such seems all wrong. To start with the dates are back to front. A good number of 'colonies' were established, according to traditional accounts (corroborated in some cases by archaeological evidence) at dates so early (the eleventh century BC in Asia Minor, and the eighth in the West) that it is difficult to believe that the parent city was itself yet clear of the pre-urban stage, or even, in some cases, in existence at all. Later on the colonial model makes better sense. In the fifth century BC rivals for the leadership of the panhellenic 'nation', such as Corinth, Sparta and Athens, needed their colonies to secure and demonstrate the breadth of their power-base. Their colonies by the same link gained authority and status in regions where they were coming under increasing local challenge.

Rome

Nation to empire

With Rome *nation-state* became *empire-state*. Rome was to become the first truly imperial and colonial power, taking the higher levels of organizational complexity seen with classical Greece to a further pitch of systematization. Like Greece, Rome was a 'secondary' civilization, a hybrid taking its components from many different sources. A major component was of course Greek civilization itself, which, as we have stressed, needs to be seen in the context of general developments in *Mediterranean* urbanization. Less directly involved were the ancient cultures of the Near East and Egypt, seen very largely through a Greek filter. Nearer home, Rome was more indebted to the civilizations of Etruria and Phoenicia on the one hand, and to the cultures of central European tribal chiefdoms (generically known to the Romans as 'Celts') on the other, than the dismissive hostility of later Roman historians would have us believe.

View of the Pantheon, a classical round temple in Rome. The building standing today is essentially that reconstructed by the emperor Hadrian in AD 118–128. The domed rotunda lit by a central circular aperture to the sky represents an early example of the adventurous use of concrete in monumental building.

Early and Republican Rome

If we use the conventional but inappropriate ethnic labels, early Rome was not Roman at all, but emphatically Etruscan. Located primarily in ancient Etruria (which corresponds very roughly to modern Tuscany), and based upon a loose agglomeration of city-states, the Etruscan civilization reached prominence in the sixth and fifth centuries BC. It left archaeological and epigraphic evidence of its expansion, notably in the Po valley to the north and on the Campanian seaboard to the south. The Etruscans were seafarers trading with the Phoenicians and the Greeks, as the vast numbers of Greek vases in Etruscan tombs testify. Etruscan technology showed considerable advancement and refinement, and resulted in highly characteristic products – notably the black fine pottery known as *bucchero*, and large- and small-scale bronzes.

The Romans found an Etruscan origin unpalatable. They saw the Etruscans as foreigners intruding into an uncontaminated farming culture – luxury-loving urban foreigners, whose dominance they had first to tolerate, but were subsequently able to break. By contrast, they liked to see themselves as guardians of a society grounded upon solid agrarian values.

There is, however, plentiful evidence of shared elements. Something as Roman as the taking of the *auspices* by studying the flight of birds has clear Etruscan and Italic parallels. Roman hydraulic engineering, which was to produce the vast aqueducts of the Empire, took its model from Etruscan water and drainage management schemes. Moreover, recent research suggests that even a distinction in language between Etruscan and Italic may not be as clear cut as was once supposed.

It thus seems that we may well be dealing with a shared cultural background, out of which arose first the Etruscan civilization, and then the Roman. By the time a recognizably Roman Rome emerges from its Etruscan period, it does so as an embryonic republic, with one of the new tentative democracies that characterized Mediterranean culture at this time.

Imperial Rome: packaged society

The new systems of land tenure encouraged by the developing Mediterranean city-states exerted similar pressures in the Roman state towards territorial expansion. From the third century BC onwards Rome grew from a modest city-state to embrace the widest geographical spread yet spanned by one civilization. At its greatest extent, during the second and third centuries AD, the new empire ringed almost the continuous line of the Mediterranean basin, pushed north through Gaul to Scotland, and reached appreciably into the Near East. The overall tendency was now towards a packaged and transferable society: the hybrid of Roman imperial civilization.

Economy and technology

The later Roman Republic and the early Roman Empire marked the final establishment of the market economy. It is from this period that the marketplace with fixed architecture, areas of shops with street frontages, and the great expansion of a cheap coinage currency all rapidly become recognizable and expected features of urban life. There was a marked

what is often thought of as a mark of Roman sophistication – the civic fountain – was in fact a symptom of this inadequacy, being one of several destinations to which temporary overflow supplies could be directed.

Perhaps as Roman, in the packaged and transferable sense, was the phenomenon of the public baths. These were built both at public expense on a grand scale for the emperor's pleasure, and on a commercial entrepreneurial basis for the diversion of the public. Over and above their social function as a meeting-place, which can be paralleled from elsewhere, the idea of state-provided or privately purchased secular *entertainment* is probably a Roman innovation. These complexes of hot and cold rooms were made possible by advances in technique and manufacture, such as the invention of a waterproof plaster, the production of the glazed tile and, above all, the introduction of underfloor central heating, the *hypocaust*. This must have been a particular advantage when it came to transferring

Left: A masterpiece of Etruscan art *c.* 300 BC and one of the few large pieces of terracotta sculpture to have survived. They may have once formed part of the façade of a temple at Tarquinia, and apart from the wing and the tail, seem to have been modelled in one piece.

expansion of trade throughout the Mediterranean, and in many cases far beyond (e.g. to the far north of Europe and to the Far East). Consumerism could be said to have arrived, bringing with it mass-production and the throw-away container. Pottery amphorae, for example, the favoured containers for the bulk transport of wine and oil, were used once only. Their smashed fragments piled up behind the warehouses that lined the commercial stretches of the River Tiber in Rome, as Rome's Monte Testaccio still testifies.

In a reciprocal cycle, economic growth favoured technology, and in turn technological advance encouraged economic activity. Especially important were advances in the construction of large public buildings and complexes. The key to a new inventive architecture was the discovery of concrete and the realization of some of its potential. This, coupled with the mass-production of fired bricks, gave Roman builders a fresh plasticity of design. The formation of concrete structures enabled much larger spans to be roofed than could ever have been envisaged with the use of timber or stone beams. Barrel vaulting made possible the construction of multi-storey public buildings and the blocks of residential apartments that were to become so characteristic of Roman imperial urban architecture.

Under the Empire, cities became dense centres of population. Vast populations had to be fed, and the movement and storage of large grain stocks across the Mediterranean area became problems that had to be confronted. Granary ships supplied enormous granary warehouses (*horrea*), which became typical features of major ports.

The provision of drainage systems, and of an aqueduct-based water-supply, also became standard aspects of the Romanized city. The distribution of water was managed privately, and never reached the individualized level of modern cities. Considering the inadequacy of this particular technology (leakage at probably well over 50 per cent, with no efficient valves and pumps) the general success of these water systems was remarkable. Paradoxically enough,

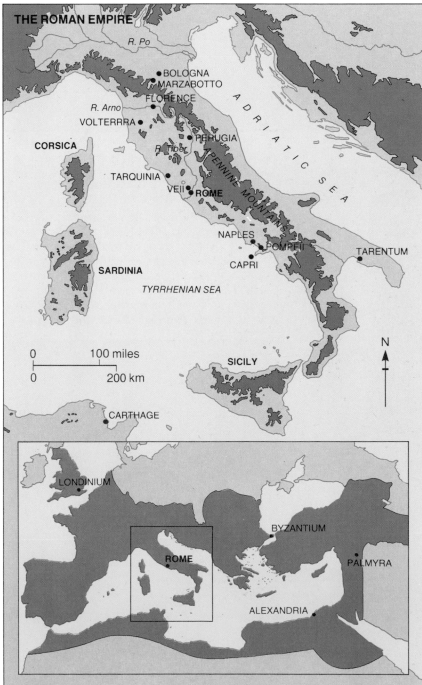

THE ROMAN EMPIRE

R. Po · BOLOGNA · MARZABOTTO · FLORENCE · R. Arno · VOLTERRRA · PERUGIA · CORSICA · R. Tiber · APENNINE MOUNTAINS · TARQUINIA · VEII · ROME · ADRIATIC SEA · NAPLES · POMPEII · CAPRI · TARENTUM · SARDINIA · TYRRHENIAN SEA · SICILY · N · CARTHAGE

0 — 100 miles
0 — 200 km

LONDINIUM · BYZANTIUM · ROME · PALMYRA · ALEXANDRIA

View of a first-century AD house decorated with fine wall mosaics at Herculaneum.

Portrait of a young man on a linen burial shroud. Although found in Italy, the piece is Egyptian and dates from the period of Roman rule in Egypt.

close connections in other spheres. Whatever its precise route, the transmission is likely to have taken place through the Etruscan/Phoenician/Greek trading centres of the Italian western seaboard.

The adoption of the alphabet and the spread of literacy took place in much the same context as we sketched for Greece, and we may assume that they had a similarly wide-ranging set of effects upon society. In the western Mediterranean, however, literacy, literature and the sciences seem to have progressed at a slower pace than they did further east, so that when in the late Republic and early Empire a sudden demand was felt for literate and educated personnel, Rome and Italy were unable to find sufficient local resources.

The political upheaval which led to the transition from Republic to Empire, and the administrative demands made by the new geographical scale of the Roman state, brought pressure for a radical reorganization of bureaucracy and state institutions. These pressures led directly to the formation of a properly constituted civil service and to a more explicitly managed system of education. Many Romans in this period felt it a national scandal that the only source of the literate staff required by the new civil service lay among educated Greeks of freedman status. These often emerged from a tradition in which literate Greek slaves were attached as 'secretaries' to influential Roman families and might be granted freedman status in return for their services. The employment of such personnel and the degree of resentment that it engendered at Rome indicate two things very clearly: the xenophobia so often typical of nation-states (the empire-state at this stage is still clearly only a geographically enlarged nation-state), and the gap between supply and demand in the new technology of literacy. Obviously literacy at Rome still fell well short of the standards that prevailed by then in the eastern Mediterranean.

Law

Much the same pressures toward greater systematization and codification led to the development of explicit state institutions, for instance of the legal profession and the juridical service. Public law as such was not new in this period: not only early Rome and Greece but also early Sumer show plain evidence of slowly accumulating bodies of law. What was new was the degree to which law and its public practice were codified and explicitly institutionalized. This finer differentiation of state institutions is characteristic of the later, evolved civilizations.

Propaganda

Another use to which language was now put was what we may call the articulation of deliberate propaganda. In a sense non-linguistic propaganda pre-dates urban civilization. Statements about the status and importance of an individual or a family could be made without any language commentary: by wealth association, or later by the construction of large and elaborate buildings. The use of explicit linguistic propaganda – public statements made to enhance and consolidate an image of military or political achievement – probably dates from the initial tentative spread of literacy, especially in the Near East. The propaganda requirements of a localized city-state, however, are of quite a different

this particular component of Roman civilization to colder northern climates.

Language and literacy

The alphabet we know as Roman came into use on the Italian peninsula possibly as early as the seventh century BC, and was first used by the Etruscans. The values given to the letters correspond roughly with a version of the Greek alphabet known as Western Greek. The Etruscans may have taken the alphabet over from the Greeks or, perhaps more probably, straight from the Phoenicians with whom they had

order from those of a nation- or empire-state. The deliberate use of propaganda as part of state management and control belongs only to the nation- and empire-state.

Furthermore, propaganda can take both direct and indirect forms. At Rome we have not only direct and official examples, such as the *Ara Pacis* ('Altar of Peace'), a monument set up by the emperor Augustus with an inscription to celebrate his achievement in establishing a stable and peaceful state, but also the deliberate creation of a state image in the arts and literature. This might involve reinforcing the idea of traditional origins by the use of material with mythological associations: Octavian, for instance, chose his new name, Augustus, intentionally for its 'archival' ring; Vergil was encouraged in his *Aeneid* to compose a suitably epic tale of Rome's origins.

State, individual and religion

Nation- and empire-states in particular throw into relief a fundamental tension between individual and state. There are many and complex reasons for this, as we have seen in our description of Greece. This tension leads eventually towards the gradual evolution of state institutions which have a critical tolerance of individualist aspirations built-in.

A city-state is not just a social or linguistic collective of its citizens. It needs its citizens as workforce, food-producers, traders and providers of all kinds of specialist services. Paradoxically, however, it can be said to have an existence and continuity of its own, and perhaps its ultimate interest lies in its own stability and continuation. Its dimension therefore is long-term. The individual, on the other hand, tends to have a short-term horizon. If unchecked or unconditioned, he may tend ultimately toward anarchy and the dissolution of the state. The state therefore has an interest in the direct management of the individual's motivation and co-operation. Such an analysis is simplistic, and would have little relevance to the early civilizations. It is plausible, however, that with 'evolved' states, such as Greece and Rome, the need for such management became explicitly recognized.

This is particularly relevant to the role of religion, especially in the context of the empire-state. The enormous extent of the Roman Empire made it necessary for Roman civilization to evolve into a multi-dimensional cosmopolitan product that could assimilate a high level of 'fringe diversity'. Present among that fringe diversity were a number of 'personalized' religions which made powerful appeal to the individual through a saviour-deity offering individual purification and salvation. Christianity is familiar to us by its survival, and by its pervasive incorporation into the institutions and conceptual structure of our own society. Mithraism (equally if not more influential in the central phases of the Roman Empire) by contrast now seems an historical oddity.

These saviour-cults were by no means new when they made their impact under the early Empire. To account for the strength of appeal that they began to exert at that time, we need to look at the changing social structure of the early Empire, the ordinary individual's greater social and geographical mobility, and his exposure and receptivity towards new ideas. In particular, Christianity was initially

the personalized religion of the less advantaged classes of society, and of the non-commissioned and private soldiers in the Roman army. For these, stationed as they usually were far from their original homes (which by now might be neither Rome nor Italy), the saviour cults articulated a protest against what they felt to be a remote, unrepresentative and corrupt state. The militancy of protest offered by the saviour cults was, however, variable. Equally significant was their role of consolation and their perspective of otherworldliness.

The final adoption of Christianity as the state religion of Rome showed a sensible appreciation not only of its success over a wide geographical and social spectrum, but also of its power to offer the individual a defined purpose in the state, and the state an obvious justification.

Top: Throughout the Roman Empire there was considerable uniformity in many aspects of urban life, including architectural style. The buildings of Palmyra, an ancient oasis town in the Syrian desert, are similar to those of Roman cities in north Africa or Gaul.

Centre: Mosaic floors are another feature found throughout the Roman Empire, decorating the houses of the wealthy. This example comes from Tunisia.

Mesoamerica

Centred on the modern states of Mexico, Guatemala, Belize and El Salvador, Mesoamerica is an area defined by archaeologists not on the basis of geography – indeed it embraces an immense environmental diversity – but on shared cultural development. The area was the setting for the first development of maize agriculture in the Americas and subsequently supported a series of advanced civilizations from the second millennium BC until the arrival of the Europeans in the sixteenth century AD.

These civilizations varied in many ways, but they shared a number of important features, which together make up the distinctive character of Mesoamerican civilization. Ceremonial centres, complexes of monumental buildings which formed the focus of religious and civil activities, are particularly characteristic of Mesoamerica. Originally it was thought that ceremonial centres were not associated with large resident populations – in other words, that they were not cities – but recent work has indicated large populations in some cases at least. The most important structures of the ceremonial centres are often truncated pyramids, sometimes of massive size, with temple buildings on top. Another trait shared by most, though not all, Mesoamerican civilizations, was the ball-game, which had great ritual significance. Played on a special H-shaped ball-court, it usually involved individuals or teams of players who had to keep a solid rubber ball in motion and, if possible, to propel it through one of the rings set high in the court wall. Some Mesoamerican civilizations also shared an elaborate hieroglyphic writing system, employed on carved stone monuments and found in its most developed form among the Maya.

The Olmecs

The Olmecs are now regarded as the earliest American civilization, beginning in the late second millennium BC and continuing for about a millennium. They occupied the swampy lowlands of south-east Mexico, flanking the Caribbean Sea. Fish and aquatic birds supplemented their diet, which was based on maize, cultivated by the slash-and-burn method of shifting cultivation, as well as domesticated dogs and turkeys. No large cities are known and the population lived mostly in small farming settlements surrounding major ceremonial centres; the three best known are San Lorenzo, La Venta and Tres Zapotes.

The Olmecs are renowned for their art, which ranges from monumental sculptures in stone, found at all the major centres, to mural painting and fine figurines in pottery or jade. Characteristic Olmec sculptures are massive basalt heads over 3 m high with down-turned mouths and thick lips, wearing tightly fitting helmets, while another recurring theme is the were-jaguar (the transmutation of man and jaguar).

The organization of Olmec society is not well understood, but it was clearly differentiated, with an elite which controlled a wide-ranging trade network in valued materials such as jade and obsidian. Craftsmen must have been specialists, probably supported by the elite. The Olmecs should perhaps be credited with the invention of writing and the technique of recording calendrical dates on stone, for a long time attributed to the Maya, since examples have been found at the late Olmec site of Tres Zapotes.

Monte Alban

Monte Alban was a large centre in the central southern highlands of Mexico, from which the Zapotecs dominated the Valley of Oaxaca, c. 500 BC to AD 700. It was supported by maize agriculture, both rain-fed and dependent on canal irrigation, practised not only on the fertile valley floor, but also on the drier, more rugged lower mountain slopes, where successful cultivation was much more difficult.

Monte Alban was long interpreted as a typical ceremonial centre, and it is certainly dominated by monumental architecture: temples, pyramids,

Above: Pottery figures of dwarfs from Teotihuacán.

The houses of officials and other wealthy citizens of Teotihuacán were often decorated with wall paintings in elaborate polychrome style. This fresco depicts the rain-god Tlaloc.

platform mounds and ball-courts surround a huge plaza. However, recent work has identified many house platforms, common burials and much domestic debris. Many now regard Monte Alban as a true city, possibly housing as many as 25,000 to 30,000 people at its peak.

Monte Alban demonstrates connections with other major Mesoamerican civilizations, beginning in the late first millennium BC with Olmec-influenced monumental art, hieroglyphs and calendar dates. Later, after c. 200 BC, Maya influence dominates, to be replaced by that of Teotihuacán after AD 200. After AD 450 Monte Alban was at the height of its power, controlling the valley through a hierarchical administrative system. After c. AD 700 the settlement went into decline, losing valley-wide sovereignty and housing a much smaller population. It was abandoned around AD 950, although it continued to be used as a burial ground.

Teotihuacán

Teotihuacán was a massive urban centre at the southern end of ancient Lake Texcoco in the Valley of Mexico. At the height of its power, between AD 400 and 600, it was the most powerful influence in Mesoamerica and occupied some 21 km^2, housing a population possibly as high as 200,000. We shall look at the city more closely in Chapter 3.

Teotihuacán controlled the Valley of Mexico, but evidence of its influence can be found further afield in almost every important contemporary Mesoamerican site, including Monte Alban and many Mayan centres. It can be charted through the architectural style adopted for building pyramids, known as *talud-tablero*, through images of the rain-god Tlaloc and through some special pottery types. After c. AD 600 Teotihuacán influence declined, although the city itself survived till the mid-eighth century, when it was apparently sacked.

The Maya

The Maya civilization of the Yucatán peninsula in southern Mexico and the Petén jungle of Guatemala was the most extensive of the early Mesoamerican civilizations. During their formative period the Maya came under the influence of Olmec culture and later they were in contact with Teotihuacán, whose influence declined only after about AD 450.

Maya civilization was at its height between AD 300 and 900. Among the best known Maya sites are Tikal, Uaxactún, Altar de Sacrificios, Palenque and Copán. These were originally thought to be ceremonial centres, providing permanent residences for the elite alone, with the peasant population dispersed in the countryside and congregating at the centres only for religious festivals. However, more recent work has shown that at least some centres, such as Tikal, did house large populations, though none on such a scale as Teotihuacán. Similarly, although the Maya were once thought to have supported themselves by slash-and-burn agriculture, it is now known that they also employed more intensive methods of cultivation.

Maya society was clearly differentiated, with an elite which mobilized a vast amount of labour for the construction of immense ceremonial monuments, and equipped its burials with prestige goods made of exotic materials, such as jade and obsidian. The Maya developed hieroglyphic writing, which is found on elaborately carved stelae and other stone surfaces, such as the 'Hieroglyphic Stairway' at Copán, which has some 2,500 hieroglyphs carved on the 63 risers. They also developed a complex calendrical system based on astronomical calculations of astonishing accuracy. Maya civilization came to an apparently abrupt end around AD 900, a date traditionally taken to mark the end of the Classic Period of Mesoamerican development.

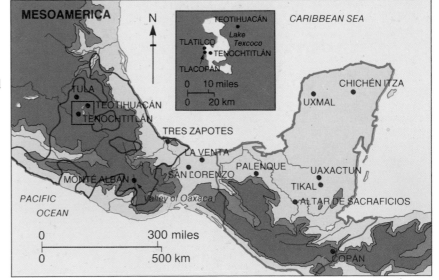

Top: Temple of the Foliated Cross at Palenque, westernmost of the Classic Maya sites, in the forest on the edge of the Chiapas Mountains.

The Toltecs

The Post-Classic Period in Mesoamerica, dated from AD 900 until the Spanish Conquest in the sixteenth century, saw the fall of many established cultures and the rise of new ones. Of these two stand out as dominant: the Toltecs, *c.* 900–1200, and the Aztecs, *c.* 1300–1520. For this period we are fortunate in having not only archaeological information, but also documentary sources, consisting of records made by Spaniards and Indian-Spanish Mestizos in the sixteenth century. In general, the period was characterized by an increasingly secular and militaristic society. Military conquest became the usual means of expansion, while human sacrifice was practised on an increasing scale; leaders and peoples were admired primarily for their prowess as warriors, and themes of war and sacrifice were prominent in art.

The Toltecs held sway over most of north central and western Mexico for some two centuries. They emerged out of the economic and political dislocation that followed the fall of Teotihuacán, to found their capital at Tula, ancient Tollan, *c.* 65 km north west of Teotihuacán. The Toltec subsistence economy was based primarily on maize agriculture, sometimes by dry-farming and sometimes by irrigation. Beans, squash, chilli peppers, amaranth and prickly pear were also cultivated. Meat came mainly from hunting deer, rabbits, rodents and birds; only dogs and turkeys were domesticated.

Tula was probably the largest Toltec settlement, and it is the only one that has been well explored archaeologically. The remains occupy some 12 km², spread over a central ridge and extending into the adjacent plain and up nearby hillsides; it may have housed between 30,000 and 50,000 people. The centre of the city was a monumental architectural complex known as the Main Civic Precinct, situated on the highest part of the ridge, containing temples, colonnaded halls, palaces, ball-courts, a skull rack (*tzompantli*) and other structures. Surface survey has shown that *c.* 10 km² of the settlement was occupied by closely packed houses, normally in groups of three or four clustered around small courtyards. The yards contain rectangular altars with burials inside them, probably of elder kinsmen, other people being buried beneath house floors. Craft production played a major role: specialist manufactures include obsidian artefacts, ceramics, textiles, wooden objects and ground stone tools and ornaments. Local trade was organized through market-place exchanges at Tula and in provincial centres, while the regional trade system, involving the whole Toltec area, was based on tributes paid by other peoples to the Toltec rulers and return gifts to local elites.

The Toltecs practised warfare on a considerable scale, and put an increasing emphasis on human sacrifice. They expanded by military conquest to dominate much of Mesoamerica, extending their control as far as Yucatán where they conquered the Maya centre of Chichén Itzá and dominated it for 200 years. Tula itself was destroyed, probably in 1178, and Toltec civilization collapsed, leaving only some fragmented groups in central Mexico, surviving at a lower level of social and cultural

Tula, the Toltec capital, is situated on an easily defensible ridge. The most important ceremonial building is the Temple of Quetzalcoatl (Pyramid B), shown here. The six 'Atlantean' stone statues which originally supported the roof take the form of warriors.

complexity. Such was the renown of the Toltecs, especially as warriors, that many other peoples claimed descent from them. Foremost among these were the Aztecs, who destroyed ancient codices and rewrote their own history in order to include a Toltec ancestry.

The Aztecs

The Aztecs flourished from about AD 1300 to the Spanish Conquest in 1520. Their origin is obscure, partly because they deliberately destroyed their own records, but they come into historical focus with the foundation of their capital, Tenochtitlán, predecessor of Mexico City, on Lake Texcoco in 1345. The formation of the Triple Alliance (with two other political centres, Texcoco and Tlacopan) in the fifteenth century allowed considerable expansion, and by the early sixteenth century the Aztecs had established hegemony over most of present-day Mexico. Their empire, which covered an area of some 300,000 km², was maintained through a system of tribute rather than direct administrative control, and within it some city-states were able to maintain a considerable degree of independence. The capital, Tenochtitlán, may have supported a population of 250,000, making it significantly larger than contemporary European capitals. It was a remarkable city and we shall describe it further in Chapter 3.

The subsistence base of the Aztecs, as of other Mesoamerican civilizations, was maize agriculture. At Tenochtitlán an extremely productive system known as *chinampa* was used, by which crop after crop could be harvested in quick succession from mats of marsh vegetation anchored in shallow water and covered with rich lake mud. Other cultivated plants included beans, squash, sweet potato, grain amaranth, manioc, avocado, tomato, cacao and various fruits. A variety of hallucinogenic plants was also cultivated, as were cotton and maguey for their fibres, and rubber trees. Meat came from wild deer, peccary and waterfowl, as well as domestic turkey and dog.

Trade was based on formal community-regulated markets, situated in centres throughout the empire. The greatest was in Tlatelolco, the northern part of Tenochtitlán. According to the Spanish Conquistador, Cortés himself, it was a colossal, splendid and colourful place, attended by some 60,000 people every day. It contained well-arranged displays of every type of merchandise found in the Aztec world, and both prices and practices were carefully supervised by appointed officials.

Aztec society was characterized by a clearly defined class system. At the top was the ruling class and below them the commoners or freemen. Below them was the group often described as serfs and at the bottom the slaves. All classes had definite legal rights and some social mobility was possible through state service, either military or mercantile.

The aspect of Aztec society that most shocked the Spanish Conquistadors was the wholesale practice of human sacrifice. Aztec religion was regulated by the calendar and dominated by sacrifice, which was thought necessary to ensure the continuation of the world, and even the daily rising of the sun. A special occasion, such as the dedication of a temple, required huge numbers of sacrifices: an

incredible 20,000 victims were allegedly sacrificed over four days at the dedication of the Great Temple of Huitzilopochtli at Tenochtitlán; the chest of each victim was opened with a stone knife and the still beating heart rapidly removed. The need for sacrificial victims led to wars solely to provide captives for this purpose, such as the so-called 'Flowery Wars' of the mid-fourteenth century. It is customary today to deplore the destruction of native cultures by European imperialists, and we have much sympathy with this attitude. However, it is difficult not to share the revulsion inspired in the Spaniards by this particular aspect of Aztec culture.

Top: The late Maya site at Uxmal in the Yucatán peninsula is noted for its elaborate architecture in the style known as Puuc; fret and lattice designs like those seen here are characteristic.

Centre: Stone head of the Aztec moon goddess, Coyolxauhqui, from Tenochtitlán.

South America

South American civilization is often thought of as synonymous with the Incas of Peru, whose huge empire and fabulous wealth, recorded by their Spanish conquerors, have caught the popular imagination. Yet this conception is mistaken: the Inca Empire flourished for barely a century before the Spanish Conquest, and was the last of a long line of Andean civilizations or near-civilizations. Some would deny the title of civilization even to the Incas themselves, since they lacked a writing system and their main settlements were not really cities.

The development of high culture in the Andes took a form that differed from Mesoamerica in a number of ways. In the first place, the subsistence base was different because of the ecology of the area, which consists of an arid coastal strip, behind which the Andes mountains rise abruptly to an average height of over 3,000 m. In the coastal zone the staple crops were maize, beans and squash, the crop complex characteristic of Mesoamerica and probably derived from there. Highland agriculture, however, depended in the main on root-crops, especially potato. Unlike Mesoamerica, domesticated animals were important here, although only the guinea pig and the muscovy duck seem to have been major food sources; of the others, llamas were kept mainly as pack animals and alpacas for wool. The co-ordination of production from two very different ecological regions was one of the challenges facing

societies in the Andes. The solution often favoured was the maintenance by societies in one zone of outposts or colonies in other zones, a pattern sometimes known as the 'vertical archipelago'.

Another difference between Andean and Mesoamerican development is in technology: metallurgy was developed early in South America and complex techniques were used, including the lost-wax method and a process known as 'depletion gilding', by which base metals are removed from the surface of alloys of gold, copper and other metals, leaving a layer of relatively pure gold.

Chavín and Páracas

Settled life based on farming became established throughout most of the region between 3000 and 1500 BC, and before very long complex societies had developed. The first stage showing signs of greater complexity lasted from about 1000–200 BC and is named after the site of Chavín de Huantar, a ceremonial centre of some size situated some 3,300 m up in the Andes in north central Peru. The Chavín culture, characterized by the dominance of the distinctive Chavín art style with its biomorphic motifs and flowing curvilinear lines, spread over the whole of northern Peru, both highland and lowland zones. It showed no evidence of marked social differentiation or organized armed conflict, and politically probably fell short of full state organization.

The Páracas peninsula, a desert region on the south coast of Peru, has yielded a series of very rich burials dating from about 700 BC to AD 200, and therefore contemporary with the Chavín culture. The most remarkable finds from these consist of sumptuous textiles used to clothe the dead and preserved by the desert conditions.

Moche and Nazca

The Early Intermediate Period that followed, c. 200 BC–AD 600, saw the rise of the first great city-states, the most important of which were Moche and Nazca. Moche, or Mochica, on the north coast of Peru, was characterized by large ceremonial centres with considerable evidence of social and economic differentiation and an administrative hierarchy. Grave goods in gold, silver and copper show a developed metal-working technology and illustrate the types of prestige goods favoured by the elite. Nazca, which developed out of the earlier Páracas culture, represents a parallel development in the southern coastal area of Peru.

Tiahuanaco and Huari

The Middle Horizon, c. AD 600–1000, saw the ascendancy of powerful regional states, especially Tiahuanaco, located on the south end of Lake Titicaca in Bolivia, and Huari, in the Mantaro River basin in the Peruvian Andes. Tiahuanaco was a large urban and ceremonial centre with huge megalithic constructions, including the famous monolith known as the 'Gateway of the Sun', which was carved from a single block of andesite weighing about 10 tonnes and featuring an anthropomorphic deity known as the 'Gateway God'. Tiahuanaco is usually thought to have been a cult centre, while Huari, a site without formal plan covering several square kilometres, became the capital of an empire that held sway over a large part of the central Andes.

Centre: Polychrome embroidered cloth from the Páracas cemetery, south Peru. These extraordinarily rich textiles of wool and cotton were found wrapped round well-preserved mummies.

Bottom: Ceremonial effigy vessel in the polychrome style characteristic of Nazca pottery.

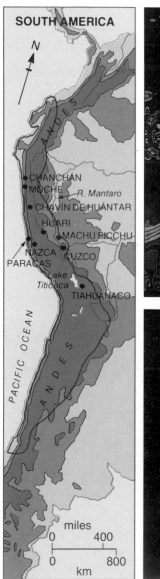

SOUTH AMERICA

N

CHANCHÁN
MOCHE
R. Mantaro
CHAVÍN DE HUÁNTAR
HUARI
MACHU PICCHU
NAZCA
CUZCO
PARACAS
Lake Titicaca
TIAHUANACO

PACIFIC OCEAN

ANDES

miles
0 — 400
0 — 800
km

Chimu

In about AD 800 the Huari Empire collapsed. A new pattern of regional autonomy then emerged consisting of numerous smaller kingdoms, and this lasted throughout the Late Intermediate Period (*c.* AD 1000–1476). The largest of these kingdoms was Chimu, centred on the north coast of Peru; its capital at Chan Chan, which we shall describe in Chapter 3, is one of the most impressive cities in the Andes. The Chimu kingdom expanded to cover an area of the northern Peruvian coast about 1,000 km long and is usually labelled an empire. Finally, in what is known as the Late Horizon (*c.* AD 1476–1532), it succumbed to the expanding power of an obscure group from the Urubamba area of Peru and was absorbed into the Inca Empire.

The Incas

Easily the largest and most powerful political unit in the whole of prehistoric America, the Inca Empire was, paradoxically, less developed in some ways than other early civilizations: the city was not the normal settlement type and writing was unknown. Nevertheless the empire, established over the period 1438–1476, stretched from the Maule River in southern Chile to southern Colombia (*c.* 4,200 km), and contained at its height an estimated six million people, in many different ethnic groups.

The highly centralized administration of this vast empire was a remarkable achievement. It was divided into four quarters and ruled from the capital, Cuzco, through a hierarchical pyramid of administrators. At the top was the emperor himself, while below him, in descending order, were the prefects of the four quarters, the governors of the provinces, lower officials and finally foremen responsible for groups of between 50 and 100 families. Most of the administrative posts were hereditary. Every social unit in the empire down to the smallest paid taxes in the form of labour service; this could take the form of cultivation of state-owned farmland, public building works or military service. This whole elaborate system, including census and tax records, was maintained without the use of writing; records were kept on *quipus*, mnemonic devices of knotted strings that were interpreted by trained specialists. The administration was made easier by an impressive system of roads (for men on foot or on animals – there were no wheeled vehicles) with way stations and distance markers.

The Incas adopted many of the political, social and religious infrastructures of the areas they conquered. Where established centres existed, they took them over, but the Inca settlement pattern was not truly urban. Most people lived in villages, and the typical administrative centre supported only a relatively small population of officials and support-ing staff. The Quechua language, however, was imposed on all conquered peoples, and five-sixths of all Andean Indians today still speak Quechua.

The emperor owned vast amounts of personal property, but none of it could be inherited by his successor; it remained under the dead king's owner-ship and could be used only to maintain his mummy in state and perpetuate his cult. Therefore each emperor had to amass his own land and other property in order to maintain his own lifestyle and reward his supporters. It has been suggested that this

extraordinary inheritance rule was the driving force behind the Incas' unrelenting territorial expansion.

Inca religion was basically a form of ancestor worship, with deceased emperors being especially honoured ancestors: their mummies were maintained in state and brought out to attend major ceremonies. The official imperial religion, the worship of the sun-god Inti, was in fact the worship of the divine ancestor of the ruling dynasty. Other deities made up a pantheon of gods. Religious ceremonies were numerous and elaborate; they usually involved animal sacrifices, but human sacrifice was practised only rarely and on a small scale.

In 1532 a mere 168 Spaniards under Francisco Pizarro brought the Inca Empire, weakened by civil war and the devastating effects of imported European diseases, to an easy end. The Inca administration was tailor-made for control by a very few: the Spaniards simply deposed the ruling elite and took over.

The 'lost city of the Incas', Machu Picchu, situated on a high ridge in the Peruvian Andes overlooking the Urubamba river, was rediscovered by Hiram Bingham in 1911.

The huge fortified complex of Sacsahuaman, adjoining the Inca capital of Cuzco, shows the massive Cyclopean masonry characteristic of Inca fortifications. The fort is thought to have taken 70 years to build.

2 The Origins of Civilization

Archaeologists and anthropologists have been studying the emergence of civilization since the late nineteenth century, and have proposed many different theories to account for this transformation in human society. We shall look briefly at the most influential of these theories before examining the whole process in greater detail. We can isolate five main groups of theories, each concentrating on a different key factor in the change.

Changes in subsistence practices

Economic practices, particularly those of the subsistence economy, are often put forward as primary factors. Particular attention has focused on the role of irrigation, prompted by the fact that the early civilizations are closely associated with large-scale irrigation agriculture. In its most developed form, as propounded by the American scholar Karl Wittfogel, this theory is known as the 'hydraulic hypothesis'. Wittfogel's basic argument runs as follows. In the arid environments in which many of the civilizations emerged, farming dependent on natural rainfall was impossible: in order to cultivate the soil farmers had to transport water to the fields. Irrigation on a large scale involves planning and constructing canals and dykes, regulating water use, maintaining the irrigation works (by dredging the channels and repairing breaches in the dykes) and protecting them against attack. The organization of all these activities necessitated some kind of central authority, whose personnel, being in control of the vital water supply, would have tremendous power.

Opposite: Irrigation can turn barren desert into fertile fields, as can be seen here in northern Sudan.

For the early civilizations of the alluvial plains the rivers served multiple purposes, as sources of water for irrigation, as suppliers of fish and as routes for water-borne transport. This Assyrian relief carving comes from Khorsabad in northern Mesopotamia, close to the river Tigris.

This provided the basis for the emergence of civilization in a particular form, known as 'oriental despotism', characterized by a single, highly centralized and supremely powerful authority, such as the temple in Sumer, or the palace in Egypt.

The prehistorian Gordon Childe also thought that irrigation was important. However, he emphasized not only the centralized organization required to run irrigation projects, but also the *productivity* of irrigation agriculture. The fertility of irrigated fields was such that a surplus could be produced and used to support full-time craftsmen – workers in metal, pottery and stone – as well as specialist food-producers and administrators. Such economic specialization is often regarded as one of the most important features of civilization.

Population pressure

A second major group of theories sees population pressure as the prime mover in the development of civilization. This is often part of a wider view, based on the principle that population expansion is a permanent feature of human evolution and is responsible for all or most major changes. Proponents of this view hold that there is a natural tendency for population to expand unless restrained by the sort of factors pinpointed by the economist Thomas Malthus in the early nineteenth century: limited food supply, disease and natural predators. This natural tendency, in the environment of the alluvial valleys (with their fertile soils and potential for highly productive agriculture) allowed a rapid and massive population expansion. Some believe that this led directly to new developments in economic and social organization, since the family-based subsistence practices and organization based on kinship relations that characterize small-scale societies could not support large communities. Others take the view that population growth in itself was not enough to trigger the emergence of civilization; they add another component: conflict.

Conflict

The American scholar Robert Carneiro, one of the main proponents of this view, argues that in a confined area, where expansion into neighbouring

areas is not possible (because of environmental factors, such as mountains, deserts or seas, or because these areas are already occupied by other people), growth in population will generate conflict between groups who are obliged to compete for land and other resources. Communities will tend to get bigger and to defend themselves against attack from outside. Leaders will be chosen to organize warfare and, if successful, may acquire more general and permanent authority in the community, eventually becoming an established ruling class. The population of defeated communities may be absorbed by the winners as a lower class, and thus the form and constituents of state society may be established.

Marxist interpretations of the origin of civilization place strong emphasis on economic factors, including agricultural intensification and craft specialization, but they too emphasize conflict. This is not conflict between different communities, however, but rather *class* conflict between the 'haves' and 'have-nots' in the rapidly differentiating society of an emergent civilization. According to this view, as propounded for instance by the Russian scholar Igor M. Diakonoff, the state emerges as a result of class conflict, and its function is to maintain the dominance of the ruling class.

Exchange

Another factor often emphasized in the discussion of how civilization developed, and sometimes considered of primary importance (e.g. by the American archaeologists Johnson and Wright), is exchange, either long distance or within the region of the emerging civilization. According to supporters of this view, the development of large-scale trade – particularly necessary in Mesopotamia, which lacked many of the materials necessary for the maintenance of civilized life (including metal, stone and timber for building) – led to the development of a centralized organization to control the procurement, transport and distribution of the raw materials and other goods. This organization provided the basis for an authority that could be extended to control other aspects of society, including subsistence activities and manufacturing crafts.

Social organization

The final group of theories sees social factors as primary, and considers that changes in technology, subsistence practices, trade and so on followed rather than preceded changes in social institutions. The American anthropologist Elman Service argues that the crucial process here is the institutionalization of centralized leadership. He believes that in certain circumstances (the special environmental conditions of the great river valleys) the authority of hereditary chiefdoms became increasingly institutionalized as both the number of people and the size of the area ruled increased. The outcome was the emergence of what may be called true government – and civilization. Others consider that there were a number of interlocking and interacting factors. The American archaeologist Robert M. Adams, for example, has argued that, in the case of Mesopotamia, economic specialization, social differentiation and the centralization of power evolved together, each contributing to the development of the others.

The timescale

Even some of the simplest questions about the development of civilization can be rather hard to answer: How long did it take for civilization to emerge in the first instance? How long did it take for later civilizations to develop? How long do civilizations last?

In order to decide how long a process took, we must first define a starting point, and this is in many ways an arbitrary process. It could be said that the first civilization took three million years to develop, taking as a starting point the appearance of the first hominids, or 30,000 years, starting with the first modern men, or 5,000 years, starting with the first farmers. However, a more meaningful starting point is the stage at which the development of the communities that were to become civilized diverged from others, in the same general area, that did not develop the same level of complexity. In the case of Mesopotamia – the world's first civilization – we have some evidence on this.

At about 6000 bc there were village communities in many parts of Western Asia, from the Mediterranean coast in the west to the central Asian highlands in the east and from the Caspian and Black Seas in the north to the Persian Gulf and the Indian Ocean in the south. The desert areas were probably unoccupied, as was the southern part of the Mesopotamian plain, which could not be cultivated without irrigation. The first settlements in the southern plain can be dated to about 5000 bc or a little earlier (about 6000 BC in real years: lower-case letters are used here for uncorrected radiocarbon dates, capitals for corrected radiocarbon dates and true calendar dates; see Chapter 11).

These settlements, of the 'Ubaid culture, are different in some important ways from their immediate predecessors and contemporaries in adjacent areas. They are often rather large (occupying about 4 hectares on average), and they are based on irrigation farming. However, both large sites and irrigation occur occasionally in other parts of Western Asia. The feature of the 'Ubaid communities that seems to be truly unique is the occurrence on all sites that have been excavated on a significant scale of a central shrine or temple – which can be seen as the forerunner of the later Mesopotamian temple. It seems reasonable, therefore, to see the run-up to civilization as beginning with the first settlement of the southern Mesopotamian plain in about 6000 BC.

What about the other end of the process? When can we say that full civilization has emerged in Mesopotamia? This is another arbitrary point, but we might take the emergence of large urban centres and the appearance of writing as suitable indicators. On the site of Uruk itself, these appear in the later Uruk period, when the city occupied c. 80 hectares and the first evidence of writing appeared as simplified pictures drawn on clay tablets.

We are short of radiocarbon dates for this period, and archaeologists have tended to accept a reconstructed 'historical' chronology which would place the beginning of the Uruk period at c. 3800 BC and the late Uruk period at c. 3400 or 3300 BC. We believe that this chronology is still too short (though it is longer than that once advocated) and that the few available radiocarbon dates, once corrected, suggest instead a date of c. 4500 BC for the beginning of the Uruk period and c. 4000 BC for late Uruk. If we accept these dates, they indicate a period of some 2,000 years (6000–4000 BC) for the emergence of civilization in Mesopotamia. This may cause some

Timechart of early civilizations The chart shows the chronological extent of the civilizations discussed in this book; it does *not* represent a history of civilization since many civilizations, especially later ones, are omitted. The maps show the civilizations under discussion, indicated by dots, and the areas where other urban civilizations occurred, indicated by hatching.

	3500 BC	3000 BC	2500 BC	2000 BC	1500 BC	1000 BC
MESOPOTAMIA						
EGYPT						
			THE INDUS			
				CHINA		
				MINOANS		
					MYCENAEANS	

surprise among scholars accustomed to traditional, shorter chronologies, but we believe that a long timespan for the emergence of the first civilization both accords with the available chronological evidence and makes good sense in terms of the processes involved.

Do we find this rather long gestation period when we look at other early civilizations? For most areas we do not have evidence as detailed as we do for Mesopotamia, but many of them show a development of around 1,000 years or more. In China the Erlitou phase, which shows the beginning of 'civilized' features such as *hangtu* palaces and bronze ritual vessels, was already in existence by *c.* 2000 BC, some 700 years before the established Shang civilization as found at Anyang. In the Aegean the entire third millennium BC can be seen as the run-up to the emergence of Minoan civilization *c.* 2000 BC. In Mesoamerica the Pre-Classic period, characterized by maize agriculture and the appearance of ceremonial centres, begins *c.* 2000 BC, almost a millennium before the emergence of the earliest Mesoamerican civilization, the Olmecs. It is likely that periods equally long were involved in the gestation of the other early civilizations that probably developed independently, in Egypt and the Indus Valley.

The later Mediterranean civilizations of Greece and Rome are different. Their gestation periods seem shorter, perhaps a few centuries, but then they developed in a context in which civilization was no longer new; cities existed within relatively easy reach and many of the individual features of civilization were available to be adopted.

Our final question is 'How long do civilizations last?' Again the answer depends upon issues of definition, and we must decide just how serious a disruption in continuity must be in order to constitute the end of a civilization. Some civilizations came to an apparently complete and perhaps sudden end, among them the Indus civilization, which lasted perhaps 600 years (*c.* 2500–1900 BC), the Minoan and Mycenaean civilizations, with a combined length of about 800 years (*c.* 2000–1200 BC), and most of the Mesoamerican civilizations: the Olmecs lasted for perhaps a thousand years (through most of the first millennium BC), Teotihuacán about 300 years (*c.* AD 400–700), the Maya about 600 years (*c.* AD 300–900), while the Toltecs and Aztecs lasted about two centuries each; but perhaps they should all be regarded as phases of one Mesoamerican civilization. The Inca Empire lasted less than a century, but was brought to an end by the Spanish conquest in 1532. By contrast, the great ancient civilizations of Mesopotamia, Egypt and China can be argued to have survived for some 3,000 years each, with essential continuity in political structure, social organization, art, architecture and writing systems.

The classical civilizations are not directly comparable. In one sense we could argue that modern western culture is simply the latest phase of classical civilization, which has therefore lasted almost as long as Mesopotamia, Egypt and China. However, we must not forget the Dark Ages, with their very tenuous hold on the continuity of civilization; and also the many contributions to modern civilization from non-classical sources.

Some civilizations seem to have qualities of considerable resilience that allow them to survive for very long periods, while others 'die young'. We shall look at this in greater detail in Chapter 10.

1000 BC	500 BC	BC/AD	500	1000	1500

CLASSICAL GREECE

ROME

OLMEC

MONTE ALBAN

TEOTIHUACAN

MAYA

TOLTEC

AZTEC

MOCHE AND NAZCA

TIAHUANACO AND HUARI

CHIMU AND INCA

1000 BC	500 BC	BC/AD	500	1000	1500

Pathways to civilization

In order to find out how civilizations emerged we must turn our attention to the pre-civilized societies that preceded them. Social evolution can be measured in a number of different ways according to whether we concentrate on, say, physical development, technology, subsistence economy or social organization. Although this may seem an arbitrary separation of actually interlocked and inseparable components of human society, it is a useful device and reflects the divergent approaches of different groups of scholars.

Physical development

The development of physiology need not delay us long, since physically modern man, *Homo sapiens sapiens*, had evolved by some 35,000 to 30,000 years ago. No significant changes in physical evolution have occurred since then, so the whole cultural development of man since that period has been enacted by men and women who were physically and mentally like ourselves, with the same range of natural abilities and skills and with the same limitations. Clearly civilization was not the product of a superior species or sub-species of man.

The technology employed by the craftsmen of the early civilizations often involved complex processes and the combination of different materials. In this example of Sumerian inlay work, from the 'Royal Standard of Ur', pieces of shell and stones of different colours were inlaid in a bitumen background.

Technology

The development of technology is one of the easiest aspects of human evolution to study. Indeed it provided the basis for the first useful division of prehistoric time into successive ages of Stone, Bronze and Iron. In this sphere we can see evolution in terms of *progress*, since it is relatively easy to develop objective tests of efficiency for tools, and technological developments like the introduction of different metal alloys can also be assessed in these terms, such as the introduction of bronze, an alloy of copper and tin, to replace copper as the main material for weapons and tools. There seems to have been fairly general progress on the technological level throughout prehistory, but within this general progression civilization is characterized by markedly greater variety and complexity. Compared with earlier communities, civilized societies exploited a far greater range of materials and used new manufacturing techniques, some involving elaborate equipment and lengthy, multi-phase processes such as the 'lost-wax' method of bronze casting, which enabled very complex objects to be produced. Such techniques imply the existence of full-time craft specialists, as they could not be organized on a part-time basis. Most early Old World civilizations had also made major technical innovations, potentially able to harness vast amounts of energy, such as the wheel and the sailing boat, although these are not found in the American civilizations.

Today scholars do not generally regard technological development as playing an important role in promoting change in society. In some ways this seems perverse, since we live in a society which is being transformed by new technology; maybe it is a reluctance to accept this that inclines us to reject an important role for technology in the past.

Subsistence economy

If we look at social evolution in terms of subsistence economy, we can see a major division between communities based on hunting and gathering (food collecting) and those based on farming (food producing). Although recent studies have shown

Most of the early civilizations increased the energy at their disposal by harnessing the power of the wind to propel sailing boats. This Egyptian New Kingdom wall painting shows a reed boat of the kind used on the Nile.

that this division is not as simple or as complete as was once thought, the distinction is still a real one. For millions of years men were foragers: they hunted game, caught fish, collected shellfish, picked nuts and fruits and gathered other plants. Over the last 10,000 years or so, however, most communities throughout the world have come to be based on farming: the cultivation of plants and the rearing of animals. This transformation took place in several different regions at different times, and it took a number of different forms. It occurred in Western Asia and the Far East from *c.* 10,000 bc, in Central America from *c.* 5000 bc, and possibly in several other areas as well. Farming is much more productive than hunting and gathering: even simple practices can support population densities of 5 to 10 people per km², while hunting and gathering – even in favourable environments – can rarely support more than 0.1 people per km².

Civilization would be inconceivable without farming. Indeed simple farming was not enough to support the kind of population densities associated with civilization; these required the *intensification* of farming techniques. Intensification is not limited to irrigation; for example, in the Mediterranean region we find the addition of olive and vine to cereals to produce the 'Mediterranean triad', or polyculture. This enabled farmers to make productive use of land unsuitable for cereals, and also provided a tradeable surplus. There was also the introduction of the plough (pulled by oxen or other animals) and what the British archaeologist Andrew Sherratt has called the 'Secondary Products Revolution' – the exploitation of animals for dairy products and wool, which is much more productive than keeping them for meat alone. Intensification of farming was a necessary condition for the emergence of civilization; but whether it was also a sufficient condition is more doubtful.

Social organization

We may be able to recognize in the archaeological record the development of different types of society, as defined by anthropologists such as Elman Service. The earliest societies associated with a hunting and gathering way of life seem to have been of the *band* type, characterized by small territorial groups held together by ties of kinship and with no division of labour or differentiation of status except by sex and age. Such bands largely lack political organization, and there are only minimal mechanisms to link bands together in larger groups.

The next stage of development, associated generally but not rigidly with the emergence of farming, is the *tribe*. Tribes are larger than bands and have developed a variety of mechanisms that cut across local residential groups and serve to integrate the larger communities; these are known as *sodalities* and include age groups, warrior groups, secret societies and religious societies. Tribes show little economic specialization and their organization remains largely egalitarian.

The *chiefdom*, the next stage, is generally associated with complex farming societies. Chiefdoms are still based on kinship, but are no longer egalitarian, being characterized by a hierarchical ordering of statuses with a central figure – the chief – at the top. The economic system is based on redistribution, associated with considerable specialization both in the subsistence economy and in craft practice. Chiefs have authority to organize economic, social and religious activities, but they lack exclusive access to strategic resources and the power to control through coercion.

The next level of organization – the *state* – is often thought to correspond to civilization, although this view can be challenged. State societies are larger and more complex than chiefdoms. They are characterized by a true class society, very strongly stratified and no longer based primarily on kinship. The power of the ruling class is based on differential or exclusive access to strategic resources and backed by force, in the form of armies and police.

We could characterize human evolution in other ways, in terms of the development of information technology, for instance, or in terms of aesthetic achievement. However, such criteria have so far not been used to provide the basis for widely used schemes of human development.

Hunters and gatherers

Man has lived by hunting animals and gathering plants for by far the longest part of his existence. The British archaeologist Desmond Collins has calculated that half the people who have ever lived have been hunters – if, for the purposes of discussion, we equate man with tool-making, which began around 2.5 million years ago. What were these prehistoric hunting communities like, and why did men give up this type of existence to become farmers? As a result of their generally mobile existence and lack of material goods as compared to farmers, hunters have left far fewer traces in the archaeological record. However, we can turn to anthropological studies of more recent communities to build up a picture of what life was like for ancient hunter-gatherers.

Above: Early hunters have sometimes left us vivid pictures of their activities in paintings or engravings on cave walls or open rock faces. This detail of a rock painting from Algeria shows part of a large hunting scene.

Right: Present-day Eskimos still live mainly by hunting large mammals and by fishing, as seen here in north-west Greenland.

Hunting communities as documented by anthropologists are essentially very small-scale societies, and they are usually organized as bands, numbering from about 25 to (occasionally) more than 100 people. These bands are made up of related nuclear families and are patrilocal – women live with their husband's family after marriage and children therefore grow up among their father's relatives. All activities take place within the family or the band and are therefore kinship-based. There is very little specialization of labour, except by age and sex, and no separate economic groups such as specialist craftsmen, or economic institutions such as markets. Authority, which exists on a very modest scale only, is vested in family heads and ephemeral leaders; there is no separate political organization – nothing at all that could be labelled a government or a legal system. Religion likewise has no separate existence; cult practice is part of total family and band activity.

The nature of the search for food itself is very variable, depending in the main on differences in the natural environment. While Inuit (Eskimo) communities live almost exclusively on fish and large mammals, the Kalahari Bushmen supplement their hunting of a wide range of game with the collection of an enormous number of plant foods, concentrating on the ubiquitous and abundant mongomongo nut. In almost all cases, however, there is no shortage of food. Population controls such as famine and disease are certainly not ever-present threats, though they may come into play in times of exceptional climatic conditions. It is likely that *permanent* famine and *widespread* epidemic disease are the creation of 'advanced' societies, not the legacy of simpler ones.

Although most hunting societies studied by anthropologists are at the band level of organization, a few are more complex. The best known of these are the Indians of the north-west coast of North America, who lived in large villages and had a social organization at the chiefdom level. It is clear that in very rich natural environments a hunting and gathering way of life can support relatively large populations and complex organizations, but in the ethnographic record at least such societies are rare.

The extent to which it is justifiable to use modern societies of primitive type as analogues for societies in much earlier stages of human evolution has been the subject of much debate. Many now feel that we cannot justify using ethnographic analogy for very early stages of development, but that with due caution we may use such evidence when studying societies of the last 30,000 to 40,000 years, that is, those associated with people physically and mentally like ourselves. The archaeological evidence for the Upper Palaeolithic and Mesolithic periods can be interpreted as giving support to this view. This evidence – taken from living sites, kill sites, manufacturing sites, burials and so on – provides information about the size of residential groups (usually small: 10–25 people), their subsistence activities, their degree of mobility (usually fairly high) and their manufacturing techniques. There is, interestingly, a general absence of evidence relating to social differentiation in dwellings or burials, which would seem to suggest an egalitarian organization of society. It is likely that these communities were organized as bands, like hunting communities of recent times.

In some cases, however, we have evidence of more complex societies with indications of hierarchy. An example comes from a series of rich burials from Sungir, some 200 km from Moscow. One burial was of an adult male who originally wore fur clothes, on to which had been sewn beads and teeth of arctic fox. Another burial was of two boys with similar clothes, with ivory fastenings for the collars. Alongside each boy was a spear made of mammoth tusk. Both graves also contained other grave goods, including animal carvings on bone and ivory. These may well have been burials of rich and powerful people, more than just family or band headmen, perhaps true chiefs like those of the Indians of the north-west coast of North America.

Since man remained a hunter for so long and took to farming so recently, we might ask why he ever abandoned the hunting economy. Until fairly recently the answer would have been thought obvious. Hunting was characterized as a 'catch-as-catch-can' existence, the life of a hunter being barely distinguishable from that of the animals he hunted – in the much quoted words of the seventeenth-century philosopher Thomas Hobbes, 'nasty, brutish and short'. It was assumed that farming was vastly and obviously superior; that once developed it would have been swiftly adopted and hunting would rapidly have become obsolete. This attitude has been labelled with some acerbity by the American anthropologist Marshall Sahlins as 'Neolithic ethnocentrism', and has recently been rejected on a number of different grounds.

First and foremost, new anthropological fieldwork has shown that the hunters' way of life is very different from the accepted 'backward' image. Even in harsh environments like the Kalahari desert of southern Africa or the Australian outback the hunting life is *not* difficult; people rarely spend more than three or four hours a day looking for food and have plenty of spare time, which they spend mostly in sleeping, talking and playing games.

Theoretical considerations have also played a part in our changing conception of hunters. In a very influential article entitled 'The original affluent society', Marshall Sahlins suggested that the lack of equipment and material comforts characteristic of hunters should not be regarded as an indication of poverty. Poverty and affluence, he argued, refer to relationships between perceived needs and the means available to meet them. The hunters are affluent because their needs are few and easily met, by means available to all. Poverty, paradoxically, is the product of an acquisitive society in which perceived needs are infinite but the means of fulfilling them are inadequate and restricted to the few. This view has been adopted with enthusiasm by many scholars; perhaps too much enthusiasm, since we can detect more than a faint echo of the 'noble savage' in the portrayal of hunting societies by some writers today. Certainly it is easy to see why people turn from the many unattractive aspects of our own society to admire the classless hunters, living for the day alone, in close communion with nature, unburdened by thoughts of the morrow, or by ownership of land or belongings, free to move at will in the forest or desert, unrestrained by the many laws and regulations that govern our own lives. But was it really so idyllic? The fact is that hunting was abandoned as a way of life in all but the most inhospitable corners of the world. There are barely 30,000 hunters left in the world today and it is unlikely that many of them will survive at the end of this century. For one reason or another, people did choose a different way of life – and it was one that became the dominant mode throughout the world.

Small groups of Kalahari Bushmen continue to live very much as their ancestors did thousands of years ago. Here a group sit around a fire in front of a hut.

Early farmers

The 'Neolithic Revolution'

In the early part of the modern epoch, which dates from the last retreat of the ice sheets some 10,000 years ago, communities in several different parts of the world changed in a very important way: they ceased to be hunters and gatherers, or exclusively so, and they began to cultivate crops and in some cases also to rear domesticated animals. In the 1920s Gordon Childe was one of the first archaeologists to appreciate the full significance of this change, which he called the 'Neolithic Revolution' or the 'Food-producing Revolution'. It has recently become customary to criticize this terminology because it implies that there was a sudden and dramatic change, whereas in fact the process was a slow and gradual one with cumulative rather than sudden effects. None the less, it was revolutionary in the sense that it brought about profound and irreversible changes.

The most obvious change was a large population increase: as we have seen, farming economies can support population densities higher than hunting economies in even the most prolific natural environments. This is probably what made the changes irreversible: once the population had increased it would have been impossible to revert to the earlier hunting and gathering way of life without causing widespread starvation.

Another change associated with farming was the adoption of a settled way of life. Although some hunting communities which depend on coastal and riverine food sources may live in permanent or semi-permanent settlements, most hunters are mobile. Most farmers, by contrast, are sedentary and live in permanent villages. This encouraged the development of more substantial architecture, not only for houses, but also for places to store and prepare food, and to perform ritual activities. Technology also developed: new techniques include the use of ground and polished stone, the manufacture of pottery and experiments with metallurgy. Trade or exchange increased in quantity and scope, with some materials, such as obsidian, being traded over very long distances. In the Near East in the seventh millennium bc obsidian from Anatolia reached Beidha in southern Jordan, about 900 km away; in America in the second millennium bc high quality grey obsidian from El Chayel in Guatemala reached Early Formative San Lorenzo in Veracruz, nearly 600 km away.

At the same time religious life seems to have become more elaborate: shrines, objects such as figurines, burial practices and other cult activities all testify to more complex ceremonial. Social organization was probably now at the level of the tribe, still organized on the basis of kinship and fundamentally egalitarian in nature, but involving larger residential groups than in the earlier bands and with more sodalities (see p. 43).

We know from both anthropology and archaeology that none of these developments is associated exclusively with farming; most or all of them are occasionally found in hunting societies like those of the Indians of the north-west coast of North America (see p. 44). However, there is no escaping the general correlation between farming and major developments in social organization, technology and ritual activity.

Where and when?

The development of farming took place in several different parts of the world at different times; it took many forms and involved various different species of plants and animals. Probably the earliest centre was in the Near East, where between 10,000 and 6000 bc communities over a wide area came to cultivate wheat, barley and a variety of leguminous plants. These communities also domesticated a number of animals: dogs, sheep, goats and, rather later, cattle and pigs.

In Eastern Asia farming seems to have developed early in a number of centres. In north China broomcorn millet, foxtail millet and various vegetables were cultivated perhaps before 5000 bc, with wheat and barley being introduced rather later. In south China, Vietnam and Thailand, by contrast, rice was the main cultivated cereal, but root crops, water-loving vegetables and fruit trees were also cultivated from around 7000 bc onwards. Domesticated animals were less important than in Western Asia: pigs may have been domesticated early, while cattle, sheep and goats were probably introduced from the west.

In Africa, the northern areas flanking the Mediterranean and the Nile Valley practised farming based on wheat, barley, sheep and goat (all introduced from Western Asia) and cattle (either introduced or domesticated locally). By 4000 bc farming was established throughout most of the area and possibly considerably earlier in Egypt, though

Above: Following the beginnings of farming and the adoption of settled village life came the development of more complex technology. The technique of firing clay to form pottery was used for a variety of objects, including figurines such as these from Vinča in Yugoslavia.

Right: Fine pottery vessels were also made, like this painted example from Lianokladi in Greece.

Rice was the dominant cereal crop throughout Eastern Asia. It was cultivated either in wet fields or on terraces similar to these present-day examples in the Philippines.

claims of plant cultivation in the Nile Valley at around 16,000 bc have now been discounted. South of the Sahara there was separate domestication of both grain and root crops, the most important crops being finger millet, sorghum, bulrush millet and yams. Dating is uncertain in this area, but it is possible that the first experiments with farming may have begun as early as the fourth millennium bc. No indigenous animals were domesticated, but cattle from north Africa eventually penetrated south of the Sahara, reaching the East African highlands by about 1000 bc.

In the Americas more than 100 native plants in various parts of the continent were domesticated before the European conquest. They included today's staple crops: maize, first cultivated in the area of modern Mexico, and potatoes, which originated in highland Bolivia or Peru. Other cultivated plants were beans, squashes, pumpkins, sunflowers, sweet potatoes, pineapples, tomatoes and cacao. The crucial plant for the development of sedentary life was maize, the only native American cereal. Maize was first domesticated as early as 7000 bc, but it did not play a very important part in human diet until about 2000 bc, when a hybridized and much more productive form evolved. No animals other than dogs, and later ducks and turkeys, were ever domesticated in Mesoamerica. Apart from these, the only other domesticated animals found in the whole continent were the llama, the alpaca and the guinea pig, which were domesticated in the Andes.

Throughout the world an enormous variety of plants and a much smaller number of animals were domesticated by man, and most of those that are eaten today were domesticated at an early stage. The

crucial plants were the cereals: wheat, barley, millet, rice and maize. Other plants could provide a useful supplement to the products of hunting and gathering, but it was only cereals, which in their later hybridized forms produced vastly greater yields than their wild ancestors, that could support significantly higher population densities. Domesticated animals did not, apparently, play a major role in the Neolithic Revolution, although they were to become important in later farming economies. Only in Western Asia were animals certainly domesticated at an early stage, and even there some communities flourished on a combination of cultivated plants and wild game.

Domesticated animals were important in Old World farming, but played only a minor role in the Americas. In the Andes llamas, seen here in highland Bolivia, were used mainly as pack animals.

47

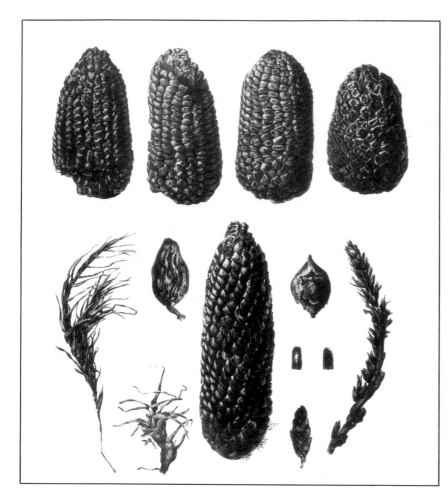

The only cereal cultivated in the New World was maize. These cobs of maize were found at Ancón on the central coast of Peru, exceptionally well preserved in the dry desert conditions.

Why?

Why did hunters all over the world abandon their apparently easy and attractive way of life to become farmers, tied to the soil and a hard, sometimes gruelling, working regime? We have already mentioned the changes that followed the introduction of farming: the settled existence, the development of technology, art and architecture, the elaboration of ritual life. Did these features offer an incentive to change? That is most unlikely: the slow pace of these developments, as indicated by the archaeological record, means that the hunters on the verge of becoming farmers would have had to be equipped with second sight – a long-distance vision of glories to come – to make a decision informed in this way. In terms of short-term changes, which we must assume is all they could actually judge, they would probably be exchanging less work for more, a more varied diet for a more restricted one, a mobile life for a sedentary one, freedom of movement for bondage to the fields and to the agricultural timetable. This is not a change that appeals to modern hunters. 'Why should we plant', say the Bushmen, 'when there are so many mongomongo nuts in the world?' Why indeed?

There is no general consensus as to why the change took place, though there are groups of theories that cluster around a few major themes. What is certain is that it was not a freak occurrence arising from a unique historical situation; if it were, the phenomenon would not be so widespread. Many consider that the answer must lie in the natural environment, and this seems sensible enough. Even the Bushmen might look more favourably on agriculture if their supply of mongomongo nuts were

to decline drastically. And certainly the changing environments of the postglacial period in all parts of the world brought about major changes in the potential food sources available to man. Most scholars, however, prefer to see the environment as allowing rather than determining the change.

Perhaps the most convincing explanation that could apply in all cases is population pressure. If population expansion is a natural feature of human (and animal) existence, then intensified techniques of obtaining food provide an alternative to starvation or possibly unpopular social population controls such as abortion, infanticide or even warfare.

Others consider that social changes – changes in the organization of society – preceded and were responsible for changes in the subsistence economy and population levels. For example, it has been suggested that the emergence of incipient elites in hunting societies might have promoted a change in the way food was regarded: where previously it had been thought of as public property, to be shared, it came to be regarded as privately owned and an indicator of wealth. This would favour the production of types of food that could be not only stored but also produced in increasing quantities; both are features of farming rather than hunting economies.

Whatever the reasons for the development of farming, the change has taken place in every area in which civilization later appeared, often several millennia before. Farming provided the subsistence base on which all the ancient civilizations arose, so it is reasonable to assume that civilization could not have developed without the prior achievement of this first 'revolution'.

Life in early farming communities

What was life like in early farming villages? How did it differ from that in hunters' camps? To get a picture of tribal life in general we must turn again to the records of ethnographers and anthropologists, while for direct, though partial, information about early villages we must look at the archaeological record, taking as examples two early farming villages, one in Iraq and one in Mexico.

Tribes, though larger than bands, are still small-scale societies: settlements rarely support more than 200 people and are often much smaller. Social relations are still dominated by kinship ties, but tribes are characterized by particular types of kinship system which occur only rarely in hunting bands. These are known as descent groups; they vary widely in the way in which descent is reckoned, but all are bodies of kinsmen united by common ancestry. The existence of descent groups is connected with territoriality and the ownership of land, which is of critical importance to sedentary farmers, but not to mobile hunters. The interest of descent groups in land is frequently reinforced by the existence of ancestor cults, with the ancestors – sometimes physically present on the land itself in their tombs – validating the claims of the living to that land. As well as descent groups there are others, such as age groups or cult associations, which cut across residential groupings, and often across descent groups as well; they are important because they counteract tendencies towards hostility and fission.

Kinship also dominates other aspects of tribal life. For instance, the basic unit of production is the

Above left: Ovens such as this, in the wall of a house at Jarmo, would have been used for the baking of bread.

Above right: Samples of grain in fired clay found at Jarmo can be identified by making casts from their impression. A comparison is made here between the impression of a spikelet of wild emmer wheat (top) and a similar fresh spikelet (bottom).

Centre: Among the new technology developed by early farming communities was the grinding and polishing of stone.

family, either nuclear or extended. This 'domestic' or 'familial' mode of production is characterized by the division of labour according to age and sex, but no other specialization. Exchange too takes place largely within a kinship context in tribal societies, particularly in the form of gift exchange. This could range from feast giving to formal exchanges such as dowries and bride prices. Cult activities also take place within the kinship structure. Indeed, as in the case of ancestor cults, they may directly reinforce and perpetuate it.

Tribal societies support a greater number of social statuses than bands, but they are still basically egalitarian. Leaders there may be – village headmen, clan leaders, cult leaders or more than one of these – but they are charismatic rather than hereditary leaders. Their positions have to be earned and maintained; they cannot be passed on to children or other chosen successors, and they can be lost through removal of popular support.

Most early farming societies were probably of this general type. Let us look at the site of Jarmo in the Zagros mountains of Iraqi Kurdistan, occupied in the seventh millennium bc, as a representative of the simple farming communities of Western Asia. Located on a steep bank overlooking a wadi (a seasonal watercourse), the village was a permanent settlement occupying between 1.5 and 2 hectares and containing about 25 houses. These were rectilinear mud-brick or pisé structures, consisting of several rooms and often a small courtyard; each may have housed a nuclear family, which would give a total population of between 100 and 200 people. The economy was based on mixed farming (einkorn and emmer wheats and barley; sheep and goats, and in the latest stage also pigs). Technology was generally

simple: flint and obsidian tools were used. Obsidian was imported from the Lake Van area of eastern Turkey, some 320 km away. The only remarkable objects were some finely worked stone bowls. Pottery was absent from all but the uppermost layers of the site, though a considerable number of unbaked clay figurines of humans and animals have been found.

We shall take the site of Tierras Largas, situated on the Atoyac river north of the city of Oaxaca, Mexico, as an example of a simple farming community in Mesoamerica in the Early Formative period. At about 1300 bc Tierras Largas occupied about 0.5 hectares and consisted of some 6 to 12 houses; by about 900 bc it had grown to cover about 1.5 hectares with some 12 to 22 houses. The houses were rectangular wattle-and-daub structures, sometimes grouped around open areas. The people lived by maize cultivation accompanied by hunting, and the fact that each house was associated with 2 to 6 storage pits suggests that the household was the unit of production. It has been estimated that each of these pits could have held enough maize to support a family for a year. Technology was simple. As at Jarmo, flint and obsidian were worked for tools. Bone needles were probably used for sewing or basketry work, while fragments of pottery indicate the use of cooking vessels. Nothing was made that requires or suggests craft specialization.

Sites like Jarmo and Tierras Largas are clearly settlements of simple tribal societies. While excavation of the sites of many farming villages in all areas of the world suggests this type of simple organization, there were also more complex settlements, especially at a later stage, and we shall look at these next.

49

Complex farming societies

The societies that immediately preceded the emergence of full civilization show significant changes from the simple farming communities that we have just discussed. They were much larger, with signs of strong central organization in the form of substantial public buildings and sometimes defences. Social differentiation was marked too; this is demonstrated most clearly in burials, which often show some very rich graves contrasting with others that are much more poorly equipped. Technology was more advanced, and some goods were almost certainly made by full-time specialists. Far-ranging trade networks brought in a wide variety of materials and goods. In the subsistence economy new plants and animals had been domesticated and more intensive methods of agricultural production were being used. Clearly, in the interval between the first appearance of farming and the development of civilization, an interval that varied in length from area to area but usually lasted several thousand years, important changes had occurred. As these changes may well be critical to our understanding of the emergence of civilization, we shall look at them more closely.

Population

An increase in population is one of the most visible characteristics, archaeologically speaking, of the period that followed the development of farming. Although the progression may not have been equally smooth in all areas and temporary phases of population decline may occasionally have occurred, population generally seems to have increased steadily. This is marked in the archaeological record both by increasing numbers of sites and by an increase in the size of individual settlements. Attempts to quantify such population increase can only be made in circumstances where very full survey data are available and there is therefore reasonable confidence that most of the sites that once existed have been found. These circumstances occur only rarely, but we do have data for the Deh Luran plain of south-west Iran, where a detailed survey was carried out by the American archaeologists Frank Hole and Kent Flannery. Their calculations indicate that the population density for the first farmers was 2.3 people per km^2, but that some 2,000 years later it had more than doubled to between 5 and 6 people per km^2. The Deh Luran plain is semi-arid and not very fertile, and figures of 10 people per km^2 or even higher have been suggested for developed farming communities in other areas, such as southern Mesopotamia.

The most important effect of this general rise in population may not have been the overall increase in population density, but rather the increase in size of the individual settlements. Once residential communities grow beyond a certain size – that at which, for instance, it becomes impossible for each individual to know all others personally – kinship bonds begin to prove inadequate to organize social life. Population increase may therefore be one reason for the development of new principles of social organization.

Subsistence

The subsistence base of complex farming societies was normally some kind of intensive agriculture. A variety of techniques was used, including irrigation, terracing, the use of ox-drawn ploughs, the development of new plant and animal breeds and the diversification of crops. These developments provided the greater yields needed to support the larger populations. They may also be closely related to developments in social organization: the so-called 'hydraulic hypothesis', as we have seen, argues that the practice of irrigation requires some kind of centralized management. It is also possible that increasing specialization in the subsistence economy could have led to increasingly centralized administration, since a central management would be needed to organize the pooling and redistribution of the various products.

Technology

Considerable advances in technology occurred in the period between the appearance of the first farming societies and the emergence of civilization, and not only in the subsistence field. In the Old World bronze metallurgy was developed; the wheel was invented and used both for transport and for throwing pottery; wind power was harnessed by sailing boats and animal power was used for a variety of purposes including ploughing and transport; a very wide range of materials was exploited for tools, weapons and ornaments. In the New World we do not find all these inventions: wheels were not used, and metallurgy was practised only in parts of South America and in the Post-Classic period in Mesoamerica. None the less, some technology in pre-civilized societies in the New World reached very high levels of complexity and skill: ceramics, obsidian and jade working fall into this category. In all areas the quality of some of the goods and the complexity of the technology involved suggests that there were full-time specialist craftsmen. The development of technology undoubtedly contributed to the increasing division

Above: Complex farming societies have left clear evidence of the existence of elites, often in the form of richly equipped burials. This gold rosette was found in a tomb at Tepe Gawra in northern Mesopotamia.

Below: Oxen were harnessed to draw ploughs, as seen in this Egyptian New Kingdom papyrus.

of labour in society. It may also have contributed to increasing social differentiation, for it made available a range of fine quality luxury items, suitable for use as status-enhancing goods in a prestige good system.

Exchange

Exchange now took place on a vastly increased scale. Materials used for prestige goods, such as precious metals, gemstones and other highly prized rocks, were traded over great distances. Lapis lazuli, for example, which appears to come from a single source in northern Afghanistan, was traded over the entire Middle East to Sumer, Egypt and the Indus from the fourth millennium BC. Intra-regional trade is also well documented, linking communities within an ecological region such as a river valley. A Mesoamerican example of this is provided by the trade in miniature iron-ore mirrors made at San José Mogote in the Valley of Oaxaca, which formed part of an elite exchange network linking Oaxaca with San Lorenzo and the Gulf Coast in the second millennium BC. More locally still, it seems as though the spread of objects and materials throughout an area was ensured through the mechanism of redistribution from a centre. This change is related to developments within the sphere of social organization.

Social organization

Very important changes had occurred in the organization of society. In terms of individual statuses, society was now clearly divided vertically: at the top a small group of 'haves' was separated from a large body of 'have-nots', or at least 'have-littles'. What the 'haves' had was certainly wealth and high status and probably also authority, and it is possible that all three were hereditary. On the other hand, what they probably did *not* have was exclusive access to vital resources: it seems likely that the producers themselves still owned the land and controlled production.

The degree of centralized organization had also increased considerably in these more complex societies. Whereas early farming societies were characterized in the main by patterns of independent and equivalent communities dispersed through the landscape, the settlements of the later more complex farming societies show a markedly different pattern. Here sites serving as 'central places', larger than the norm and usually displaying special features in architecture or artefacts, or both, are surrounded by other sites that are smaller and less rich in architectural and other remains. The 'central-place' sites often have large ceremonial buildings, evidence of manufacturing activities and a wide selection of imported goods; they clearly served as administrative, economic and religious centres for their local regions.

How and why did these complex farming societies evolve? Explanations range over the same gamut of theories as do explanations of the origin of farming itself, concentrating on the same key areas: the environment and the subsistence economy; population increase; the role of trade; and changes in social organization. Increasingly, however, many scholars have come to favour multi-causal explanations involving several interacting factors. Such explanations are often placed into a systems framework – a view of human culture as a system with sub-systems such as economy, technology, social organization, and so on. Change is seen as coming initially from outside the system, for example through environmental change or contact with other areas. However, such external factors only bring about *major* changes in the system if more than one sub-system is affected and if different sub-systems interact to exaggerate the change rather than to minimize it. This approach has been applied by the British archaeologist Colin Renfrew to the emergence of the Minoan and Mycenaean civilizations, and by others to Mesopotamia and Mesoamerica.

As organization became more complex, special sites came to serve as centres for administration and storage. This Egyptian tomb painting shows grain being transported, presumably to such a central storage place.

51

The elaboration of social life in complex farming communities is shown by this group of pottery figures from San José Mogote. They had been buried beneath a floor, deliberately arranged so as to form a scene, presumably of ritual significance.

Craftsmen at San José Mogote worked in a variety of different materials. Shell workers produced ornaments such as those illustrated here; the one at upper left was probably a holder for a magnetite mirror.

Life in complex farming societies

If we turn again to the records of anthropologists in a search for enlightenment about these ancient communities, we find that the most comparable societies are those described by some anthropologists as chiefdoms. Chiefdoms are intermediate in complexity between segmentary egalitarian tribes (the simple farming societies that we have already discussed) and centralized stratified states. They are characterized by the presence of centres to co-ordinate economic, social and religious activities. In the economic sphere we find specialization in production, with different communities or sections of communities concentrating on particular aspects of farming, hunting or fishing. Associated with this is the concentration of the different products in the controlling centre, whence they are subsequently redistributed: this kind of economic organization is described as *redistributional*.

A striking feature of the social structure of chiefdoms is the pervasive inequality of both persons and groups. At the apex of the social pyramid is the chief himself; his position is hereditary, usually according to the rule of primogeniture. In the rest of society people are ranked according to their genealogical proximity to the chief. The chief is surrounded by a whole series of rules and taboos which serve both to set him apart from everyone else and to sanctify or otherwise legitimize him. Hawaian chiefs, for example, have exclusive rights to wooden bowls decorated with the teeth of their enemies, while Maori chiefs have to eat and sleep separately from everyone else – they even have to be separated from the earth lest their power seep into it inopportunely.

Chiefdoms also exhibit a higher population density than that found in tribes, and this is associated with greater productivity in the subsistence economy. Religion is markedly different from that of tribes in a number of ways. Ceremonies and rituals serving wide social purposes increase in importance, and many are associated with the office of the chief himself. Priests are often full-time specialists and may have both high status and authority; frequently, though not always, the chief is himself the high priest. The supernatural beings that are worshipped seem different from those of tribes: they may still be ancestors, but now 'great' ancestors – approaching our conception of 'gods' – rather than the 'spirits' or 'shades' that more accurately characterize the earlier stage.

In all these ways chiefdoms differ from tribes, but they fall short of state organization, which is characteristic of civilization. They are still organized on the basis of kinship and they lack both the legitimate use of organized force and the division of society into economic or political classes, which are defining features of civilization. In spite of the control over economic activities wielded by the chief through the mechanisms of redistribution, the land is still owned by the producers; so we do not yet see the alienation found in the landless classes of civilized societies.

As examples of complex communities from the past which fall short of full civilization, we have again chosen one site in Mesopotamia and one in Mesoamerica, both of which have been well explored archaeologically.

The Mesopotamian site is Tepe Gawra, situated near Mosul in northern Iraq (north west of Jarmo, our example of an early farming village). In what is known as the 'Gawra period' of the fourth millennium bc, before the emergence of full civilization, the settlement had a number of ceremonial buildings. These included several temples, rectangular in shape with a separate portico, as well as a circular building described as the 'Round House', which had a diameter of about 18 m and a thick outer wall enclosing 17 rooms; its function is unknown, but it is clearly a special structure and it is assumed that it was a public building of some sort. Unfortunately we know very little about the size of the settlement at this stage, but the public buildings indicate that the site probably served as the centre of a settlement hierarchy. We also lack direct evidence of the subsistence base, but it is likely to have been intensive cereal agriculture assisted by irrigation. Evidence for social differentiation comes from the burials, a number of

which, assumed to be those of the elite, were in mud-brick or stone-built tombs. Three of these tombs were particularly richly equipped with goods of gold, electrum, lapis lazuli and ivory, all materials that had to be imported, some from great distances. One tomb had more than 200 gold objects and some 450 lapis lazuli beads, suggesting that differences in wealth, and presumably status, were great.

The Mesoamerican site we shall look at is San José Mogote, situated in the Valley of Oaxaca, north of Tierras Largas (which we took as an example of a simple farming village). This site started as a small village, but by about 900 bc it had expanded to cover some 20 hectares and contained between 80 and 100 households. At this stage it was ten times the size of the next largest site in the valley, indicating that there was at least a two-stage settlement hierarchy in the area. San José is not only larger than the other sites, but it is the only one of this period to have public buildings. There is also evidence of social differentiation, not in the form of burials as at Tepe Gawra, but in the dwellings: it seems that high-ranking people lived in commodious houses built on platforms, while the bulk of the population lived in one-roomed structures with walls made of cane covered by mud and plaster. As at Tepe Gawra, trade brought in a wide variety of materials, some from considerable distances: obsidian, turtle-shell drums, conch shells, oysters, stingray spines, shark teeth and blue macaws, whose wing feathers were used in dance costumes. Craft activities took place in special workshop areas. One such specialist activity was the manufacture of tiny mirrors (about the size of a thumbnail) from the iron ores ilmenite and magnetite. These mirrors were produced for export, as was fine pottery, and were traded all over Mexico.

It seems likely that both Tepe Gawra and San José Mogote, as well as other sites in both areas, represent the central settlements of chiefdoms. The evidence of settlement hierarchy, social differentiation and craft specialization all support this interpretation. The evidence from other areas where early civilization developed is less well known, but it is probable that in all regions the immediate precursors of the first civilizations were chiefdoms.

View of the Round House at Tepe Gawra while under excavation. The function of this structure is unknown, but its size and unusual form indicate that it was a special building of some sort.

The fact that at least four (and the earliest four) of the ancient civilizations developed in great alluvial valleys has already been mentioned several times. Indeed, as we have seen, the 'hydraulic hypothesis' supposes that the environment played a major role in the emergence of civilization, possibly even a determining one. Here we shall look at these environments in rather greater detail.

Egypt

In popular imagination Egypt symbolizes the benevolent river regime, with the river itself accomplishing most of the work of watering and fertilization. This popular image is in fact fairly accurate: the Nile floods at the right time of year for agriculture, in August, and it deposits about the right amount of highly fertile silt on the fields. It did this with almost unfailing regularity every year until the construction of the Aswan dam in this century. Although major irrigation schemes were therefore unnecessary, there was still a considerable amount of work to be done by the ancient Egyptian farmers: the re-establishment of the field boundaries after the inundation subsided in September, as well as the normal sowing, weeding and harvesting. However, compared with the difficulties encountered with other river regimes, the Nile created few problems: as Herodotus said, Egypt was truly 'the gift of the Nile'.

Mesopotamia

The farmers of Mesopotamia had far greater problems. The Tigris and the Euphrates (and it is the Euphrates that is really relevant here, since the Tigris was probably not exploited for irrigation until Sassanian times in the first millennium AD) carry their maximum volume of water in spring and naturally tend to flood then. The farmers, however, needed water on their fields not in spring but in late summer and autumn. They were faced therefore

with the dual problem of holding the water back in spring and releasing it in the autumn. In fact it seems as though most of the irrigation depended not on stored seasonal flood water, but on the water that flowed normally in the rivers throughout the year. Massive artificial irrigation works were constructed and had to be constantly maintained. Moreover there was a serious problem with salination of the soil over time, for the irrigation process delivered slightly saline water to the fields and the natural rainfall was inadequate to wash it away. The soil became increasingly salty and increasingly difficult to cultivate: the farmers changed from wheat to barley, which can tolerate higher levels of salt in the soil, and they also grew many date trees, which can tolerate still higher levels. But all to no avail: the soil became increasingly unusable, first and worst in the far south, spreading gradually north. Inexorably the political centre of gravity shifted north too and the far south was eventually abandoned.

The Indus

We know far less about the agricultural system of the Indus civilization, though there is no doubt that it depended on the annual flood of the Indus River. No ancient irrigation works survive, but one would not expect them to, since alluvial deposition has raised the land surface some 10 m since the third millennium BC. We simply do not know whether the Indus population practised large-scale irrigation or not, but several authorities have pointed out that it would not have been necessary. If wheat and barley were sown at the end of the annual flood in the autumn and reaped in the spring, the farmers could simply have used land submerged by the inundation, as they did in Egypt. This system is still employed in the Indus Valley today and the land requires no ploughing, manuring or additional watering during the growing season. The area under cultivation could have been extended by simple lift irrigation using the *shaduf*, which is depicted on Indus seals.

China

Chinese civilization also arose in a river valley, and we may assume that Shang agriculture was dependent on the annual flood of the Yellow River. However, we lack evidence of irrigation works on any considerable scale before the Eastern Zhou period (770–256 BC), when major irrigation canals were constructed. It is sometimes claimed that irrigation was practised in the Shang period on the grounds that double cropping would not have been possible without it, and the oracle bones indicate that millet was grown in the first half of the year and wheat in the second. There is no need, however, to postulate a very developed system of irrigation for this purpose.

The Aegean

The Mediterranean civilizations – both the second millennium BC civilizations of the Minoans and Mycenaeans and the later classical civilizations – flourished in a very different environment from the great alluvial valleys of north Africa and Asia where the earlier civilizations developed. The Mediterranean climate has a rainfall regime that can support dry farming in most areas, although the most arid regions, such as south-east Spain, are marginal in this respect. Moreover, most of the

The landscape of alternating marsh and open water in the Tigris and Euphrates delta, exploited today by the Marsh Arabs, resembles that encountered by the first settlers of southern Mesopotamia. Drainage and irrigation could turn it into fertile agricultural land.

Mediterranean lacks rivers large enough to allow irrigation on a grand scale. Of all the Mediterranean rivers, perhaps only the Po qualifies as a great river in this sense – and the Po plain has a rainfall regime with annual precipitation of 600–800 mm and higher rainfall in summer than in winter, which is fine for dry farming. In any case the Mediterranean civilizations did *not* emerge in such large plains as the region boasts; they arose in typical Mediterranean landscapes of alternating mountains, small plains and coastal strips on the island of Crete and in the peninsulas of mainland Greece and Italy. As we have seen, the economy of the Mediterranean civilizations was based on the Mediterranean triad of cereals, olives and vines, cultivated without irrigation. Agricultural intensification could be achieved by the combination of the different crops and the fact that olives and vines can be grown on hillsides unsuitable for cereal cultivation.

Mesoamerica

The environment of the Mesoamerican civilizations and their economic base have attracted considerable study in recent years. The environment includes both highlands, which are arid with a topography of alternating mountains and valleys, and lowlands, which are hot, humid and covered with forest. The early civilizations occupied both zones, although the earliest centres may have been in the lowlands. It used to be thought that Maya civilization was based on simple slash-and-burn agriculture, known in this area as *milpa* agriculture (a Maya word meaning 'cornfields'). Recently, however, archaeological opinion has tended to discount the view that this type of agriculture could support the population densities of the great Mayan centres. Moreover fieldwork has begun to show evidence of various intensive farming methods, such as canal irrigation, terracing and raised fields. Irrigation agriculture was also practised in the vicinity of Teotihuacán.

South America

Civilization in the Andes was based on a very different environment from Mesoamerica. The area consists of contrasting ecological zones: an arid coastal strip and the Andes mountains themselves. In the coastal zone the Mesoamerican crop complex – maize, beans and squash – provided the basis for agriculture and irrigation was widely practised. In the highlands a variety of root crops, including potatoes, were grown, and domesticated animals – guinea pigs, muscovy ducks, llamas and alpacas – were kept. Most of the civilizations or near-civilizations in this area depended upon systems of integrating the food resources of the different zones by wide-ranging exchange networks or colonization.

It is clear from even this simple survey that there is not a single type of environment in which civilization develops. This in itself is a strong argument against simplistic environmental determinism. However, it is also clear that the natural environment did play an important role. What we can say is that early civilizations developed (perhaps could only develop) in a restricted number of environments. What these environments have in common is their capacity for productive increase. This capacity for intensive food production was a necessary condition for the support of the high population densities associated with civilization.

It was only with the passage of time and, more importantly, the development of new technologies, that civilization could be supported in other environments. Today, with the help of modern technology, we can support some form of civilized life at the North Pole, or on the sea bed, or in outer space: the ultimate stage of a very long development from the first civilizations that flourished on the fertile soils of the great alluvial valleys.

Above: Olive trees in southern Greece. Olives, cereals and vines formed the triad of crops exploited from the third millennium BC. *Below:* Maize, beans and squash in coastal areas and root crops in the highlands formed the agricultural base of early South American civilizations.

3 Cities

The concept of civilization is intimately linked with that of the city, as we saw in Chapter 1. And the city is a *familiar* concept, something that we feel we know and understand. More than a third of the world's population today is city-dwelling, and the proportion in developed countries is two-thirds or more. The chances are that you live in a city now, or have spent part of your life in a city. At the very least you will have spent some time in a city and will be familiar with the nature of city life. But what is *your* image of the city? New York? London? Paris? Rome? Calcutta? Whatever your answer, it is likely that you will be thinking of a huge metropolis, housing a million people or more, humming with a multitude of activities – political, administrative, industrial, commercial and recreational – all used by a population of strangers linked only by their mutual residence in the same city. But were the cities of the early civilizations like this? Can we find a definition of a city that covers both ancient and modern examples? Are we, indeed, dealing with the same phenomenon at all?

When we try to define a city we find ourselves in difficulties. If we look at urban geographers' definitions, we find that they refer specifically to the modern world, that is to societies in which we may find hamlets, villages, towns and cities, but all are linked together within the organizational framework of the nation-state. In this context it is reasonable to use simple numerical differences in population size to separate villages from towns and towns from cities. Additional criteria may be employed: some require a city to serve as an administrative centre, while others define a city as a settlement in which a significant proportion of the population (sometimes specified) is engaged in activities other than agriculture. Definitions of this kind serve well enough to distinguish different types of settlement within the framework of the modern nation-state, but they do not help us very much in our search for the basic nature of the city: that which makes a city fundamentally different from all other types of settlement and which should apply equally to ancient cities and to modern ones. In this chapter we shall look at some examples of ancient cities. These may seem to demonstrate the differences between cities more clearly than any underlying shared unity, but we nevertheless believe that there *are* shared characteristics and that it is possible to define a city in a useful way.

Opposite: Aerial view of the citadel at Mycenae showing the strong defensive walls and closely packed buildings characteristic of cities.

Below: Plan of the centre of the Teotihuacán complex, showing the principal religious monuments situated along the 'Street of the Dead'. The plan shows an amazing concentration of religious buildings – many of the smaller constructions along the street are also temples or shrines of some kind.

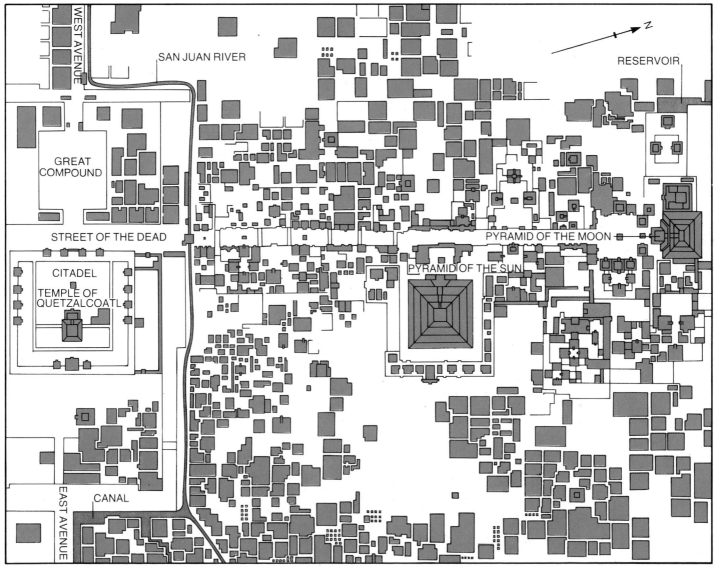

size anywhere. We are on safer ground if we take *relative* size, relating the size of a particular settlement to the overall population of the area and the size of other settlements round about. We could then say that a city must have a considerable population in relation to the population of the area and in comparison with other settlements of the same period. For the earliest cities we might also include a chronological element and expect a city to be larger than any settlement of the preceding – pre-urban – period. Such a definition would allow us to classify settlements of a few thousand, maybe even a few hundred people, as cities within their own contexts – whereas in our own society communities of this size would count only as villages.

Another relevant factor is the number of different activities that take place within a settlement. We expect cities to be centres of arts and crafts, because only within a city economy would we find the intense division of labour and the diversity of resources needed to support such activities. We also expect fewer people in cities than in rural settlements to be engaged exclusively in agriculture and more to be specialists – craftsmen, merchants, priests or administrators. These developments might be less apparent in ancient than in modern cities, but both should be present in some degree.

Another important aspect to be considered is the function of the city within its region. A self-sufficient city, unconnected with any other community, is inconceivable. A city has to be the *centre* of an area, whether a small region, a city-state, a nation-state or a vast empire. Within its area the city is the organizational centre, providing services such as central storage, craft products and supplies of raw materials. It also receives from its area supplies of food, raw materials and manpower, whether voluntarily contributed or forcibly exacted. If the services provided include protection from external threat and maintenance of internal law and order by means of legalized force, then we can also define a *political* role for the city. For this would make the city the principal centre of the type of political organization known as the state. Many would in fact include this political role in their definition of a city.

To sum up, we can define a city as a community of substantial size and population density, supporting a range of non-agricultural specialist activities and serving as the political, administrative and economic centre of a state or part of a state. Such a definition is valid for both modern and ancient cities, including those described in this chapter.

But what about towns? Are they any different from cities and, if so, in what ways? In fact, many authorities use the terms town and city interchangeably. If we wish to make a distinction, the most useful is one that corresponds to everyday usage: a town is a lower-order settlement within a larger system, serving equivalent political, administrative and economic roles to the city but on a smaller regional scale, and being itself dependent on the primary settlement, the city. In this sense we should not use the term 'town' for the emergent cities of the first civilizations, even if they were small and had restricted civil functions. Instead they should be called 'proto-cities' to distinguish them from the towns that formed part of larger systems in the fully developed civilizations that followed.

Top: Wheeled vehicles wore deep ruts in the paved streets of Roman towns, as here at Pompeii.

Centre: Houses still stand two storeys high at Herculaneum, preserved by the mud that engulfed the town after the eruption of Vesuvius in AD 79.

Clearly, one significant factor is size: cities are large, dense settlements, housing many people. Equally clearly, if we wish to find a definition that embraces both ancient and modern cities, we cannot take some absolute population figure as an index. For instance, in 1970 there were some 1,725 cities in the world housing 100,000 or more people, yet in 1000 BC, when civilization was already more than 2,000 years old, there may have been no city of this

Previous page: Unlike most other cities, the Chimu capital of Chan Chan in northern Peru was not densely built up. The centre contained nine large compounds spread over 6 km² of land.

Right: Some ancient cities were provided with well developed drainage and sewerage systems. The Indus cities had systems of brick-built covered drains, like this one at Mohenjo-Daro.

Below: Communal lavatories are found in some Roman towns. This well preserved example is at Dougga in Tunisia.

Ancient and modern cities

Now that we have decided what a city is, can we assume that the similarities between cities are more important than the differences? Would you, as a citizen of London or New York or any other modern city, feel at home in third millennium BC Uruk or Mohenjo-Daro, first millennium AD Teotihuacán or the other ancient cities described here? The answer is almost certainly no: the differences would most probably outweigh the similarities in your impressions.

The physical form of the city probably would not dismay you too much: although the precise forms of the buildings and the building materials might be unfamiliar, you would recognize the city walls and the great public buildings, predominantly though not exclusively religious in type – particularly if you are familiar with some of the older cities of Europe or the Middle East. The street systems too would be recognizable, whether of the narrow winding pattern found in medieval city centres or the straight wide regular boulevards of planned new towns. Systems of water supply, drainage and sewerage would be familiar too, and the range from rudimentary to sophisticated found in ancient cities is still paralleled today. Private houses and craft workshops also would be not unlike those of some modern or recent cities.

What would be strange, however, is the *absence* of many features of modern cities. This arises from differences in both the economy and the society of ancient cities compared to those of today. Many, perhaps all, of the early civilizations were characterized by monolithic state organizations, often theocratic in nature, which controlled all or most activities, including production, trade and recreation. Round the core of the state economy there would initially have been little room for private enterprise, though this appears to have increased over time and is certainly more apparent in later civilizations, such as Greece and Rome, than in earlier ones. If we consider also that before about the fourth century BC there was no money economy in operation anywhere and exchange either took place through the state redistributive system or was conducted between individuals by barter and gift exchange, we can understand why ancient cities lacked such characteristic modern features as shops.

Markets there may have been, but shops appear regularly only in Roman and later cities in Europe and are absent from the Mesoamerican centres. Entertainment was also organized by the state in early cities. This is not without parallel today: the ball-courts of Mesoamerica, the theatres of Greece and the amphitheatres of Rome may be compared in some respects to, say, sports stadia in modern European and American cities, or state-run theatres and opera houses. However, privately organized places of entertainment, such as cinemas, discotheques or clubs, had no parallel in ancient cities, at least before imperial Roman times. Bars, restaurants, tea and coffee shops, or their equivalents, were also largely lacking in the ancient cities, again becoming established only in the imperial Roman period. Absent too from early cities was industry as we have known it since the Industrial Revolution, with production based predominantly not on human energy, but on machines powered largely by fossil fuels and recently nuclear power. In ancient cities production was based overwhelmingly on human energy, supplemented only by the use of animals and occasionally some modest use of wind and water power. There were workshops, and in some cases extensive quarters devoted to production, but no factories. Directly related to this is another difference: ancient cities were free of industrial pollution. Crowded, insanitary and disease-ridden they may have been, but they did not have to endure smog or acid rain. Only the Romans seem to have achieved a significant degree of chemical poisoning, not through industrial practices, but through the widespread use of lead for water-pipes.

Perhaps most unfamiliar of all to a modern observer would be the social systems of early cities. Although these varied, they were all far more rigidly divided into classes than modern society. With powerful elites at the top and slaves at the bottom, and with social roles and behaviour often prescribed by law, social mobility was extremely restricted. Such modern ideals as individual freedom, universal suffrage and equal rights for all were not only unachieved, as indeed they are today, but literally unthinkable.

Clearly, of the features typical of city life today, some are ancient while others are historically recent developments. To put it another way, some features of ancient cities are familiar, while others are strange and difficult to understand. The American scholar Kingsley Davis has likened our appreciation of these cities to the way in which we view mythological monsters: 'A familiar and recognizable part of their body was joined to a mysterious and incredible other part.'

Civilization without cities?

In Chapter 1 we looked at the close semantic link between the words 'city' and 'civilization', and we have seen that cities are certainly characteristic of several of the early civilizations. But can one have a civilization without cities or, for that matter, a city without civilization? The answers to these questions are largely matters of definition, but they are not pointless questions and we shall attempt to answer them briefly here.

To take the second question first, it seems to us that a city implies civilization. It is true that some scholars have used the terms 'town' or 'city' to

describe large and complex farming communities such as Jericho and Çatal Hüyük, but we think this usage is misguided. Complex these communities certainly were, but in each case they lacked some of the features of true cities. Neither had large public buildings or a street system, which are found in all true cities and are indicators of the highly centralized administration characteristic of city organization. Moreover they fall short of city status since neither can be plausibly argued to have been the centre of a state society, though they may have played central roles within their areas. We think it sensible to preserve this aspect of the definition of a city. It is clear that pre-civilized societies can sometimes support large and elaborate settlements with some 'advanced' features such as complex division of labour and some degree of centralized organization, but they invariably lack some of the characteristics of true cities.

The case for civilization without cities is, at least on the face of it, stronger. It could be argued for at least three of the civilizations discussed here: Egypt, the Minoans and Mycenaeans, and the Olmecs. The term 'a civilization without cities' has been applied specifically to Egypt, and it is certainly true that we have little evidence of urban settlements in the early phases of Egyptian civilization. However, many authorities would argue that this reflects modern ignorance rather than ancient reality: early cities probably existed in Egypt, they reason, but have not been discovered and investigated by archaeologists, probably because they lie buried deep beneath the silt of the Nile delta.

In the case of the early Aegean civilizations the settlements are known, but it is debatable whether they can be considered cities. They are generally very small, some occupying only a few hectares each;

The Cloaca Maxima was part of the ancient drainage system of the city of Rome. Its construction began in the period of Etruscan domination in the sixth and fifth centuries BC, but most of the surviving structure is of late Republican date.

Ancient cities were important economic centres, and there are many indications of economic activity in the archaeological record. In this tomb model from New Kingdom Egypt men are loading grain in a granary while a scribe keeps records.

countryside. In recent years, however, surveys have shown that some of the Maya centres, as well as Teotihuacán, were in fact large cities housing populations of thousands – in the case of Teotihuacán, 100,000 or more. This has cast some doubt on the whole concept of the ceremonial centre, but it may be that it is still applicable to the early centres of the Olmecs, if not to the later Maya and Teotihuacán civilizations.

The whole problem of 'civilizations without cities' may be resolved by looking at it in chronological perspective. It seems that cities are characteristic of all *developed* civilizations, but may not appear in their very earliest phases. Both the Olmecs, with their ceremonial centres, and the Mycenaeans, with their 'castles', represent early phases of civilization in their respective areas. It follows from this that although cities are characteristic of civilization, they do not play a critical role in its evolution. While trying to avoid the implication that this is inevitable, we can probably conclude that civilization leads to cities, rather than the other way round.

The origins of cities

Do all ancient cities, particularly the earliest cities in any area, have similar origins? When considering the cities of today and of recent history we are accustomed to thinking in terms of different types of city. There are great capital cities, like London or Tokyo, which are both administrative and commercial centres and frequently also house very large populations. There are also much more specialized cities, such as Mecca and Jerusalem; primarily religious centres, often with relatively small resident populations periodically reinforced by influxes of pilgrims. Other cities are primarily industrial and trading centres, like Detroit or Manchester; some concentrate specifically on trade with relatively little local production, like Bristol in its heyday. There are imperial cities established in the outposts of empire, often both administrative and commercial centres, but dependent

only the largest, Knossos, occupies an area comparable in size to the cities of Mesopotamia or the Indus, and then only if one includes the so-called 'outer city', which may not have been fully occupied by buildings. The small Mycenaean sites, like Mycenae itself or Tiryns, seem to consist largely of heavily defended citadels containing public buildings (palaces) and only a small number of houses; it is difficult to see them as having housed large populations. To look for parallels in more recent history, they seem closer to the motte-and-bailey castles of Norman times than to the true cities of medieval Europe.

As far as Mesoamerica is concerned, it has often been argued that the earliest manifestations of civilization were associated not with urban agglomerations of population, but rather with 'ceremonial centres', where the main buildings were religious and administrative, only a relatively small religious elite was in permanent residence, and the bulk of the population was dispersed in the

The Minoan palaces were centres of redistributive economies and provided large areas for storing produce. The west magazines at Knossos, shown here, had lined cists in the floor as well as rows of large pottery jars, probably 400 originally. These would have held either grain or oil. The total capacity of the jars and cists together has been calculated as 1.25 million litres.

In the market economy of the Roman Empire there were both true markets and shops. This well preserved market is at Leptis Magna in Libya.

Below: Good examples of shops have been excavated at Pompeii and Herculaneum. This food shop at Pompeii has a counter with inset containers.

fundamentally on the homeland rather than the local area, like New Delhi, capital of British India. It would be easy to add to this list, but we have mentioned enough to indicate the variety. What we must consider now is whether these different types of city represent variants that developed late on or whether they were different in origin.

This question arouses controversy even in relation to at least partly documented history, that is to the re-emergence of towns in Europe after the Dark Ages. In that particular case it seems likely that there was more than one route to city development. Some cities, like Southampton, grew up as trading centres on the coast; others, like Northampton, developed as administrative centres around the residences of 'kings' (chiefs); others, such as Winchester, may originally have been primarily religious centres.

It may be that with further work we shall find similar variety in the genesis of the first cities, but this is not apparent on the basis of the evidence we have now. In all cases where we have good evidence, the primary role of cities seems to have been as *administrative* centres. In many cases they were important religious centres too, but we must remember that these were societies in which power and authority were invested in religious elites; this is true of the Sumerians in Mesopotamia, the Egyptians, the Chinese and the Mesoamerican civilizations (the religious element is less conspicuous in the Indus and the early Aegean civilizations, but may nevertheless have played an important role). This is not to say that cities of more

specialized types did not exist in the ancient world – they almost certainly did – but on present evidence these seem to have been secondary creations, which arose only in the context of already urbanized societies. The cities that were created for the first time from a non-urban background developed as ceremonial and administrative centres.

Uruk

The site of Uruk, modern Warka, in the far south of Mesopotamia has a long and evocative history. Abandoned today and largely buried under the sands of the desert, it was once a large and thriving city. Home of the epic hero Gilgamesh, now identified as a real king of the city's first dynasty, it appears in the Bible as Erech and flourished for some 4,000 years until the Parthian period early in the first millennium AD. Most significant of all, it has a good claim to be the world's oldest city: on present evidence it was the first to reach urban size and the first to practise writing.

Historically, Uruk figures in the 'Sumerian King List' (actually a composite list compiled from about fifteen different documents), where the First Dynasty of Uruk is recorded as the second dynasty to rule Sumer after the Flood. It is difficult to know what weight to give to this part of the King List as a historical source, since the twelve kings of the Dynasty are allotted a combined reign of 23,100 years, with the earlier kings having reigns of several hundred years each! None the less it is likely that it preserves the names of actual rulers, including the four kings of Uruk who appear as heroes in the Sumerian epics: Enmerkar, Lugulbanda, Dumuzi and Gilgamesh. The real formative role of Uruk in the emerging Sumerian civilization, documented by archaeology, is reflected in the role played by the city in Sumerian mythology: the myth known as 'Inanna and Enki: The Transfer of the Arts of Civilization from Eridu to Uruk' can be seen as symbolizing the emergence of Uruk as the main city of Sumer.

Unfortunately we know little about the lay-out of the city except for its central ceremonial buildings – massive temples built mostly of mud-brick – where the German archaeologists who excavated at Uruk both before and after the Second World War concentrated their efforts. We know the extent of the settlement, since most of the city wall can still be traced.

Uruk seems to have started as two separate settlements, Kullaba and Eanna, each with its separate temple complex, that at Kullaba dedicated to the sun-god Anu, that at Eanna to the goddess of love, Inanna. In the fifth or fourth millennium BC the two communities coalesced to form a city occupying some 80 hectares and probably housing several thousand people. Field survey in the area around Uruk has shown that this expansion coincided with a widespread abandonment of rural settlements in the region. Thus this first urban expansion was fuelled by immigration from the countryside, as has happened so often since in so many different parts of the world.

We do not know whether this first city had a surrounding wall, but it had two large temple complexes with successive temple structures, including the White Temple in the Anu sanctuary and the Limestone and Pillar Temples in the Eanna sanctuary. These buildings were impressive in scale and construction and highly decorated, often in the technique known as clay cone mosaic, in which clay cones with tops painted in red, white and black were pressed into the mud plaster to produce an elaborate polychrome effect. The 20 m deep trench excavated in the Eanna sanctuary has produced some of the site's most important finds: several hundred clay tablets impressed with simple 'pictographic' symbols, ancestral to the cuneiform script found later. These early tablets indicate the existence, at least in rudimentary form, of a temple bureaucracy, for they record lists of commodities, materials and rations. They suggest strongly that the temple was not simply a religious centre but, as we know was the case later, the economic and administrative centre too. It may also have been the centre of craft

Left: Fine carved stone objects are characteristic of the later Predynastic period (later fourth millennium BC) at Uruk. This striking female mask is made of white marble.

Right: A jug, carved out of yellow limestone, depicting a lion struggling with a bull. This and the mask above were found in the Eanna temple precinct.

activities; certainly some of the finest objects of this period have been found in the temples, though there is no clear evidence of manufacturing processes. Later on, in the third millennium BC, the combined roles of the temple – economic, administrative, manufacturing and trading, as well as religious – are very clearly manifested. This phenomenon seems strange to us, though perhaps the Vatican provides a modern parallel: the aptly named Vatican City serves economic, political and cultural interests as well as religious ones.

In the Early Dynastic period in the first half of the third millennium BC the city of Uruk grew to cover 450 hectares, outstandingly large in the ancient world, and may have housed 50,000 people or more. In this period the city wall was constructed, allegedly in the reign of king Gilgamesh himself. It had a circumference of nearly 10 km and consisted of a double rampart, the inner one 4–5 m thick. A late version of the Gilgamesh Epic sings the praises of this wall, proclaiming its great strength and comparing its appearance to burnished copper. Less is known about the temples of this time than those of the earlier period, but late in the third millennium BC a great ziggurat, or staged temple tower, was built by king Ur-nammu of the Third Dynasty of Ur, close to the earlier Eanna sanctuary. This monument, which has now been restored, dominates the site today.

Because of the lack of excavation in areas outside the temple enclosures, we know very little about private houses or indeed any buildings other than temples. Moreover we are largely ignorant of the lay-out of the city, its street system or the extent to which it was deliberately planned. If it was similar to other south Mesopotamian cities, like Ur, there may have been few elements of deliberate design, with streets and buildings being added as necessary. This would have produced a pattern of irregular

winding streets and buildings of various shapes and sizes, rather than a grid plan with carefully laid-out blocks of buildings. However, it is clear that both the temples and the city wall did require considerable central planning, and it may be that the city's development was characterized by organic growth, interphased with episodes of conscious urban planning.

Above: The mud-brick structures in the foreground were once splendid temples dominating the Sumerian city.

Below: A wall decorated in three-colour 'clay cone mosaic', an ornamental technique used at Uruk in the fourth millennium BC.

Tell-el Amarna

This Egyptian city cannot be regarded as typical: by any standard it is exceptional, not only in Egypt but among cities anywhere. It was founded by a heretic king in revolt against the orthodox religion of his land, as his new capital and the seat of his new religion. This experimental city did not outlast its founder and was occupied for less than twenty years. The city is Tell-el Amarna and the rebel pharaoh was Akhenaten, famous far beyond the bounds of the scholarly world as the husband of the beautiful queen Nefertiti and predecessor of the boy-king Tutankhamun. Akhenaten was a pharaoh of the Eighteenth Dynasty of Egypt's New Kingdom and reigned *c*.1364–1347 BC. We know comparatively little about the other, more permanent, cities of Egypt. This is because the most widely used building material was mud-brick, which does not survive well; in the cities of Thebes and Memphis we know much about the great stone temples, but little about domestic architecture. In the abandoned city of Amarna, however, the footings of the mud-brick houses were never built over and have survived to be studied by archaeologists.

The city that Akhenaten called Akhetaten, 'Horizon of the Aten' (Aten was the sun-disc deity worshipped by Akhenaten), was founded on a desolate stretch of the Nile about half way between the capital cities of Memphis and Thebes in the fourth year of the king's reign. A series of boundary stelae cut high in the cliffs on the east bank of the Nile set the limits of the city in its desert-filled bay. Within these limits the city straggled along the edge of the river, while sprawling suburbs developed inland. The city was not very rigorously planned, lacking any overall street system, but individual building complexes do show signs of central planning.

At the heart of the city was the official royal complex, which was located in the central zone, while court officials and servants were accommodated in nearby settlements. The complex included a series of temples dedicated to Aten, ceremonial palaces and residential areas, both for the pharaoh and his family and for high officials such as the vizier, high priest, police chief and mayor. The complex also contained government offices and police headquarters, and it is thought that the close association of the royal residence with government offices and official residences indicates that the pharaoh exercised direct supervision over central government. A broad avenue led from the northern royal complex to another complex of buildings in the south, comprising shrines, pavilions and artificial lakes.

Away from the royal centre were residential suburbs, some a mixture of rich and poor dwellings; others, further away, exclusively for workers. Houses of both rich and poor were built of mud-brick, though rich houses had stone door frames inscribed with their owners' names, and also incorporated pillars of wood – a precious material in the largely treeless Nile Valley. The houses of the wealthy, together with their gardens, were enclosed in rectangular walled compounds, and shared a common design. Behind the hall, which was for visitors, was the chief reception room, containing an altar in a niche; the room was often decorated white and painted with garlands of flowers. Behind the reception room was the principal bedroom, with a raised platform for the bed, and adjoining the bedroom a bathroom and lavatory. Some of the larger houses had an upper storey with loggia facing north, where the family could sleep in the open in the hot Egyptian summer. Servants had separate

Tell-el Amarna lacks impressive standing buildings, but the plan of much of the city has been reconstructed from the mud-brick footings that survive, like those of the northern palace shown here.

accommodation within the compound, near the kitchen and bakehouse. In general these dwellings do not demonstrate the economy in the use of space that is characteristic of typical town houses; they resemble rather the houses in which the nobility lived in their country estates.

One suburb was devoted to the workers employed in the state necropolis. We know their occupations – stone-masons, painters and foremen – from their own graves, which were near their settlement. This suburb was surrounded by a square compound wall and, except for a warden's house near the entrance, all 74 dwellings were quite small and laid out in straight terrace blocks separated by narrow alleys. The houses, though small, were not slums, and each had several rooms: entrance halls, living rooms, bedrooms and kitchens have been identified.

In the cliffs behind the city were the tombs of the court officials; two main groups of these, all unfinished, have been found. These tombs, as well as many of the houses and palaces, were decorated with stone carvings and paintings in the Amarna style. This is characterized by a more naturalistic style than is usual in Egyptian art and by an overwhelming concentration on depictions of the royal family. The best known single object from Tell-el Amarna is the bust of Queen Nefertiti, which was found in a sculptor's workshop.

An important discovery, which has thrown much light on international diplomacy at the time of Akhenaten and his predecessors, was a group of clay tablets of Mesopotamian type inscribed in cuneiform in the Akkadian language, which was the *lingua franca* of international correspondence at this time. Known as the 'Amarna letters', they are indeed letters sent by rulers of states in various parts of Western Asia, some client states, some independent, to the pharaohs of the Eighteenth Dynasty, from Tuthmosis III to Akhenaten himself. They record the diplomatic side of what was clearly an extensive international exchange. To the Babylonians, for example, the Egyptians sent gold, receiving in return various precious gifts and women of the royal families to join the pharaoh's harem.

Akhenaten's city did not survive his reign; his successors returned to the earlier capital at Thebes and to the old religion of Amun. The whole episode represents but a hiccough in the long development of Egyptian civilization. It is likely enough that the city was atypical in both form and function, but it gives us an opportunity, rare in Egypt, to study domestic architecture and the lives of people outside the ranks of royalty and the aristocracy.

Left: In the Amarna period fine vessels were made of the vitreous paste called faience. This flask would have been used as a container for the cosmetic kohl.

Right: The wall frescoes decorating the houses and palaces of Tell-el Amarna were more naturalistic in style than most Egyptian art. This example shows pigeon and shrike among the papyrus reeds.

Centre: Relief carving showing the heretic king Akhenaten and Smenkhare, who was probably his half-brother and may have reigned jointly with him between 1364 and 1362 BC.

Mohenjo-Daro

Mohenjo-Daro, situated in the upper Sind district of Pakistan on the right bank of the Indus, was one of the two major cities of the Indus civilization, the other being Harappa. In fact it is the largest of all the Indus cities, covering c.100 hectares, of which almost one third has been excavated in successive excavations in the 1920s by John Marshall and E.J.H. Mackay, in the 1940s by Mortimer Wheeler and more recently by George Dales and others. Since 1979 a German-Italian team has been carrying out a mapping and field survey project which has added greatly to our knowledge of the city. As a result of all this work we know more about the plan of the mature city than we do about most ancient settlements. On the other hand, none of the excavations has been able to investigate the early phases of the city's development. This is because alluvial deposition has raised the level of the plain by many metres and the water table has risen accordingly – wells drilled on the site have revealed traces of occupation an astonishing 18 m below the present surface of the flood plain.

The surviving plan and buildings belong to the mature phase of the civilization, c.2400–2000 BC. At this stage Mohenjo-Daro took the form of a large lower town to the east, overlooked by a fortified citadel built on an artificial mound to the west, a plan recorded at several other Indus sites, notably

Stoneworkers at Mohenjo-Daro worked in a variety of materials. These necklaces are made of carnelian, a form of chalcedony found in the Indian Ocean.

Below: The inhabitants of the Indus cities, like those of other Old World civilizations, used wheeled vehicles. This clay model shows a cart pulled by two oxen.

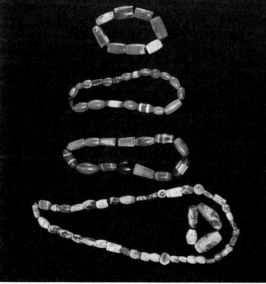

Harappa, Kalibangan and Sutkagen Dor. Recent survey work has discovered two massive mud-brick platforms, one under part of the Lower Town, the other under the Citadel. These must have required an enormous investment of labour and imply the existence of tight central control over the planning and construction of the city. This is also suggested by its highly organized lay-out: the Lower Town was built on a grid-iron plan of main streets running approximately north–south and east–west and dividing the area into rectangular blocks measuring about 250 × 370 m. Parts of seven blocks have been excavated, and there were probably originally twelve, with the citadel mound situated in the central western block. The main streets were up to 10 m wide, while the blocks were subdivided by narrow lanes 1.3–3 m wide. It has recently become clear that the different blocks were laid out on slightly varying orientations, although each block was internally consistent. Houses were first built along the main streets, the areas behind being filled in later. The streets were provided with brick drains and brick man-holes with stone covers. Waste was discharged from the houses into these drains through earthenware pipes and purpose-built chutes. Fresh water was obtained from numerous wells throughout the city, both in houses and in public places. The standard of the drainage and sewerage works in the Indus cities far surpassed those found anywhere in the ancient world before Rome.

A high proportion of the buildings seem to have been private houses, and large comfortable houses at that, originally two storeys high. They consisted of ranges of rooms clustered around a courtyard. Most houses had a well room and adjoining bathroom connected by drains to the street drain outside; some had remarkably modern-looking latrines with proper seats. The building material was normally true baked brick, although mud-brick was sometimes used internally and timber may also have been

employed. As well as houses, there are a few buildings which might have served commercial or industrial purposes. The new survey has located a workshop area in the south-eastern part of the Lower Town, producing among other things stoneware bangles fired at very high temperatures (1050–1100°C) and sometimes inscribed in the Indus script. Some buildings have been tentatively interpreted as shrines, but the evidence for this is slight. Others look rather like barracks, and it has been suggested that they housed slave or serf labourers.

The fortified Citadel, dominated today by a ruined Buddhist stupa of the second century AD, has produced remains of several important public buildings. The Great Bath, measuring 12 × 7 m and 2.5 m deep, with its associated complex of bathrooms and other rooms, may have served a religious purpose. Next to it is the Granary, a massive structure originally covering about 46 × 23 m and subsequently extended; it was probably used to store the collective agricultural wealth of the community. The function of other structures on the Citadel, labelled by the excavators the 'College' and the 'Assembly Hall' are unknown, but their location as well as their size and impressive appearance suggest that they were public buildings of some sort. They may have included residential quarters for the elite, but it is noticeable that the Indus cities lack the unequivocal palaces found in other early civilizations. Obvious temples too are lacking.

All the excavations have brought to light evidence of periodic serious flooding of the city, and similar evidence appears at other southern Indus sites such as Chanhu-Daro. These floods were probably not due in the main to the annual flooding of the Indus in summer; rather periodic uplifts of land between Mohenjo-Daro and the sea, caused by earthquake movements, created a barrier which

Mohenjo-Daro was dominated by its citadel, a large artificial mud-brick structure supporting the city's main public buildings. It is surmounted by a later building, a Buddhist stupa of the second century AD.

Indus craftsmen worked mainly in terracotta, but among the few stone sculptures is this limestone figure of a bearded man from Mohenjo-Daro, often labelled – though with little justification – a 'priest king'.

dammed up much of the river water. Whether such environmental problems were responsible for the city's final abandonment is uncertain, but in the latest phase of its life there was a decline in both town planning and building standards, with many houses being subdivided into slum-like tenements.

The outstanding impression we receive from Mohenjo-Daro and the other Indus cities is of a remarkable degree of central planning and control. The city was laid out like a modern 'new town', and supplied with impressive defences. The drainage and sewerage arrangements imply a highly organized municipal service. We know little about the nature of the city rulers' authority, but about its extent we need have no doubt.

Zhengzhou

The modern city of Zhengzhou, south of the Yellow River in Henan Province, China, lies over the remains of a large Bronze Age city, probably a capital of the early Shang dynasty in the first half of the second millennium BC. The site has been under excavation since 1956, and work has concentrated on the city wall and a number of sites outside the walls; because of the modern buildings, relatively few structures have been identified inside the city. Zhengzhou has been tentatively identified with the city of Ao named in the historical tradition, abandoned by king Pankeng about 1400 BC when he moved his capital north of the river to the site now called Anyang. This identification is lent plausibility by two radiocarbon dates for the city wall at Zhengzhou, which fall around 1600 BC, and by the fact that the archaeological evidence indicates a considerable decline in importance of the settlement by the Anyang phase.

The city wall is a remarkable construction. With an overall length of 7.1 km, it is laid out in the form of a fairly regular rectangle, with walls measuring nearly 2 km in the north–south direction and c.1.7 km east–west. The area enclosed is some 320 hectares, comparable with the larger cities of ancient Mesopotamia and more than twice the size of the modern walled city of Zhengzhou. The wall is built in the technique known as *hangtu*, in which earth was packed between wooden forms in successive layers, 7–10 cm thick, each layer being

pounded hard before the next was added. The wall is c.20 m thick at the base and is estimated to have stood 10 m or more high originally; in places it still survives to a height of 3–4 m. It has been suggested that the work of constructing this massive wall would have occupied 10,000 men for nearly 20 years – eloquent testimony to the power and centralized control of the early Shang rulers.

Inside the walled enclosure only a few house walls have been excavated, and so far no unequivocal palace has been found. One structure was larger than any yet found outside the walls and has been interpreted as a public building of some sort. Nearby was a ditch in which about a hundred human skulls were found, most of which had their upper portions sawn off at about eyebrow level. To the north was a large *hangtu* platform, which has been interpreted as a possible altar. The alignment of the buildings inside the walls suggests that the interior was divided up into regular rectangular blocks. Together with the lay-out of the wall itself, this indicates a high degree of central planning: the city seems to have been laid out according to design, rather than developing by organic growth from a smaller settlement.

Outside the walls residential zones, workshop areas and tombs have been found. The settlements, apparently simple villages, had dwellings of semi-subterranean type. Some of the villages were built directly up against the enclosure wall, others up to 3 km away. The site of Erligang, which has given its name to the stage of the north Chinese Bronze Age when Zhengzhou was at its height, lies about 0.5 km from the enclosure wall.

Workshops have been found both within these settlements and in separate areas around the enclosure. The main industrial activities were pottery manufacture, bronze-casting and bone-carving. On the western side, 1,200 m from the walls, was a pottery with no fewer than fourteen kilns, together with the houses of the potters; other potteries on a smaller scale have also been identified. Two bronze foundries have been investigated: an earlier one to the south, occupying more than 1,000 m^2, and a later one to the north, which has associated houses for the metal-workers. The bronze smiths were already using the distinctive Chinese section-mould technique to produce elaborate cast ritual vessels, some of considerable size. The scale of the operations at Zhengzhou makes it highly probable that the smiths were working under royal patronage, as we know was the case at the later Shang site of Anyang. Also in the northern area was a bone workshop, producing arrowheads and hairpins from the bones of cattle, pigs and deer, as well as cups made from human skulls. In the Erligang settlement a possible distillery has been identified from a white deposit found on the inside of large jars. This, if correctly interpreted, may represent another example of specialist production.

Areas of burials have also been found, all at some distance from the walls. These include both poorer and richer examples, indicating a considerable degree of social differentiation. The richest burials do not compare in splendour with the rather later great shaft tombs of Anyang with their abundant human sacrifices, but many contain fine bronze ritual vessels, and two have elaborate furnishings and human sacrifices.

Cast bronze ritual vessels were produced in the foundries outside Zhengzhou. This tripod form is a *jia*; it is decorated with two bands of face-like designs known as *taotie*, the favourite motif of Shang bronze-casters.

One interpretation of this site is that the walled enclosure represents a ceremonial and administrative focus for a group of surrounding villages and hamlets. According to this view, only royalty, the priesthood, a few selected craftsmen and perhaps some sort of royal guard would have lived in the walled centre, while the peasants and the majority of the artisans lived in villages in the surrounding countryside. This interpretation is plausible, but it lacks any strong supporting evidence: only the hypothetical public building and a hoard of finely worked jade hairpins support the idea of elite occupancy of the site. The existence of villages outside the walls does not preclude the possibility of intensive occupation within them. It is possible that only 'overflow' population and the more anti-social crafts (noisy, smelly or otherwise offensive) were located outside. Until further information becomes available from inside the walls, an alternative interpretation – that the city was a major residential centre for a large and dense population – must remain a possibility. The changing interpretations of some of the major Mesoamerican sites, such as Teotihuacán (see p. 78), must serve as a warning against too ready acceptance of the 'ceremonial centre' idea.

Other goods produced in the bronze foundries include weapons, such as this halberd blade decorated with a whirligig design.

Pottery manufacture was another area of specialist craft production. A small proportion of the vessels were finished with a high-fired leadless glaze, like this jar from the pottery at Minggonglu, outside Zhengzhou.

Mycenae

Mycenae is a name to conjure with: city of Agamemnon, according to Homer the most powerful of the Greek kings to go into battle against Troy, and, in apparent confirmation of Homer's story, the site where in 1876 the German scholar Heinrich Schliemann excavated a series of astoundingly wealthy royal burials. The city that Schliemann excavated was in truth Mycenae, even if the royal burials turned out to belong to a period several centuries before Agamemnon. Yet, in spite of its renown, of all the cities described in this chapter Mycenae is both the smallest and the least urban in character. Like most of the other Mycenaean centres, it took the form of an imposing fortified citadel – a castle – which contained the royal palace, religious buildings and perhaps the houses of important people. However, this citadel occupied less than a hectare and did not house the bulk of the population, who probably lived in a series of undefended villages on hills around the citadel; this assumption is supported by the fact that the name in Greek has a plural form (*Mykenai*).

The most impressive feature of the citadel at Mycenae is the defensive wall. First built *c.*1400 BC and rebuilt in the thirteenth century BC, it was constructed in the Cyclopean style (so called after the mythical one-eyed giant Cyclops) of very large blocks of stone fitted closely together. It has a maximum thickness of 6.7 m and is entered through the monumental Lion Gate, a massive trilithon entrance of three stone slabs surmounted by a triangular relief showing a column supported by two lionesses. The gate would have been closed by wooden doors and barred by additional timbers.

From the Lion Gate a road led up the acropolis to the entrance of the palace, which was approached by a monumental staircase. The palace itself, high up on the acropolis, survives less well than most other Mycenaean palaces, for it has succumbed both to erosion and to robbing for later buildings. However, it seems to have been similar in plan to the better-known palaces, with a main building in *megaron* form, preceded by a vestibule and porch fronting onto a large courtyard. All these survive in part at Mycenae, but the usual storerooms, archive rooms and royal apartments are missing.

Just inside the walls is the Shaft Grave Circle excavated by Schliemann (known as Circle A).

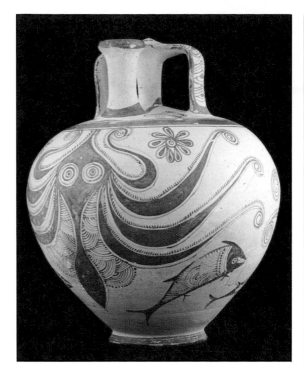

These graves date to the sixteenth century BC and were originally outside the settlement, but in the thirteenth century, when the defences of the citadel were enlarged, they were separated off from the rest of the cemetery (including Shaft Grave Circle B) and incorporated within the new walls. By this time the royal tomb form at Mycenae had changed, and the kings of the fifteenth, fourteenth and thirteenth centuries BC were buried in magnificent tombs of *tholos* type outside the citadel walls; the most splendid examples of these are the monuments known as 'The Treasury of Atreus' and 'The Tomb of Clytemnestra'. The wealth of the goods from the shaft graves is well known, but the tholos tombs were all robbed in antiquity, so we know little about the burial customs associated with them; we may safely assume, however, that the kings for whom such large and elaborate monuments were erected would have gone to the next life in wealth and splendour.

Excavations in the last twenty years have brought to light two cult areas at Mycenae, both at the foot of the acropolis, just within the citadel walls south of Shaft Grave Circle A. The two areas were adjacent but not connected, and they seem to have served two different cults. One building is described as a temple, in which a female clay idol stood on a platform, while a small room at a higher level had been used to store a collection of 23 clay idols in human form (both male and female) and 17 clay snakes. The other cult area to the west was different. The main room contained a bath-tub, a long bench and an altar, and the east wall was decorated with a painted fresco portraying three goddesses of clear Minoan inspiration. A small adjacent room was used as a shrine and contained a dais on which stood a small female idol. Other rooms nearby also seem to have served as shrines, and clearly the whole area was a religious centre of some importance, though not comparable in scale or magnificence to the great temples of other early civilizations.

Other buildings have been excavated within the citadel, but because of their poor state of preservation it is difficult to determine their function; they may have been residences of priests and other important people. One of the most remarkable features on the citadel is a secret water cistern, constructed at the end of the thirteenth century BC, when Mycenae apparently came under attack from outside. Three flights of steps led down to the hidden reservoir which it is assumed was fed through an underground channel (not yet discovered) from a spring situated outside the citadel on higher ground.

A number of buildings have been investigated lower down the hill, outside the citadel. Labelled, according to their main finds, 'The House of Shields', 'The House of the Oil Merchant' and 'The House of Sphinxes', they are interpreted by some as merchants' houses. However, as there is no documentary evidence for independent traders in Mycenaean society, it is more likely that the buildings were the workshops of the palace household. This interpretation is supported by the fact that most of the 70 Linear B tablets so far found at Mycenae came from these buildings.

Mycenae suffered serious destruction by fire on at least three occasions – c.1250, 1200 and 1150 BC; the palace succumbed to either the second or the third of these disasters, which were part of widespread destructions affecting Mycenaean centres at the time. Mycenae continued to be inhabited during the succeeding Dark Age, but at a lower level of organizational and cultural complexity.

Left: Among the most attractive products of the Mycenaean craftsmen were pottery vessels, like this twelfth-century BC jar decorated with a characteristic octopus motif.

Right: The later kings of Mycenae were buried in great *tholos* tombs, built of Cyclopean masonry with corbelled vaults. The mis-named 'Treasury of Atreus' is one of the finest examples dating from the fourteenth century BC.

Centre: Whereas the *tholos* tombs had been robbed in antiquity, the older shaft graves, excavated by Schliemann, produced rich grave goods, including this gold diadem found in Shaft Grave III.

Athens

In classical antiquity Athens was one of several brilliant urban centres that typified a developed 'Greek' culture (see pp. 22–3). Other examples are Corinth, Thebes, Ephesus and the greater cities of Magna Graecia (southern Italy) such as Syracuse and Agrigentum. At the height of their prosperity, in the fifth and fourth centuries BC, all these cities showed a competitive enthusiasm for erecting decorative public buildings, experimented with varying political systems, and gave active encouragement to the fine arts, literature and learning.

Athens' geographical position was not particularly favourable. Situated on a coastal plain about 7 km inland, the city gradually developed a separate port community, the Peiraeus. In the fifth century BC Athens protected its communications with this port area by building a series of long walls. As resources, the city had silver from the mines of Laurium near Cape Sunium, marble from Mount Pentelikon and Mount Hymettus (also renowned for its honey), and local supplies of potter's clay.

Early Athens

Unlike Rome, Athens had to watch her political dominance come and go several times during her history. For the earliest phase of that history we may discount both the 'foundation' literature, which would like to push the origin of the city back to a mythical King Cecrops in the middle of the second millennium BC, and the pro-Athenian bias of many classical authors and modern scholars. In particular, the traditional preoccupation with tribal migrations during this early period, and the great debate as to whether the Athenians should be regarded as 'autochthonous' (i.e. originally indigenous to the area) or not, are both unrewarding as models of analysis. The issue of indigenous status is particularly vacuous, since if we press the matter back far enough, virtually everyone arrives from somewhere. Archaeologically, there are some isolated pieces of evidence for an occupation of the acropolis area in Neolithic times. In the Mycenaean period what we find seems to amount to a modest fortified settlement, again on the acropolis. This evidence might be associated with what appear to be references on some Linear B tablets to a 'Lady (Goddess) Athena'.

The crucial issue, however, is that of urbanization. On other evidence, and on general grounds, a truly urban Athens is unlikely much before the end of the eighth century BC.

Periclean Athens

The conventional picture of Athens is that of the mid-fifth-century BC city under the rule of Pericles. The 'high' period is very short – say twenty years from 450–430 BC. At the battles of Marathon (490 BC) and Salamis (480 BC) Athens had been able to organize Greek national resistance to the Persian invader. The boost given to her status by these successes, and Pericles' vision of a Panhellenic unified Greek nation, brought about a brief period of imperial glory. Enormous sums were spent on large-scale redevelopment, especially on the new showpiece, the complex of super-size buildings on the acropolis – notably the Parthenon, or temple to Athena Parthenos (virgin goddess); the Propylaea, or monumental gateway to the complex; and the Erechtheum, or temple to the mythical king Erechtheus.

The mood among the governing elite at this time was one of conservative idealism and pride in their achievements. This is seen clearly in Pericles' 'Funeral Oration' in honour of those who had fallen in battle early in the First Peloponnesian War, recorded by Thucydides in Book II of his history: 'Athenian institutions are a model to other states. We need always to respect our well-established principles of freedom, tolerance, and equality before the law. There does exist a love of the beautiful, and of the things of the mind, that brings not weakness but strength to one's character.' Plato was later to look back to this period with similar sentiments, and mourn the lost greatness of this Golden Age.

In reality all was not so perfect. Although money was spent laying out the streets of the Peiraeus to the design of the Miletian architect Hippodamus, expenditure on the cheaper residential areas of the main city was probably low. The great plague of 430 BC probably resulted from the hot, airless and insanitary conditions of down-town Athens.

What Athens saw as her benign and enlightened leadership of the nation was resented by others as rank presumption and self-enrichment. In the ensuing friction, Sparta sent a final embassy to Athens with the simple message: 'Sparta wants peace; peace is still possible if you will give the Hellenes back their freedom.' However, a stubborn Athens embarked upon a lengthy saga of ill-judged decisions that resulted in the tragic events of the Peloponnesian

The greatest development of the city of Athens took place in the mid-fifth century BC under the leadership of Pericles. He is shown here wearing a helmet pushed back off his face, emphasizing the military aspect of his power.

Above: Under Pericles' rule the main buildings of the acropolis were constructed, as a monumental representation of the city's glory.

Left: The most magnificent of the monuments on the acropolis is the Parthenon, which was originally decorated with a sculpted marble frieze. This frieze, now known as the 'Elgin Marbles', was transported to Britain by Lord Elgin in 1816, and is now displayed in the British Museum. In this scene from the north frieze riders are preparing for a procession.

War (431–404 BC). At the end of the war Athens faced the disgrace of subjection to Sparta.

Subordination to Sparta was followed, with brief interludes of uncertain independence, by domination first by Macedon and then finally by Rome. The ultimate disaster was the plundering of the city and its works of art by that epitome of anti-culture, the Roman general Sulla. Under the Roman Empire Athens had to be content with a latterday role as cultural centre and venue for a fashionable education. This continued until the sixth century AD,

when the emperor Justinian finally closed down the schools of philosophy.

What remains today of the monuments of classical Athens reflects the vicissitudes of the intervening centuries. The Erechtheum was converted for a time into an harem by the Turks, and their use of both the Propylaea and the Parthenon as arsenals resulted in catastrophic damage. In 1687 the Parthenon was struck by mortar fire which ignited a massive explosion, leaving the temple a burnt-out ruin, torn into two dismembered halves.

The city of Rome

Traditionally the city of Rome is associated with its seven hills: the Capitoline, Quirinal, Viminal, Esquiline, Aventine, Palatine and Janiculum. The majority of these are grouped in an arc to the left of the River Tiber, the poet Vergil's *Tiberinus flavus*, or tawny-yellow Tiber. The midstream island (Isola Tiberina) offered a fording-point, and archaeological evidence suggests that some occupation (of the Apennine Culture) began here around the middle of the second millennium BC. The subsequent ancient city, and to a large extent the modern city, has tended to echo this beginning and favour left-bank occupation. The area enclosed by the hills – the later location of the Forum Romanum – was marshy and troubled by frequent flooding. A partial solution was found at an early date by the construction of the Cloaca Maxima, or Great Drain – a work traditionally attributed to the engineers of the Etruscan king, Tarquinius Priscus.

Imperial Rome: image of eternity

Our visual image of Rome, however, is likely to be that of the imperial city of the first two centuries AD. This is partly because earlier Republican structures were fewer in number, and because many were removed to make way for imperial redevelopment schemes. The effect is also due, however, to the success of Roman image-builders. Monumental construction on this scale has an obvious propaganda value. Emperors from Augustus onward wanted to create a capital city with an image appropriate to the dignity of the Empire (*urbs pro maiestate imperii ornata*), as the historian Suetonius was to remark. Julius Caesar himself had set an example by introducing widespread re-planning of the major areas of the city. Nero was to take the process one step further. On the night of 18 July AD 64, a great fire broke out which was to burn for nine days. Extensive areas of the central city, which had been

constructed largely of timber, were burnt to the ground. Nero, suspected by some of complicity, claimed not to have been in Rome at the time. Rumour, however, told of his having indulged in a stage performance of the burning of Troy while the fire raged. On the credit side, Nero reacted vigorously with grants for rebuilding, and by publishing new fire regulations to apply to house construction. Whether planned or not, the fire amounted to a radical clearance scheme for a part of Rome that was choked with cheap and crowded accommodation, and cleared the way for some remarkable new buildings.

The Domus Aurea

The great shift to typically Roman imperial building styles and shapes seems to have begun at about this time. One of the most striking of the new buildings is Nero's palace, the Domus Aurea (Golden House) – situated, conveniently enough, largely in the area cleared by the fire. Suetonius' description undoubtedly contains much exaggeration, but an excerpt is worth quoting:

> Its vestibule was large enough to contain a colossal statue of the emperor 120 feet high; and . . . a triple portico a mile long. There was a lake too, like a sea, surrounded with buildings to represent cities; also vineyards, woods and large numbers of wild and domestic animals. There were dining-rooms with fretted ceilings of ivory, whose panels could turn and shower down flowers and were fitted with pipes for sprinkling the guests with perfumes. The main banquet hall was circular and constantly revolved day and night, like the heavens. When the palace was finished, . . . he said nothing more than that he was at last beginning to be housed like a human being.

One of the two surviving rooms of Nero's Golden House, built after the fire of AD 64. Originally, the palace comprised many buildings, lavishly equipped, and set in *c.* 50 hectares of landscaped parkland.

The Colosseum

The emperor Vespasian later made most of the buildings and the parkland available to the ordinary people – a popular move. The site of Nero's lake was occupied by an amazing and colossal new structure (hence its medieval title of Colosseum), the Flavian Amphitheatre. This was built specifically to provide 'entertainment' (virtually a new concept from about this date) for the mass of the population. The building measured about 188 m by 156 m and was nearly 50 m high. The main exterior structure was built of concrete and faced with travertine marble. The impression upon the city's inhabitants must have been dazzling. All kinds of technical innovations were incorporated, including awnings which partially shaded the audience, and were winched into position (traditionally, it is said, by sailors). Modifications to the original central arena produced a timber floor, beneath which was hidden a labyrinth of service corridors, cages for animals and pre-tensioned lifts which were capable of shooting wild beasts out onto the arena through trapdoors, in amusingly unpredictable locations.

Aqueducts

Imperial Rome had many contrasts. The lavish use of water, for example, to supply bath complexes and fountains might be thought to indicate automatic benefits for public health. Unfortunately this did not always follow. What is certain is that the level of water consumption led to the construction of an ever-increasing network of aqueducts to maintain the supply. Already in the fourth and third centuries BC, Rome had started with subterranean tunnels on the Etruscan model, the Aqua Appia and the Anio Vetus. Water conduits carried on arches marching across the countryside – our usual image of an aqueduct – were first attempted with the Aqua

Marcia in 144 BC. By the time of the established Empire, the city was served by a 'spaghetti junction' of such structures, some carrying more than one conduit.

Insulae

Flowing fountains, however, were balanced by downtown squalor. While new techniques emanating from the discovery of concrete (see Chapter 8) facilitated decorative architecture, they also enabled a new density of urban building to be achieved by the introduction of the apartment block, or *insula*. Some of the best surviving remains of these are to be found at Ostia, the port of Rome. In Rome itself, these new structures were built to unsafe heights (collapses were not uncommon) and introduced appalling hazards of fire risk and poor sanitation. As Umbricius said in Juvenal's third Satire, it was safer to live outside Rome than in it!

The best known Roman monuments were built under the Empire, but the Romans were already accomplished engineers in the Republican era. These are the remains of the Pons Amilius, the oldest stone bridge across the Tiber, built in the second century BC.

Triumphal arches, erected to commemorate military victories, are among the most characteristic Roman monuments. The arch of Titus in the Roman Forum was constructed after the emperor's death in AD 81. It was situated on the Sacred Way, shown here in the foreground, which was used for religious processions.

Teotihuacán

The Temple of Quetzalcoatl, the Plumed Serpent deity, was one of the main religious monuments of the city. The facade was elaborately decorated with relief sculpture and paint.

Situated in the Valley of Mexico, 50 km north east of Mexico City, Teotihuacán was the largest city of the New World, and at the height of its power in the mid-first millennium AD may have housed 200,000 people. The city occupies a strategic position astride the narrow waist of a valley linking the Valley of Mexico and the Valley of Puebla, which in turn gives access to the lowlands along the Gulf of Mexico. The valley in its lower part is a rich alluvial plain, which, with irrigation, produced rich harvests; it also had deposits of obsidian which was in demand throughout Mesoamerica as a raw material for tool-making. The settlement started life as one of a number of agricultural villages around the shores of ancient Lake Texcoco in the last few centuries BC. After the destruction of Cuicuilco, a rival centre at the southern end of the lake, as the result of a volcanic eruption c.150 BC, Teotihuacán began to expand rapidly, reaching its zenith between AD 400 and 600.

Teotihuacán was for a long time interpreted as a ceremonial centre and thought to have housed only a relatively small administrative and religious elite. However, a mapping project carried out in the 1960s under the direction of René Millon demonstrated just how wrong this conception was: it revealed 21 km² of continuous structures, meticulously recorded by Millon and his team. It became clear that Teotihuacán was a huge city; the area occupied was larger than that of imperial Rome, though the population estimates – in the range 100,000–200,000 – represent less than a quarter of the figure usually estimated for Rome in the early imperial period. This vast area was not enclosed by a continuous city wall, though parts of the city were surrounded by walls or platforms which would have provided some defence. In any case its great size, especially in comparison with the small settlements elsewhere in the valley, would for long have given it unchallenged supremacy.

Teotihuacán was a planned city, and planned on a remarkable scale. Not only the centre, but almost the entire occupied area, was laid out on a grid system aligned approximately north–south. The basic modular unit measured about 57 m, and many distances were multiples of this. Not content with a rigidly regular street system, the planners insisted that even the river should conform to their design: it was canalized to run through the city along one of the lines of the grid.

At the heart of the city was a magnificent architectural complex which still survives to a considerable extent. Two sets of structures, the Great Compound and the Citadel, stand on either side of the Street of the Dead, the main north–south axis of the city (these names are all those given by modern investigators, not the original names, which are unknown). The Great Compound may have been a market, whereas the Citadel contained one of the city's largest religious monuments, the Temple of Quetzalcoatl. Together these structures probably also represent the administrative centre of the city. To the north of them were two other large temples, the pyramids of the Sun and the Moon. The Pyramid of the Sun, the largest single building in Mesoamerica, occupied an area comparable in size to the Great Pyramid of Cheops in Egypt (though it was only half the height). Both monuments were classic stepped pyramids, built in the style labelled *talud-tablero* that is characteristic of Teotihuacán: each step consists of an upward-sloping apron (*talud*), surmounted by a rectangular slab (*tablero*) with a recessed outside vertical face.

The residential structures of Teotihuacán – more than 4,000 of them – took the form of clusters of rooms around a central patio; only one storey high, they have been described by Millon as 'ranch style' rather than 'high rise'. Walls were made of stone and mortar or of mud-brick; floors and roofs were constructed of a sort of concrete made of the local

Right: Painted earthenware jar depicting in abstract form the rain-god Tlaloc, one of the most important deities of Teotihuacán.

porous volcanic rock crushed and mixed with lime and earth. Floors and walls were usually finished with gleaming polished plaster. The buildings demonstrate some social differentiation, although they share the same basic design: the finest have been described as 'palaces', the poorest as 'slums'.

Some areas of the city were used for industrial purposes: stone, obsidian and pottery workshops have been identified, and there were probably others concerned with more perishable materials such as cloth, leather, feathers and wood. As time passed some of the crafts became increasingly specialized. For example, from the third century AD onwards two different kinds of obsidian workshop can be identified, one concentrating on blade tools struck from prepared cores, the other on tools made by shaping the core itself.

As well as serving as a massive residential complex and an administrative and commercial centre, Teotihuacán was clearly a holy city: in addition to the three major religious structures already described, more than 100 smaller temples and shrines lined the Street of the Dead. The city attracted pilgrims not only from the Valley of Mexico itself, but from distant areas as far away as Guatemala.

After c.AD 600 Teotihuacán influence in other areas declined, although the city itself flourished until c.750 when it was detroyed by fire. A greatly reduced population lived on in the ruined city for a further century or so, and even after its final abandonment as a residential centre it was revered for its religious associations: the Aztecs were still worshipping at its sacred monuments at the time of the Spanish Conquest.

View of the ceremonial centre of Teotihuacán showing the Pyramid of the Sun, the largest of the city's many temples.

Stone masks, including this alabaster example, are among the most accomplished products of Teotihuacán craftsmen.

Tenochtitlán

The Aztec capital, Tenochtitlán, unlike Teotihuacán, does not exist as a ruined city. Very little survives today of this predecessor of Mexico City, although remains of the Great Temple came to light during construction work in 1978, and a major excavation was undertaken between 1978 and 1982. Apart from this we must make do with the descriptions – vivid enough by any account, but of uncertain accuracy – and the maps made by Spanish observers in the sixteenth century, outstanding among whom was a priest, called Bernadino de Sahagún.

The ancient city was situated in a very different environment from its modern successor, for it was founded in 1345 on an island in Lake Texcoco and remained waterbound throughout its life – a sort of New World Venice. Since the sixteenth century, however, the lake has evaporated steadily, leaving modern Mexico City high and dry. It requires a mental effort to imagine the great hydraulic exercise undertaken by the Aztec engineers, who converted the swampy land around the island into the highly productive *chinampas* (see p. 33) which supported the dense population of the city. Great drainage ditches were constructed together with complex flood control devices incorporating dykes and sluice gates.

The Aztec capital was a twin city, originally two separate centres on two different islands: Tenochtitlán itself to the south, which became the main administrative centre of the Aztec Empire, and Tlatelolco to the north, which housed the main market complex. According to surviving plans and descriptions, three giant causeways linked the island to the mainland, and the city was served by a network of eight large canals. At its height it contained some 60,000 dwellings and housed a population variously calculated as between 100,000 and 300,000 people.

Sahagún has left us a vivid picture of the ceremonial centre of the city, which contained twenty-five pyramid temples, nine priests' quarters, seven *tzompantli* (racks for displaying victims' skulls), two ball-courts, various arsenals and plazas, all dominated by one very large plaza and the twin temple of Tlaloc (god of water, rain and fertility) and Huitzilopochtli (warrior god and chief deity of Tenochtitlán, at whose temple dedication some 20,000 victims were sacrificed). The accuracy of Sahagún's description of this monument has been largely confirmed by the recent excavations. The temple stood on a massive platform and consisted of four main elements, two stairways leading up to two sanctuaries, that of Huitzilopochtli on the south, that of Tlaloc on the north. The main facade faced west. Seven major building phases have been recognized, the first dating to before 1390, the last being that destroyed by the Spaniards in 1521. Although the temple was razed to the ground, a surprising amount survives of earlier building phases, including some splendid sculpture. The most spectacular is the Coyolxauhqui Stone, the discovery of which in 1978 initiated the excavation of the Great Temple. It is a huge circular monolith, 3.25 m in diameter, bearing on its upper surface a sculpted representation of a decapitated and dismembered naked woman, identified as Coyolxauhqui, a lunar goddess who, according to myth, was murdered by her brother Huitzilopochtli. Other discoveries include altars, statues of gods, humans and serpents, and the sculpted decoration of the platforms and stair-cases. These recent excavations also unearthed a staggering 7,000 artefacts, representing offerings to the gods.

Splendid as the ceremonial centre undoubtedly was, it occupied only 36 hectares, less than half the size of the great ceremonial centre of Teotihuacán. Some authorities have suggested that Tenochtitlán

Among the goods produced by Aztec craftsmen were fine mosaic masks. This example, thought to represent Quetzalcoatl, is made of turquoise, with eyes and teeth of white shell.

Below: The Spanish priest, Bernadino de Sahagún, recorded in words and drawings the Aztec culture encountered by the Conquistadores in the sixteenth century. This plan of the ceremonial centre at Tenochtitlán appears in his book, *Historia general de las cosas de Nueva España.*

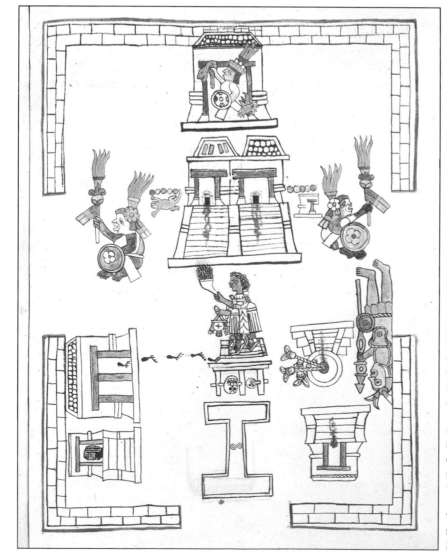

may have had a more secular orientation than Teotihuacán, and this is supported by the fact that the palace of Moctezuma II (the last Aztec emperor, popularly known as Montezuma), as described by the Spanish conquistador Cortés, occupied nearly 2.5 hectares – much larger than any non-religious building in the earlier city. It seems that by this stage less labour was being invested in ceremonial buildings and more in secular architecture and agricultural projects, such as creating and maintaining the *chinampas*.

According to reconstructions, the houses of Tenochtitlán were small, typically inhabited only by a nuclear family. They were architecturally free units, each with direct access to streets and canals and juxtaposed to other buildings rather than incorporated into larger complexes (like the compound houses of Teotihuacán). They showed greater variety in architectural ornamentation too, with individual houses distinguished even from their immediate neighbours; these variations are interpreted as status markers.

Several Spanish observers described the great market in Tlatelolco, including Cortés himself, who claimed that it was attended by some 60,000 people every day. Bernal Diaz wrote: 'We were astonished at the number of people and the quantity of merchandise that it contained, and at the good order and control that was maintained.' The market contained well-organized displays of the enormous variety of merchandise available in the late Aztec world, and was controlled by state officials, who enforced the regulations and settled disputes on the spot, from a building in the centre of the market place. The market was open every day of the week, but every fifth day was the official market day, especially devoted to commerce. Business was generally conducted by barter, but cacao beans and cotton mantles of standard sizes were also used as fixed units of value. Aztec merchants were professionals, organized into political units rather like medieval European guilds; they lived in their own section of the city, had their own leaders and worshipped their own particular deities. They conducted long-distance expeditions, both for state and private purposes, to bring back to the capital the products of all corners of the Aztec Empire and beyond. The Aztec market system was nearer full commercialization than any previous economy in Mesoamerica, although there was still a considerable degree of state control.

Tenochtitlán fell to the Spaniards in 1521 after a siege which lasted 90 days, ending in a battle which left the city a flattened and smoking ruin. Apart from the newly discovered temple, few archaeological discoveries of importance have been made in Tenochtitlán. However, two outstanding stone sculptures were unearthed in 1790, when an underground aqueduct was constructed in the city centre: a huge statue of the goddess Coatlicue and the so-called Calendar Stone. The statue is nearly 2.5 m high and weighs some 12 tonnes; it depicts a grotesque figure, decapitated and streaming blood (represented by snakes), wearing a necklace of severed human hands and hearts and a skirt made of intertwined rattlesnakes. The Calendar Stone is an even more remarkable sculpture: 4 m in diameter and weighing 20 tonnes, it was commissioned by the emperor Axayacatl in 1479. The Aztecs believed that they were living in the fifth of a series of eras, or suns. The central figure on the Calendar Stone represents Tonatuih, the fifth sun, and is surrounded by a series of concentric bands containing symbols for elements of the universe. These two immense sculptures aptly symbolize both the power of the Aztec emperors and the cruel and demanding religion that motivated them.

Top: Stone carving of a *tzompantli*, a skull rack used to store the heads of slain enemies.

Bottom: Stone statue of the goddess Coatlicue.

Chan Chan

The cities of the Andean civilizations were very different from those of either Mesoamerica or the Old World: although they sometimes occupied large areas, they did not house dense populations and served mainly as administrative and ceremonial centres. We should have liked to take as our example the Inca capital, Cuzco, but this city is still a thriving community and has undergone little archaeological exploration. Instead we shall describe Chan Chan, capital of the earlier Chimu (or Chimor) Empire, which has been the subject of a major international archaeological project.

Chan Chan is situated at the mouth of the Moche Valley on the north coast of Peru. Founded, according to tradition, in the thirteenth century AD, it was incorporated into the Inca Empire in about 1470; by the time of the Spanish Conquest in 1532 it was no longer an important settlement.

The site covers an immense area, more than 20 km^2: about the same size as Teotihuacán, the largest city in Mesoamerica. In strong contrast to Teotihuacán, however, at Chan Chan the area is not densely built up: instead there are open spaces, empty enclosures, isolated mounds and small structures. The American archaeologist Michael Moseley, one of the directors of the excavations at Chan Chan, has described the settlement as characterized by 'great architectural sprawl but minimal nucleation'. Large tracts of farming land were locked up in high-walled enclosures; they contain remains of canals and field systems, laid out in a highly standardized way. The labour and planning involved in these enclosures suggests that they were built by the state, but they are without known parallel and their purpose is not understood.

The sprawling city of Chan Chan does have a ceremonial centre of sorts, occupying some 6 km^2, but it is very unlike the ceremonial centres of the cities of Mesoamerica or indeed some of the cities of South America. There are, it is true, two pyramid mounds in the area, but these are not the most conspicuous buildings in the centre: that distinction goes to a series of nine very large rectangular compounds with massive external walls of mud-brick, 200–600 m long and in some cases surviving to a height of more than 9 m. Inside the compounds much of the space was given over to plazas, courtyards and sunken gardens. Of the roofed floor space, the largest area was apparently occupied by storeroom complexes. Other rooms seem to have been residential, while now open areas in the southern parts of the compounds originally contained dwellings built of perishable materials which housed service personnel or retainers. Both inside and outside the compounds, are the U-shaped *audiencias* situated in small courts; their function is unknown, but it is thought that they were used for official formal activities of some sort.

The largest structure in each compound was a rectangular platform enclosed in a high-walled court. The platforms contain rectangular cells which were used for burials. All the platforms had been extensively robbed long before archaeologists investigated the site, but enough survives to suggest that the burials were originally equipped with an abundance of rich grave goods and sometimes accompanied by sacrificial burials of attendants (91 young females, in the case of one excavated example). The excavators believe that each platform was a royal tomb, and that the compounds were the administrative quarters of the heads of state. Each king would have built a compound to serve as his seat of government during his life and his mausoleum after death. This interpretation is lent some support by the fact that the number of compounds is, as the excavators say, 'a close but imperfect fit with the number of Chimor monarchs mentioned in the Colonial king list' (which in fact lists ten independent monarchs and a further three who served under Inca jurisdiction).

Outside the compounds there are two other classes of structure. One, labelled 'intermediate architecture', consists of well-made mud-brick structures which may have housed the aristocracy. The other is described as 'small irregular agglutinated rooms' (SIAR for short) which housed most of the populace. These occur mainly in marginal areas, especially in the south and west of

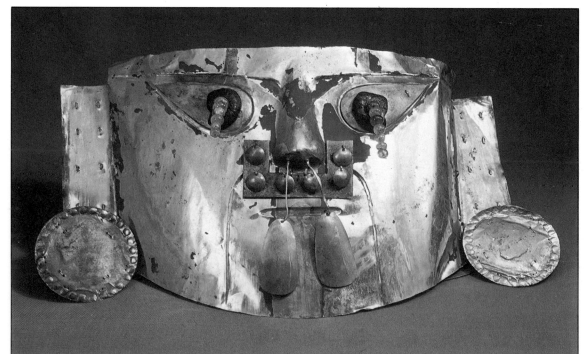

Chimu dead were often equipped with fine funerary masks. This example is made of gold and emeralds and retains traces of red paint decoration.

View of one of the *audiencias* in the *Cuidadela Tschudi*, one of the nine large compounds in the centre of Chan Chan. The building is made of *adobe* (sun-dried mud-bricks).

the city. They are variable in plan, characteristically consisting of a mixture of roofed and open areas; the building material was usually cane and mud on cobble or mud-brick footings. They commonly contain a hearth and a variety of storage facilities: pits, brick bins and large pottery vessels. They are grouped in compounds which seem to have been occupied by single families. Some may have been used as workshops for metal-working, stone-working, the manufacture of textiles and wood-working, but there is no indication of mass-production: the evidence suggests cottage industries rather than centralized production.

While the individual large compounds and the empty agricultural enclosures provide abundant evidence of central planning, there is very little evidence of overall city planning. There is a general tendency to adopt a single orientation (approximately N12°E) which provides some degree of overall organization, but there is little standardization of measurements or angles of lay-out. The SIAR in particular seem to have been built in haphazard fashion without any central planning, for they lack any organized street system.

It is difficult to calculate the population of Chan Chan. It is clear, however, that it was relatively small. Of the total 20 km², about 7 were occupied by empty enclosures, and of the nine large compounds in the centre, only one would have been an active administrative centre at any one time; if the theory is correct, the others would have been either not yet constructed or mausolea. Only the SIAR seem to indicate a high population density, and they occupy only about 1 km², including no more than 20,000 individual rooms. Even at the height of its power as the capital of the Chimu Empire, Chan Chan may not have housed more than 25,000–30,000 people.

The excavators believe that the labour force that built the great monumental compounds did not in the main live in the city. Instead, they suggest, the labourers came from outside the capital and were mobilized by means of a labour tax system, of the kind that we know was employed by the Incas. The relatively small resident population of the lower class would have consisted mainly of retainers, service personnel and craftsmen. Chan Chan was a city built exclusively for governmental purposes, and its facilities were designed for the aristocracy and the state, not for the mass of the populace.

A priest in ceremonial dress, wearing a deermask, holds two staffs in each hand. This figure is made of thin hammered gold and is only 5 cm high.

Cities, states and empires

We have argued that all civilizations, except perhaps in their earliest stages, have cities. However, the role played by cities within the different settlement systems varied considerably.

One pattern that is well documented is that of the primate state, in which there is one single urban centre and all other settlements are very small, entirely subordinate to the main city. Such systems lack any significant spatial hierarchy, with all the main administrative functions concentrated in the single city. One of the best known examples of this is the Greek city-state, the *polis*, which characteristically consisted of the main city itself surrounded by very small rural settlements; intermediate-sized settlements with local administrative functions, comparable to our county towns, were apparently lacking. A New World example is provided by Teotihuacán which dominated the Valley of Mexico c.AD 200–700. During this period some 50–60 per cent of the total population of the valley resided in Teotihuacán itself, with the remaining populace dispersed in small rural settlements; there seems to have been very little development of secondary administrative or economic centres.

A contrasting pattern demonstrates a clear hierarchy of settlements. The chief city, usually the largest and also usually centrally placed, houses the central administration of the state and the residence of the main ruler. It is surrounded by a series of smaller secondary centres, which in turn may be surrounded by still smaller tertiary centres. Each of these centres serves administrative and economic functions for the rural settlements in its local area, but is subordinate to its nearest higher-order settlement. Thus a hierarchy of settlement around a central place – the chief city – can be discerned. Examples of this hierarchical settlement pattern can be found in southern Mesopotamia in the period of the emergent civilization of Sumer (the Uruk period). Field survey in the area of Uruk has demonstrated the existence of secondary and tertiary centres around Uruk itself. New World examples can be found in Mesoamerica, both among the Maya and in the Valley of Mexico in late Aztec times. In strong contrast to the primate system that operated earlier when Teotihuacán dominated the valley, in late Aztec times there was a hierarchy of settlement with at least three levels. At this time, only some 20 per cent of the valley population lived in the main

city – Tenochtitlán – compared to the 50–60 per cent that had lived in Teotihuacán. The three levels of settlement were the 'supraregional' centres of Tenochtitlán and Texcoco at the top, then some fifty semi-autonomous 'city-states', each based on a regional centre, and finally a third level of numerous local units, housing of the order of 1,000 people, providing ritual centres and elite residences for small local areas.

Unfortunately, because of lack of research, especially field survey, in the areas of many ancient civilizations, it is not possible to establish their pattern of settlement. Indeed, it is not clear whether we are dealing with two clearly opposed settlement types or with a continuum of varying degrees of spatial hierarchy, of which we have recognized only the two extremes. This might prove a profitable direction for future research.

What possible explanations are there for these differences in settlement pattern? One reason could relate to *scale*, that is to the size of the state, measured in terms of either area or population. One might imagine that small-scale states would experience little need for a hierarchy of settlement, for all necessary administration could easily be accommodated in a single centre. This would fit the case of the Greek city-states, which were small by any standard: barely a *polis* boasted a territory of more than 1,000 km^2, and some, especially on the islands, occupied less than a tenth of that area. The populations of these classical city-states could be as small 1,500 people, and the majority of city-states may have had populations of fewer than 10,000. It is difficult to see how there could be much scope for an elaborate spatial hierarchy in states of this size.

The situation in the Valley of Mexico is different, however, for the same geographical area seems to have supported a primate system in the first millennium AD, but to have developed a centralized hierarchical pattern by the mid-second millennium. However, though the area occupied was the same in both periods, the population density certainly was not. One estimate puts the valley population in the period of Teotihuacán dominance as between 200,000 and 250,000 with some 100,000 or more living in the city itself. Even if these figures represent conservative estimates, there was clearly a vast increase in the late Aztec period, when the population of the valley increased to about a million. It is likely that such a greatly increased population would require a more hierarchical administrative system.

Another factor which might be relevant to the degree of hierarchy found is the amount of information that had to be processed by the state machinery. In those states where economic activities, especially agricultural production, were closely controlled by a central bureaucracy, a very large volume of information had to be gathered and collated before decisions could be made and then passed back from the centre for action. This would require a complex administrative organization with a hierarchy of personnel. One might also expect that this hierarchy would have a spatial dimension: thus one might imagine a system where information was gathered by local leaders and passed to regional governors, who would in turn pass it to the central authority; decisions about appropriate action would

Ownership of land was settled by law in some ancient civilizations. This Babylonian boundary stone, showing the king and landowners, was erected in the tenth century BC.

travel in the opposite direction, that is *down* the social ladder and *outwards* from the centre. Such an explanation would fit the cases of Mesopotamia and the Minoans and Mycenaeans, where centralized bureaucratic control of the economy is well documented; it could explain why hierarchical settlement patterns are found in these contexts, although neither the areas of the states nor their populations may have been particularly high, especially in the case of the Minoan and Mycenaean civilizations.

In the case of true empires, the hierarchical character of the settlement pattern is still more marked. Indeed it is difficult to see how any large empire could function without a highly developed administrative hierarchy of both people and places. The organization of the Roman Empire is well known: each province was run like a state in its own

right, but with the provincial governor in the provincial capital directly answerable to the central authority, indeed to the emperor himself, in Rome. A less well known but equally hierarchical system, described in Chapter 1, controlled the Inca Empire of Peru.

To sum up, we can see that there is a correlation between the degree of hierarchy shown in any particular settlement pattern and the complexity of the state organization. This complexity can derive either from the size of the state, especially its population size, or from the amount of information that has to be processed by the administration. It is salutary to remember, however, that some states – including the archetypal city-states of classical Greece – could and did function for long periods without developing any marked hierarchy in spatial organization.

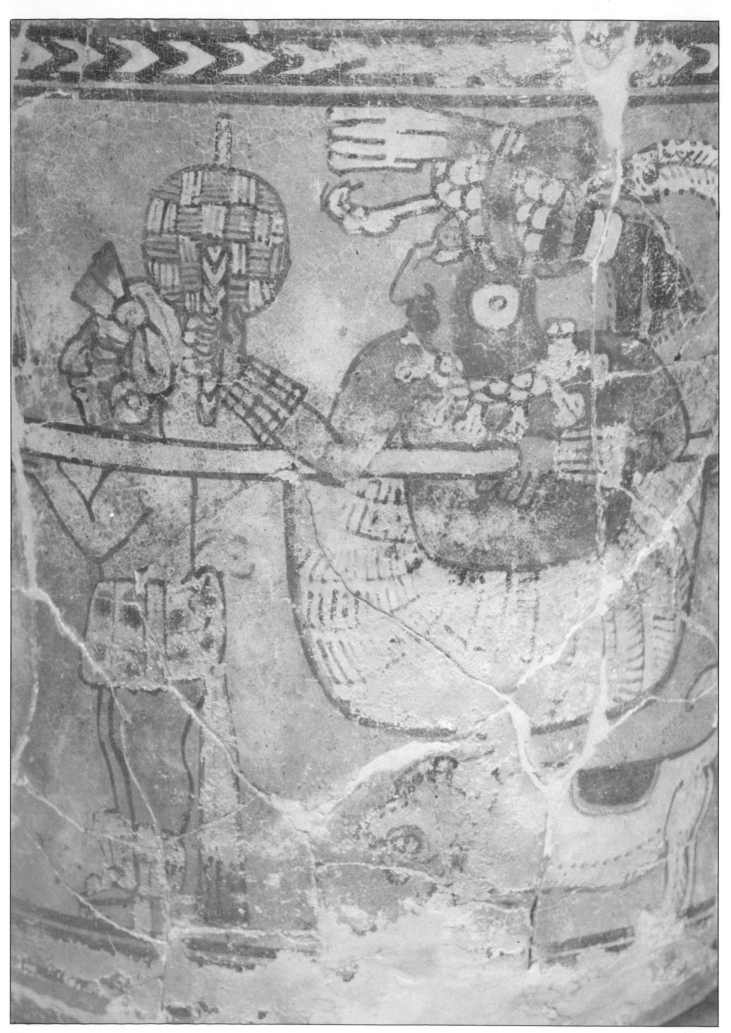

4 Rank, Authority and Power

The existence of powerful elites is one of the salient characteristics of ancient civilizations, and there is often abundant evidence of their presence in the archaeological record. Furthermore, many would agree that the emergence of pervasive inequality in society is one of the most important aspects of social evolution. There is, predictably, far less agreement on the reasons for these phenomena, although there are a number of dominant theories. In this chapter we shall look at the role of elites, how and why they developed, and the traces they have left in the archaeological record.

First, however, we must define three concepts that are often confused: rank, authority and power. It is important to realize that these are different attributes, although they may be (and frequently are – hence the confusion) vested in the same individual or group.

Rank refers to hereditary status; it may be associated with both privileges and obligations, but it does not necessarily confer either authority or power. Marshall Sahlins has described very clearly the role of the hereditary headman or petty chieftain in tribal societies: 'the Chieftain is usually spokesman of his group and master of its ceremonies, with otherwise little influence, few functions and no privileges. One word from him and everyone does as he pleases.'

Contrast this with the definition of *authority*

offered by the American anthropologist Morton Fried: 'the ability to channel the behaviour of others in the absence of the threat or use of sanctions.' This definition coincides with our use of the term to describe experts in any field. Someone may be described as an authority on, say, sewage systems: as a result his or her views on sewage will be listened to with respect and it is likely that any advice he or she offers on the subject will be followed; however, he or she cannot force people to follow the advice if they choose not to. Society has invested such an individual with authority but not power.

In complex societies authority is generally multiple and subdivided, with different authorities for different purposes. In simple societies there are usually only a few different sources of authority, though there are sometimes separate secular and religious authorities and there may be authorities of a restricted kind on particular activities, such as hunting or stone tool manufacture. Authority *may* be associated with rank, but in many simple societies it is directly related to an individual's personality and abilities. Such a person cannot pass on this achieved authority to his or her descendants. Indeed it may not even last a lifetime, since it can be undermined by unsatisfactory performance in the relevant role or by a switch in allegiance of the group recognizing the authority to a rival. Leadership based on such authority is sometimes described as charismatic.

Opposite: The elaborate headdress and other insignia indicate the high status of this Mayan dignitary on a vase from the Late Classic site of Ratinlixul in north-east Guatemala. He is being carried in a litter in what may be a funerary procession; the dog following the litter is a symbol of death. The hieroglyphs probably give the name of the dignitary.

Below: In many early civilizations the aristocracy provided the elite troops of the army. These marching warriors, in one of the frescoes from Akrotiri on Thera (Santorini), appear to be wearing leather helmets with boars' tusks attached, a type known from the Mycenaean mainland. They carry spears in their right hands, while long rectangular shields, probably of leather, hang from their necks and conceal their bodies.

Right: A nomadic camp of the Hadza, a strongly egalitarian East African hunting and gathering people. The Hadza often camp among baobab trees whose fruit they eat.

In egalitarian societies the few possessions are constantly circulating. These Hadza men are playing *Lukucuko*, a traditional gambling game which is an important means of circulating arrows, stone pipes and other possessions.

Power is different again, being defined by Morton Fried as 'the ability to channel the behaviour of others by threat or use of sanctions'. Sources of power are varied, but among the most compelling are the use of brute force on the one hand and, on the other, the ability to deprive an individual of the source of his livelihood by control of critical resources, such as agricultural land, water for irrigation or restricted raw materials. Whereas authority is conferred by others, power is usually acquired by the would-be powerful. Even where it is acquired with the consent of others, it cannot normally be removed with ease; although in complex societies power may be restricted by law, it can

rarely be removed altogether without a political revolution. Like authority, power may be associated with rank, but it does not have to be. Power is often vested in hereditary leaders, but it can also be seized by outsiders. These are frequently military leaders, especially in the case of state societies with organized armies, which provide a ready-made instrument for the seizure of power. The history of many an ancient civilization is characterized by the frequent seizure of power by usurpers from the ranks of the military: the Roman Empire springs to mind, but parallels also occur among the Aztecs and the Incas. In almost every case, however, the usurper goes on to make his position hereditary, to allow him to pass on his power to his descendants, and thus it becomes associated again with rank. In a situation of this sort, rank does not necessarily confer power, but power, whether inherited or illegally seized, brings rank. The late Shah of Iran was wont to claim for his country 'two and a half thousand years of continuous monarchy' going back to Cyrus the Great, but those millennia saw the throne occupied by a succession of Greeks, Parthians, Sassanians, Arabs and Mongols – to name but a few – while the Shah's dynasty began only with his father in 1921 and ended with his own overthrow in 1979. The monarchy may have been continuous, but the line of descent was broken time and time again.

Power is closely related to authority. Whereas authority can clearly exist without power, it is rare for power to exist without some degree of authority. There are only two instances in which we can say that power really exists without authority. One is the case of the brutal totalitarian regime which retains its power only by the regular use of force against its own citizens. All other types of government have *some* authority to govern, though this authority may be partial and restricted. The second instance refers not to the central leadership of society, but to smaller

Tlanjalaga, a Hadza man, and his family in their hut. They are surrounded by most of their possessions: arrows, an axe, a sleeping hide, a cloth, two tins and a metal cooking pot as well as some meat from a recently killed zebra.

power groups within a more complex community. In our own society it could be argued that the City, or the Unions, or both (depending on your political views) exercise power without authority.

In the early civilizations, or at least in those that have provided sufficient evidence for us to judge, rank, authority and power are normally vested in the same people, who form the central government. This frequently, though not invariably, leads to monolithic state institutions, although the earliest civilization of all, that of Sumer, seems to have had a dual power base in the Temple and Palace respectively. Only with the Greeks do we find serious attempts to divorce power and authority from rank, and even these experiments were partial and geographically localized.

But even if rank, authority and power do coincide in most ancient civilizations, we need to separate the concepts clearly in order to examine their *origins* in the simpler societies that came first.

Is inequality natural?

What is the origin of inequality in society? Of all the problems that have engaged archaeologists in recent years few are as relevant to us today. We live in a society in which inequalities are pervasive and entrenched. Around us in the world we see other societies organized in different ways but none without marked social inequalities (despite some politicians' claims to the contrary). In some societies such divisions are more marked and more rigid than others, but none is free of them. History shows us the same story: societies divided into rigid castes or classes, or societies with a 'sliding scale' of social statuses, but all markedly differentiated. Where and why did this start? Or is it an inevitable part of the human condition? These questions are important not only for those who study the past, but also for those who wish to build the future.

It is often argued in popular discussion that there is no such thing as an egalitarian society. In any group of people, however small, the argument runs, there will be those that lead and those that are led. Men are not equally endowed: some are bigger, stronger, braver, wiser or more cunning than others, and those best equipped to do so will be chosen to lead. In larger-scale societies there is greater scope for a hierarchy of leaders, but some degree of division will be present even in very small-scale societies. This argument sees inequality as 'natural'; associated with this view is the idea that competition and rivalry are also 'human nature'.

This, though often propounded as self-evident truth, is in fact an ethnocentric view: what we regard as 'human nature' is in reality the nature of our own society. It is part of our validating ideology, one of many attitudes, often subconscious, that support and reinforce the structure of our society. In fact anthropologists have shown us very clearly that there *are* societies which are to all intents and purposes egalitarian, at least as far as men are concerned (a much stronger case can be made that there has never been a society in which men do not dominate women, but that is not the issue here). In these egalitarian societies, which are mostly associated with hunters but also found among simple farmers, the emphasis is on co-operation and collective decision-making, rather than on competition and individual leadership. And we can see here where the popular misunderstanding lies. Competition and leadership are indeed part of 'human nature', but then so are co-operation, mutual support and decision by consensus. The differences between societies are related to these different qualities, which are emphasized in some cases and played down in others.

In our own society aggressive competition is dominant (a distinctively human characteristic, perversely known as the 'rat race'), but even we encourage the opposite attitudes in some situations and groups: in the family, for instance, or in team games, where of course there is competition with the other side, but members are expected to suppress their individual egos in the interests of the team as a whole. Among egalitarian hunting societies humility and self-effacement are prime virtues, while bossiness, boasting and showing off are intolerable. According to Elizabeth Marshall Thomas in *The Harmless People*,

> A Bushman will go to any lengths to avoid making other Bushmen jealous of him, and for this reason the few possessions that Bushmen have are constantly circulating among the members of their groups.

> No Bushman wants prominence, but Toma went further than most in avoiding prominence, he had almost no possessions and gave away everything that came into his hands.

If, as seems to be the case, most surviving hunters and gatherers live in egalitarian societies, and if we are right in arguing, as we did in Chapter 2, that Palaeolithic hunters would have been similarly organized, then for the majority of our long history our ancestors lived in egalitarian style. It follows that social inequality is no more 'natural' to man than equality.

We can also dismiss another notion that is often associated with the 'human nature' view of hierarchical organization – that those who are the actual leaders of society are in fact those best equipped to lead. This is clearly not necessarily the case, whether leaders are hereditary, appointed or elected. Even a cursory glance at history reveals too many mad monarchs, weak generals and ineffectual politicians to allow us to sustain this view. Not only is hierarchy not the inevitable condition of mankind,

but when it does occur it does not necessarily correspond to the real differences in abilities between individuals.

Big Men, chiefs and kings

Where then did hierarchy come from? How did the egalitarian hunters become citizens of societies headed by extremely powerful, immensely wealthy, hereditary kings, emperors or high priests, like most of the early civilizations described in this book? Two points are clear. First, the development was certainly a gradual one, with slight inequalities being succeeded by stronger ones, through a series of steps culminating in the institutionalized hierarchy of the state. Secondly, it is clear that the beginnings of the process occurred far back in prehistory, for not only are all historically documented societies markedly hierarchical, but the archaeological record demonstrates that many prehistoric societies were so too.

In fact, as we saw in Chapter 2, the archaeological record seems to show the evolution out of simple egalitarian societies of first markedly ranked communities, probably organized as chiefdoms, and subsequently class societies, organized as states. So we really need to pose two questions. First we must ask how hierarchy began, leading to the emergence of ranked societies (chiefdoms); secondly we must enquire how hierarchy became institutionalized in the bureaucratic state. For we would argue that the differences between egalitarian and ranked societies on the one hand, and between ranked societies and states on the other, are not simply differences of degree, but differences of kind.

Tribal societies, basically egalitarian in organization, may none the less have leaders, but these are 'charismatic', their influence dependent upon personality and reputation. Such leaders, often described as 'Big Men', have authority, but they lack coercive power. They normally also lack rank, for they owe their positions to ability rather than birth. In the terms used by anthropologists, they possess *achieved* rather than *ascribed* status.

In chiefdoms, by contrast, the leaders have both rank and authority: they are the heads of societies characterized by a hierarchy of hereditary (*ascribed*) statuses. None the less they lack power in the sense in which we have defined it: they have no instrument of forceful repression, no police force or army. And although they do have sanctions at their disposal, such as the withdrawal of protection or services, or simply social disapproval, they lack the most powerful – those provided by control over the means of production, normally agricultural land in the early civilizations.

A further contrast is provided by state societies, at least by primitive states (later states have in some cases developed other modes of organization), whose leaders have rank, authority *and* power: this power is based in many cases on ownership of or control over the means of production, and backed by legalized force, i.e. by state armies and police.

The germs of hierarchy

In any kind of evolutionary perspective the germs of hierarchy must lie in the earlier egalitarian societies. Indeed, as we have seen, such societies often do recognize leaders of sorts, as well as individuals

Religion provided one route to hierarchy in the evolution of society. The influential religious leaders of pre-civilized societies may have evolved into the powerful priests of the early civilizations. This ceramic portrait of a Maya priest comes from the island cemetery of Jaina.

expert in specialist skills. According to Elman Service, 'it is a fact that segmental societies, however equal their parts, do exalt individuals. They follow war chiefs, accept advice from wise men, and believe in the unequal access of persons to supernatural power'. However, the influence of such warriors, wise men and priests is restricted in scope and cannot be passed from a man to his heirs. If a chiefdom is to develop, two changes must occur: the scope and extent of the individual's authority must increase, and the position must become a hereditary one.

The first change might occur in a number of ways. One possibility is that a particularly successful war leader might establish a leadership that extended to non-military matters, and that he might then retain his position in peacetime. If war were particularly prevalent, and if it led to territorial expansion and especially to the conquest of another people, it would enhance considerably the influence of such a leader. At the same time, the incorporation of a conquered people into society might provide the basis for a fundamental division into two social groups. The newcomers might well have a permanently subordinate position: in Africa in particular, patron–client relations are well documented between members of dominant and minority or conquered groups.

If war and conquest provide one route to permanent enhanced authority, another, it is often suggested, is through the managerial roles required in some societies. These occur particularly where redistribution plays a major role: the collection and redistribution of goods requires administrative skills and considerable application on the part of the organizer, who therefore has significant potential influence. Yet another type of person who has the potential to expand his influence is the priest or religious leader. Such figures may serve many roles in society, but two are particularly relevant here. First, they are frequently appealed to for advice when society is faced with difficult decisions. Secondly, they often serve as arbitrators in disputes between individuals or groups. In certain circumstances – for instance, if outside threats are prevalent or internal dissension increases – a successful religious leader may achieve widespread influence. Clearly this list does not exhaust the possible ways in which an individual might extend his influence in an egalitarian society: they have been chosen because examples of all of them can be found in the ethnographic record.

The second major change that has to occur before a chiefdom develops is that the leadership has to become hereditary. We can imagine how this might happen. The hereditary principle is always present in some form, even in egalitarian societies, since social organization is based on kinship and descent is a major aspect of kin relations. There may even be hereditary positions in egalitarian societies, though these generally carry few privileges and little authority, like the petty chieftains described by Marshall Sahlins (see p. 87) There may also be a belief that the character of a parent is transmitted to his offspring: so if a man is a good warrior, organizer or priest, there may be some expectation that his son will be so too. If these general tendencies exist in a situation where an individual is extending his influence, then there is the basis for the emergence of

Above: In chiefdom societies officials are generally close relatives of the chief himself and this situation occurs also in the early phases of civilization. In Egypt in Old Kingdom times high officials were usually members of the pharaoh's own family. As time passed these offices became separated from the royal family and a distinct class of officials emerged; the high chiefdom had evolved into the bureaucratic state. This statue is of a high official of the Eighteenth Dynasty.

Left: Some of the earliest leaders were probably war chiefs, and the role of the head of state as leader of the army remained important in later periods. This Egyptian painted wall relief shows soldiers on an expedition to the land of Punt (somewhere on the East African coast). It comes from the mortuary temple of Queen Hatshepsut, who ruled as a pharaoh in her own right from 1503 to 1482 BC, at Deir el-Bahri across the Nile from Luxor.

a true chiefdom, with authority consolidated in a hereditary office.

We have indicated the kinds of tendencies and situations which could lead to the development of hierarchical organization from egalitarian societies. What actually happened in the prehistoric past is another matter: what we have described are 'Just So Stories', not historical accounts. For the latter we need to examine the archaeological record for each area in detail in the light of particular theories, and we shall look at some work of this kind later in this chapter.

The emergence of the bureaucratic state

The next stage in the development of hierarchy sees the transformation of the kinship-based chiefdom into the class-based state, with formal institutions of government and true law, backed by the use of force. How did this second change come about? Morton Fried's scheme of social evolution has a stage, labelled 'stratified society', which follows ranked society and is the immediate prelude to the emergence of the state. According to Fried, a stratified society is 'one in which members of the same sex and equivalent age status do not have equal access to the basic resources that sustain life'. This new criterion for social inequality – economic advantage – is not found in definitions of chiefdoms or ranked societies.

Those groups that have superior access to basic resources (frequently, though not invariably, good agricultural land) will certainly become wealthier than others. If those others have not simply inferior, but actually inadequate access to basic resources, they may have to pay in some form or another to acquire them, thus becoming dependent on those

The developed civilizations had a class of slaves at their base, which provided at least part of the manpower for public building works, as well as for extractive and manufacturing industries and agricultural production. This Assyrian relief from Nineveh shows slaves building the palace of Sennacherib (704–681 BC).

All state societies have bureaucratic institutions supporting a hierarchy of officials. This relief at Saqqara in Egypt comes from the tomb of Ptahhotep, who was the vizier or chief of the civil service in the reign of king Djedkare Isesi (c.2380 BC). The vizier himself controlled a body of lesser officials, one of whom – Ihy, the overseer of linen – is shown in this relief.

with superior access. Variable access to basic resources could come about in a number of ways: through population pressure for instance, or through the development of new technology that enhances inequalities in the value of farming land – irrigation is the prime example. It could also come about through military conquest, with conquered people being deprived of their land and thereby becoming totally dependent on those who control it.

In classic Marxist theory such economic stratification would lead to class struggle and the emergence of the state as a repressive structure to maintain the dominance of the upper class. However, one does not have to accept this interpretation: the facts would as easily, perhaps more easily, support a gradualist view, with the distinctions of wealth and power based on differential access to basic resources gradually becoming more important and superseding those based on kinship. This is the more plausible when one considers that the same people were probably involved: the people with superior access to resources would in all likelihood be the chiefs and other high-ranking persons of the chiefdom, by virtue of the rights and privileges of their positions. Thus the king whose power was based on control of vast tracts of land might be the lineal descendant of the chief whose authority was based on his hereditary position as head of the clan. State armies, developed for protection against external attack, might also be used to maintain internal order, but they need not be seen primarily as instruments of class repression. This suggested evolution of state society is of course another 'Just So Story': later in this chapter we shall be looking at the archaeological evidence for the emergence of some ancient states.

Elites – good or bad?

Although it may seem inappropriate to ask such a loaded question, particularly one framed so simplistically, we put it this way to underline the point that many writers, consciously or otherwise, do adopt subjective stances on this matter, and that these views affect their interpretations of the origins and nature of elites.

The British archaeologist Graeme Barker has argued tellingly that a person's view of elites in past societies depends on whether he feels he was a 'Chief' or an 'Indian' in any previous incarnation. The 'Chiefs' will point to the achievements of hierarchically organized societies: the technological inventions, the scientific discoveries, the great works of art and architecture, the invention of writing, the development of literature, the institutions of government, the rule of law. They see elites as benefactors, serving the community as a whole, presiding over harmony within and defending a united society against attack from outside. The 'Indians', on the other hand, argue that for the mass of the population all the achievements of civilization are but a poor exchange for the loss of freedom, equality and control over their own economic means enjoyed by hunters and simple tribal farmers. They therefore regard elites as fundamentally exploitative – if not always grinding the faces of the poor, at least keeping them in perpetual economic servitude. Elites do not work in the interests of a united society, but in their own interests by domination of a divided society.

As far as we can judge these views objectively, there seems to be some truth on both sides. It is true that strongly hierarchical societies have produced incomparably more great art and architecture and new discoveries and inventions than egalitarian ones. On the other hand, it seems true that well-established elites, with secure power bases, act in their own interests and not in the interests of those they rule. We can see this developing through the evolutionary stages of emerging hierarchy. The charismatic 'Big Man' has to act in the interests of his followers; otherwise he has no followers. The chief is on stronger ground in pursuing his own interests against those of his people: his hereditary position makes him harder to depose than the Big Man. None the less, lacking coercive power, the chief still rules basically by consent – if he becomes too unpopular he will be deposed, usually to be replaced by another chief. The head of the true state, however, has the law and coercive power at his disposal; he can be a true tyrant, exacting forced labour, levying crippling taxes, confiscating land and forcing people into slavery. This is not to say that all kings or emperors are tyrants: some are benign and well-loved. However, they wield vast power over a permanently subordinate population, and such a relation is clearly one of exploitation. Such were the leaders of all the earliest civilizations for which we have adequate evidence; only with later societies, exemplified in this book by classical Greece and Rome, do we find attempts to curb the power of rulers through the use of law.

The hierarchy of Mayan society is well illustrated in this relief from Palenque. A priest and priestess offer gifts to a king or lord, who is seated on the backs of two subordinates, either slaves or defeated enemies.

Ancient elites: the basis of power

The positions of elites in pre-industrial societies have been based on three main sources: religion, coercive force and the ownership of land. An examination of their role in the ancient civilizations will enable us to isolate important trends in the development of power.

In Egypt most buildings were made of mud-brick, but two classes of monument – royal tombs and temples – were built of stone and on a massive scale. They exerted a dominating presence and were intended to last for ever, representing the power of the god-king in society. This view is of the Temple of Isis at Philae.

Not only temples and tombs but statues were built on a huge scale in ancient Egypt. This statue, in front of the temple of Amun at Karnak, shows a princess, perhaps Bent'anta, standing between the feet of a colossal statue of her father, Ramesses II.

Religion

The evident importance of religion in the ancient civilizations has led many to regard it as the basis of power in these societies, which they have therefore described as theocracies. The foremost proponent of this view is Elman Service, who believes that the earliest civilizations were in fact not state societies, but highly developed chiefdoms. In chiefdoms, as we have seen, government is largely not by coercion, but by consent – consent that is forthcoming partly because of the chief's authority as religious leader of the community. According to Service, all chiefdoms are theocracies in which religion permeates all aspects of society and the chief is also high priest: 'A priest-chief can be an awesome figure, his supernatural powers augmented by the powers of his ancestors who are now gods in an hierarchical pantheon.' The authority of such a chief is based on his ability to mediate with these ancestral deities, for good or bad.

If we look at the archaeological evidence for the early civilizations, there are certainly some that lend support to this view. Mesopotamia provides the best example, for in Sumer the temples were the first monumental buildings, already impressive sanctuaries on large terraces in the fourth millennium BC, many centuries before any other identifiable public buildings, such as palaces, appear. Moreover by this stage the temples were already not only religious buildings but administrative centres in which economic records were kept. It seems clear that the temple was the main institution of early Sumerian civilization, and it is likely that the high priest was the supreme ruler.

The role of religion seems to have been strong in Mesoamerica too, where all the major centres had massive ceremonial complexes serving both religious and administrative purposes. The same case could probably be made for the pre-Incan civilizations of Peru, particularly Chavín and Tiahuanaco.

In the early stages of both Egyptian and Chinese civilizations temples do not figure prominently, although the elites built magnificent monuments of other types. These civilizations may nevertheless have been theocracies, with religion as the main integrating force in society: both had characteristic religions based on ancestor worship, and in Egypt the pharaohs were themselves gods. We should perhaps make a distinction here between two types of society, both theocracies but conceived in rather different ways. One type, exemplified by Mesopotamia at an early stage, was headed by the gods themselves. Consequently the high priests, whatever their real powers, were notionally just servants of the gods like everyone else. In the second type, of which Egypt is an example, the king was himself the god and was thus set further apart from the people than the high priest of the Sumerians. Egyptian religion seems to have been as much a personality cult of the living pharaoh as a cult of supernatural deities. Personality cults, in which the king's divinity is sometimes simply another aspect of temporal power, are also found in later civilizations: among Roman or Inca emperors, for instance. These emperors were also gods, or became gods after death, but their power was based on coercive force rather than religious authority alone. This may not have been the case in Egypt at an early stage, but it is

In Roman cities the forum was the physical focus of the power centres of the state, containing the main religious, administrative and commercial buildings. This view of the forum at Sbeitla in Tunisia shows three adjacent temples along one side of the square.

Below: The basis of power in Mesoamerica is indicated by the scale of building and lavish decoration of the ceremonial centres, which served both religious and administrative functions. At the centre of the Classic Maya site of Tikal, situated in the rain forest of lowland Guatemala, is the Great Plaza, with Temples I and II at either end and the associated North Acropolis complex, seen here from the air.

possible that the institution of divine kingship provided a smoother path from religious to secular authority than could occur in societies of the Sumerian type. Incidentally, both types of theocratic state can still be recognized in the modern world: Hailie Selassie's Ethiopia was a good example of the 'Egyptian' model, while Vatican City can be compared in some ways to an early Sumerian city-state.

In the case of the Indus civilization we lack the evidence to identify the type of authority wielded by the rulers. No clearly identifiable temples have been recognized; the suggestion that this society was also theocratic is based only on the rather weak argument that there is no clear evidence for the use of military force.

Coercive force

All the early civilizations became more secular as time passed. Secularization involves two main changes. First, there is growing differentiation between secular and religious functions in the bureaucracy, leading eventually to total separation with one set of bureaucrats controlling utilitarian affairs and another organizing religious activities. Secondly, there is the introduction of the rule of law, backed by coercive force. As we have seen, these features are often taken to define the state; if they do not appear at the beginning of civilization, then, as Elman Service suggests, the early civilizations may not have been fully-fledged state societies. Indeed we might go further and say that if they were not states, then they were not fully-fledged civilizations either.

Ownership of land provided a source of wealth and power that became more important as time passed. On this stele the Babylonian king Merodachbaladan II is shown investing an official with land. The official is depicted as smaller in stature, with his left hand raised in a gesture of respect.

Below: In later civilizations the power of the rulers was invariably backed by the use of force. As well as large armies for use in war, a small highly trained group would serve as the personal bodyguards of the king. The Roman Praetorian Guard, shown here in a sculpture of the Hadrianic period, served this purpose for the Roman emperors from 27 BC to AD 312.

It does not much matter which definition we accept; what is important is that we recognize that not all aspects of civilization appear at the same time. Just as in Chapter 3 (pp. 61–2) we saw that some civilizations – notably Egypt, the Minoans and Mycenaeans, and the Olmecs – did not have cities to begin with, so we now see that some were not initially states. By the time these civilizations had reached their mature or classic stage, however, state organization had evolved. In the archaeological record secularization can be recognized in a number of ways: by the occurrence of non-religious bureaucratic institutions, by increased emphasis on military force, and by documentary evidence for civil law. In Mesopotamia all these are present from *c.* 2500 BC at the latest: palaces are found, functioning as economic institutions like the temples; weapons appear commonly, and references to military prowess figure prominently in the documents; law codes and other legal records form an important category of clay tablets.

The secularization of power in other early civilizations is less well documented: in particular, we lack the written evidence for law which has given the Mesopotamians their reputation as the world's first law-givers. Of course we know a lot about the laws of classical Greece and Rome, but these were late civilizations and secular from the beginning. It is not always easy to document the secularization of the administrative bureaucracy. In Mesopotamia the study is made easier because a new institution was involved, and we can chart the rise of the Palace against the decline of the Temple as the major institution. But this was the exception rather than the rule; in the other ancient civilizations the change probably occurred within a single institution and could therefore only be followed if very full records survived.

It is easier to document the increasing use of force, through the presence of fortifications, increasing prominence of weapons, the appearance of warlike motifs in art and documentary records of war. All these can be found in the later stages of the Mesopotamian, Egyptian and Chinese civilizations and among the Toltecs, Aztecs and Incas in the Americas. We should distinguish, however, between the use of force against outsiders and the use of force within society to back up the rule of law. The archaeological record is rarely explicit about the second type of use, and it is usually assumed that if a head of state has force at his disposal, he will use it both externally and internally – an assumption that may not be justified.

Yet another way of documenting secularization is to look at its mirror image: the decline of religious authority, which may perhaps be charted by the decline in number, size and splendour of temples. Such an argument on its own is weak, as there is no straightforward correlation between the size of a temple and the importance of religion in society, but it may add weight to other arguments for secularization. The whole issue is confused by the fact that religion is never absent from society and rulers of all periods have tended to claim divine support. This, however, is not in itself sufficient evidence for a theocracy: even an emperor whose power was based on ruthlessly enforced military control might well proclaim that he was acting on god's instructions.

Ownership of land

Power based on the ownership of land is familiar to us, for it characterized European societies until the Industrial Revolution. Whether in the feudal form based on serf labour, or the later variety based on paid labour, it involved a class of landless poor dependent on the big landowners, who were also the ruling class. However, land-owning aristocracies of this type were not characteristic of the earliest civilizations. Instead, most of the land was probably still owned by the farmers who worked it, while the management of production, collection and distribution was in the hands of the central bureaucracy. Private transactions in land were not important initially. This is not to say that there were no differences in the quantity and value of farming land owned by different families. There almost certainly were, but while the ownership of plentiful fertile land might bring wealth, it would not necessarily bring power. For land-ownership to become a power base there must be people *without* land who are perforce dependent on those with it. The existence of such people is not typical of chiefdoms, though it is of state societies. According to Marshall Sahlins, 'As an *economic* rule, there is no class of landless paupers in primitive society. If expropriation occurs it is accidental to the mode of production itself, a cruel fortune of war, for instance, and not a systematic condition of the economic organization. Primitive peoples have invented many ways to elevate a man above his fellows. But the producers' hold on their own economic means rules out the most compelling history has known: exclusive control of such means by some few, rendering dependent the many others.'

As time passed, however, private ownership of land became more important and a class of landless poor emerged. These were not true slaves, who formed only a small proportion of society in the early civilizations, but more like the serfs of feudal Europe – not owned by, but economically dependent on the nobles whose land they worked. Again the best evidence comes from Mesopotamia. After *c.* 2500 BC we find documents recording sales of property by individuals. The Russian scholar Igor Diakonoff, studying documents from the Mesopotamian city of Lagash, concluded that although the temple was a major landowner, most of the land was privately owned, either as large estates by the king and the nobles or as small plots by commoners. For Diakonoff this information supports the Marxist view of the emergence of the state as an instrument of class repression. However, as we have said, it is more likely that land-ownership gradually increased in importance as a source of power, as the numbers of dispossessed and dependent grew. This change, together with the introduction of coercive force, only gradually replaced the earlier authority based on religion.

The evidence for Egypt is less clear but fits the same pattern. After *c.* 2500 BC both nobles and priestly foundations were major landowners, but before this the pharaoh may have been the only large landowner, with the farmers still in possession of their own plots. A similar development may have occurred in China. By the first millennium BC in the Western Zhou period a system akin to European feudalism existed. The evidence for the preceding Shang period is less clear, but it is likely that it saw the transition from a society in which the rural people were still free farmers to one in which some people at least were landless and dependent on the noble families. We know nothing about land-ownership in the Indus civilization and little about it in the earlier American civilizations. By Aztec times, however, private ownership of land was well established; the nobles owned lands which were worked for them by commoners, some of whom were tenants without land of their own. In Peru, by contrast, private ownership of land did not develop to any considerable extent.

We know something about land tenure in Mycenaean society from the tablets fround in the palace at Pylos. Both publicly and privately owned land was leased to tenants who, we assume, had no land of their own. If this is correct, land-ownership was at least part of the power base in Mycenaean society. By the time of the classical civilizations of Greece and Rome, land-ownership was unequivocally the basis of power; by this time the main labour force was composed of slaves.

Thus we can identify a number of trends in the development of power. Initial theocracies, functioning by consent based on religious authority, became increasingly secular and increasingly militaristic, finally functioning through the twin sanctions of coercive force and economic dependence. Later civilizations were secular from their beginnings.

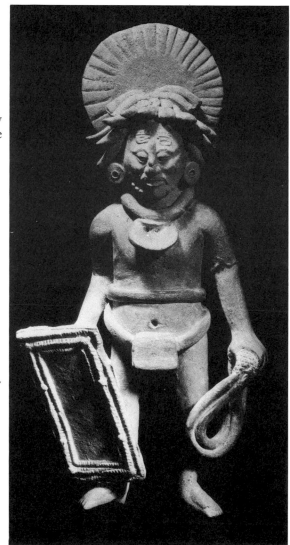

In the Maya civilization power may have been based mainly on religion, but military prowess was also important. This sculpted ceramic warrior comes from the island cemetery of Jaina.

Ancient elites: the archaeological evidence

Elites are generally more visible in the archaeological record than other sections of society, and this is especially true of the supreme rulers themselves. Kings and queens build themselves splendid residences and equip themselves with the finest goods their merchants and craftsmen can supply; often they take these goods with them to their graves. They build temples to the glory of their gods and goddesses, or more directly to themselves. They may erect public notices, statues and other monuments; they may even borrow each other's monuments, as the Romans did with Egyptian obelisks, which they transported to Italy to erect in their own public places.

Buildings and monuments

The public buildings and other monuments of the early civilizations are large, elaborate and impressive, and one of their purposes was propaganda. This may be explicit in words or pictures, as when the Persian king Darius I carved an inscription high up on the rock face at Bisitun in north-west Iran, proclaiming his achievements in three different languages; or when the Roman emperor Trajan, under whom the Empire reached its widest extent, erected a column 38 m high in Rome, depicting his successful military campaigns in Dacia, north of the river Danube, by a relief carving running in a continuous spiral from the base to the top. Other monuments may be less explicit, but they make the same point: the pyramids of Giza, the great ziggurat at Ur, the Temple of the Sun at Tiahuanaco all proclaim the greatness and power of their builders. Great size, splendour of design, elaboration of ornament, use of rare and precious materials, all contribute to the message. In life the message would have been reinforced in other ways, for instance through elaborate ceremonial, but such manifestations are essentially ephemeral. The monuments by contrast are permanent; they were built to last and in many cases they have indeed survived for many millennia.

The Great Pyramid of Cheops and the Sphinx at Giza still speak forcefully of the power of the pharaohs of Egypt's Fourth Dynasty.

The ball-court at the Maya site of Copán in western Honduras. The Mesoamerican ball-game involved opposing teams attempting to keep a solid rubber ball, up to 2 kg or more in weight, in motion without using their hands or feet. Although it was a public spectacle, the game was not simply for entertainment – it was also an important religious ritual. On some occasions at least the losing team was sacrificed.

Temples are among the most common buildings of ancient civilizations, as befits societies organized as theocracies. Even in the later civilizations, where power had a more secular base, temples were still important public buildings: this is as true of the Aztecs and Incas as it is of classical Greece and Rome.

The size of the temple complexes and the amount of work involved in their construction was often prodigious. The Pyramid of the Sun at Teotihuacán, the largest single-period building in prehistoric America, was a four-stage truncated platform supporting a small temple. The platform was constructed of mud-bricks with external walls of stone faced with lime stucco and plaster, with a total volume of close to one million cubic metres. In Mesopotamia as early as the fourth millennium BC the city of Uruk boasted a vast terrace surmounted by monumental buildings; the American archaeologist Adam Falkenstein calculated that it would have taken 1,500 men working a ten-hour day five years to build the terrace – before any temple buildings were even begun! In both Mesopotamia and Mesoamerica the temple was not only the religious centre of the city, but the administrative centre as well, associated with storage facilities, workshops, record offices and residences of the temple staff. In civilizations where power was less closely associated with religion, temples were more modest in scale: Greek and Roman temples, impressive though they are, represent a much smaller proportion of the state's 'labour budget' than those of the early theocracies. A similar change probably occurred in the late Mesoamerican civilizations: the major temple pyramid of Tenochtitlán, the Aztec capital in the Valley of Mexico, was only one quarter of the size of the Pyramid of the Sun at Teotihuacán, the valley's capital a millennium earlier.

Palaces form a second major category of elite buildings. In most ancient civilizations royal residences were large, well-equipped and elaborately decorated, but the most impressive occur, as one would expect, in those civilizations where the palace was the administrative centre, like the later Mesopotamian civilizations or the Minoan and Mycenaean civilizations. The Great Palace at Mari on the middle Euphrates in Syria early in the second millennium BC occupied 2 hectares and had 250 rooms, including an audience chamber and other reception rooms, residential and administrative quarters, an archive of some 25,000 clay tablets, and a school. The palace of Knossos on Crete during the period *c.* 1750–1450 BC occupied an equivalent area and provided the same kind of accommodation and facilities. The fine wall paintings and the domestic equipment, such as baths, of the Minoan palaces are well known, but similar features occurred in the Near Eastern palaces too. The palace at Ugarit on the Mediterranean coast of Syria in the later second millennium BC had piped water laid on to some of its 90 rooms.

Places of public entertainment were also prominent structures in some of the early civilizations. However, entertainment is probably not the right word to describe the Mesoamerican ball-game, which had a ritual significance. The ball-court at the Maya centre of Chichén Itzá, the largest in America, was 128 m long and I-shaped. It was flanked by playing walls 8 m high and surrounded on three sides by temples which provided 'grandstand' views of the game. Below each of the playing walls was a low inclined wall decorated with relief carvings of scenes from the game, with the leader of the victorious team holding in his hand the severed head of the defeated leader. Whether the losing team always paid with their lives is unknown, but

Left: In the civilizations of the Minoans and Mycenaeans, among others, the dominant public building was the palace, which was both the residence of the ruler and the seat of the state bureaucracy. Part of the palace at Knossos on Crete is seen in this view; the standing section is part of the reconstruction undertaken by Sir Arthur Evans.

Below: Temples were among the most important monuments not only of the early theocratic states, but also of the later civilizations of Greece and Rome which had a more secular base. This small temple of Athena Nike was erected on the Athenian acropolis in the later fifth century BC.

certainly the ball-game was an important religious ceremony.

Other places of entertainment include Greek and Roman theatres and amphitheatres. The last were characteristically Roman constructions, consisting of oval areas surrounded by tiers of seats, designed to accommodate huge numbers of spectators and to stage complex and spectacular events such as gladiatorial contests; at the grand opening of the Colosseum a full-scale sea-battle was enacted in the flooded arena. The purpose of these events was to glorify the emperor and entertain the people; such entertainments were the circus component of the 'bread and circuses' which, according to the Roman satirist Juvenal, reconciled the masses to their position in society.

In the later civilizations *civic buildings* of various sorts appear, which in earlier phases had no identity separate from that of the temple or palace. These include market-places, public baths, council chambers and law-courts. However, these are not buildings of elites in the same sense as the other monuments described here; they are public buildings but not for the exclusive use of the elite.

Kings and emperors frequently erected *commemorative monuments* to celebrate their achievements, such as statues, stelae, obelisks and columns. Maya stelae, for instance, have a portrait of a ruler on one face, while the back and sides bear hieroglyphic inscriptions recording his genealogy and achievements. The most elaborate monuments are probably the triumphal arches developed by the Romans. Consisting of one to three arches and decorated with relief panels and attached sculptures, they commemorate military victories or the restoration of peace.

Equipment

As one might expect, elites of all periods equipped themselves with splendid goods, often made of rare materials traded from distant sources and worked with all the technical skill their craftsmen could offer. These are among the best-known remains of the ancient civilizations, now to be found in the great museums of the world. It is in the nature of archaeological evidence that most of them were discovered in burials: precious objects are unlikely to survive in abandoned buildings or deserted streets. Only in the case of the Aztecs and the Incas, where sixteenth-century Europeans encountered living civilizations, do we gain an idea of the immense wealth which the elites disposed of in life. The Spanish king's share of the Inca treasure, sent back to the Spanish court, comprised 30 gold jars with an average weight of *c.* 20 kg each, 28 gold statues of men, women and 'sheep' (i.e. llamas) weighing *c.* 18 kg on average, 29 silver jars and 15 silver statues.

Of particular interest are the objects chosen as specific symbols of status and power, commonly head-gear (crowns, head-dresses), clothing, seats (thrones, stools) and weapons. The crowns of the Egyptian pharaohs are one example. In predynastic times there had been two separate crowns, a 'white'

Above: Among the hundreds of goods in the tomb of the second-century BC Chinese princess Dou Wan at Mancheng were these gilt bronze leopards, inlaid with silver and garnets.

For the elite of ancient Egypt the correct funerary ritual was as important as the mummification of the body and the preparation of the tomb and grave goods. This scene from the funerary papyrus of the Royal Scribe Hunefer, *c.*1300 BC, shows the 'Opening of the Mouth' ceremony performed on the coffin outside the tomb.

crown of Upper Egypt and a 'red' crown of Lower Egypt, while the historical pharaohs wore a double, combination crown. The Mesoamerican rulers wore elaborate headgear: Maya stelae show rulers wearing animal-head head-dresses topped by quetzal feathers. Other examples of symbolic equipment include the double-axe of the Minoans and the *fasces* (bundles of rods bound together by thongs) which the Romans inherited from the Etruscans as a symbol of power. Axes were originally attached to the *fasces*, but from the early Republic they were removed within the city boundary.

Burials

Royal burials are the ancient remains that have most captured the imagination of the modern world. Indeed one great tomb – that of king Mausolus at Halicarnassus in south-west Asia Minor – was one of the Seven Wonders of the Ancient World and has given us the term mausoleum for all grand burial structures. The *monumentality* of the tombs, the treatment of the body (especially mummification), the richness of the grave goods and the occasional practice of human sacrifice all speak powerfully of the manpower and the wealth at the disposal of the dead monarchs. In monumentality nothing exceeds the two huge pyramids of Cheops and Chephren at Giza, but the burial complex of the first Chinese emperor Qin Shi Huangdi, who died in 210 BC, must represent a comparable investment of manpower: it consists of a huge tumulus in two walled enclosures, the outer one more than 6 km long, as well as burial pits containing an estimated 7,000 life-size terracotta figures of officers, infantry, cavalry, chariots and charioteers. By contrast the royal burials of civilizations such as the Mycenaeans, though they are impressive enough, represent a much smaller investment of labour, appropriate to the smaller scale of the Mycenaean state.

The process of *mummification*, designed to preserve the body, was developed to its highest extent in Egypt, but was also practised by the Incas. In Egypt at an early stage it was restricted to the king himself, whose survival was thought to be essential to the whole of society, though later it was extended to other classes. Among the Incas the emperor's mummy was maintained in state by his attendants; it was brought out to attend ceremonies and consulted in times of difficulty. The Chinese did not practise mummification, but they believed, wrongly, that jade had the power to preserve the body. The second-century BC prince Liu Sheng and his wife Dou Wan were buried in jade suits made of more than 2,000 pieces each and sewn together with gold thread.

The dead were normally buried with *grave goods*, and those of the royal family and nobles were wealthy in proportion to their status. What has survived for the archaeologists, however, is rather arbitrary, depending both on what has been excavated and what has escaped the depredations of tomb robbers, ancient and modern. The goods found by the British archaeologist Sir Leonard Woolley in the Royal Tombs of Ur are well known, as are those from the shaft graves at Mycenae, though none are as famous as those from Tutankhamun's tomb in Egypt's Valley of the Kings. Less well known, though becoming more familiar, is the material from Chinese tombs, such as those of

Gold mask of the god Xipe Totec, cast by the lost-wax method, from Tomb 7 at Monte Albán, Oaxaca. The tomb, of the Mixtec culture (AD 900–1494), is one of the richest ever found in Mesoamerica. It contained nine bodies and more than 500 objects of gold, jade, onyx, rock crystal, shell and bone.

Liu Sheng and Dou Wan, excavated over the last twenty years. The tomb of the Marquess of Dai, which dates from the mid-second century BC, contained a body buried in three nested coffins and a wealth of objects, including vessels and chopsticks of lacquer, 162 wooden figurines of the Marquess' household retinue, many clothes and more than 50 rolls of silk. The whole contents of the tomb were inventoried on 312 slips of bamboo.

Elites in various parts of the world sometimes practised *human sacrifice*. Some of the best known examples were found in the Royal Tombs at Ur: 11 in Queen Puabi's tomb, 63 in the 'King's Grave' and 74 in the 'Great Death Pit'; they included court women decked out in gold and lapis lazuli jewellery, musicians with their instruments, courtiers, soldiers and drivers of chariots, which were also buried in the tombs together with the oxen that drew them. Human sacrifices also occurred in Shang China, sometimes accompanying the burial, sometimes made later as offerings to the reigning king's ancestor, as at Anyang. Human sacrifice was common in the Americas, especially among the Toltecs and Aztecs (see pp. 32–3), but it is usually found in association with religious ceremonial rather than with burials. However, tombs containing sacrificed retainers have been found at the highland Maya site of Kaminaljuyú near Guatemala City, and also, as we have seen, in the Chimu capital of Chan Chan (see p. 82).

Human sacrifice was never the rule even among the most powerful elites, and instead retainers were often represented in tombs by statues or figurines; this practice was particularly common in Egypt and China.

Elites are not equally visible in all civilizations and at all times. If we see the monuments and the display in terms of public statements about the power of the leaders, it is possible that the greatest visibility occurs at times when power is being established or when it is threatened in some way. If power is well-established, wide-ranging and unchallenged, there is less need to devote so many resources to this purpose.

5 The Economy

Subsistence economy has already been mentioned in connection with theories about the origin of civilizations, their environments and the role of elites. Subsistence is indeed a crucial issue: all societies must feed their populations in one way or another, and in the early civilizations these populations were much larger than in any earlier era. The population density for mid-third-millennium BC Sumer has been estimated as about 20 people per km^2 (over all inhabited land, town and country together); for the Classic Period Maya (AD 300–900) the comparable figure is between 40 and 80 people. These figures compare with estimates of between 1 and 10 people per km^2 for early farmers. Moreover, until a relatively late date all food had to be produced locally: it is unlikely that any early civilization was dependent on imported staple foodstuffs. Fifth-century BC Athens was probably the first city-state to rely on imported grain, and it was exceptional in this respect. The Romans imported grain in large quantities, from Sicily, Egypt and north Africa, but these areas were all within the Roman Empire; the Romans were not dependent on trade with areas outside their own control.

The primacy of cereals

The early civilizations needed both fertile land and high-yielding crops in order to produce enough food within their own territories to feed their growing populations. The only plants that were sufficiently productive were the cereals: wheat and barley in Western Asia, Egypt and Europe, millet and rice in South-East Asia and maize in the Americas. Cereal agriculture is about 22 times more productive than rearing domesticated animals for meat. It is no exaggeration to say that without cereals civilization could not have developed. Indeed, cereals are still by far the most important sources of plant food today: try to imagine a world without bread, rice or pasta!

Agricultural intensification

As we have seen, various techniques were used to increase agricultural yields, of which the most important was irrigation. Sometimes this involved simply taking advantage of the natural flood regime of large rivers, as in Egypt and perhaps also the Indus Valley and Shang China; this might be supplemented by the use of water-lifting devices such as the *shaduf*. At the opposite extreme were massive irrigation works, great canals and dykes, involving centralized organization and large labour forces. We have good documentary evidence of these from both Mesopotamia and China, but not before a developed stage of the civilization (late Early Dynastic in Sumer and Eastern Zhou in China). Far from being the cause of civilization, as Wittfogel suggested, huge hydraulic enterprises followed the development of civilization and were only made possible by the organizing power of the new bureaucracies. Irrigation was practised in the New World as well as the Old, but in Mesoamerica it was never employed on a very large scale. In the Andes canal construction is documented from the last centuries BC, but sizeable programmes of terracing and canalization occur only after the emergence of the Inca state.

Irrigation undoubtedly increased crop yields, but it could also cause problems. These are particularly well documented for Mesopotamia, where it seems that long-term irrigation agriculture in conditions of inadequate drainage led to increasingly saline soil. In a well-known study, the

Opposite: The introduction of the ox-drawn plough was an early improvement in agricultural practice. Early farmers in Western Asia used plough teams very similar to this one, photographed in northern India today.

First-century AD Roman mosaic from Tunisia showing a similar ploughing scene.

Below: Mediterranean civilizations were based on the combination of cereal agriculture with the cultivation of olives and vines, often grown together, as seen here in southern Italy.

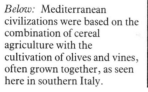

In Mesoamerica, a variety of techniques was employed to augment production, including terracing, the use of humid bottom land and the 'floating gardens' or *chinampas* (described on p. 33). Other methods of improving production, used in the Old World but not in the Americas, include the application of animal manure to the fields and the use of ploughs drawn by animals.

Other plants

Between them the early civilizations cultivated an enormous variety of plants: root crops, pulses, green vegetables, fruits and nuts. Indeed, most of those grown today were cultivated in early times. Cereals were probably the main source of both proteins and carbohydrates, but other plants contributed as well. Some – particularly peas, beans and lentils and, to a lesser extent, potatoes and manioc – were high in both proteins and carbohydrates. The oil-producing plants such as olive, soya and sunflower were also major providers of energy, while nuts provided protein, oil and starch. Other plants were important for their mineral or vitamin contents (citrus fruits and green vegetables for Vitamin C, for instance), while sugar-rich fruits such as figs and dates were an easily digested source of energy. Apart from food, some plants were grown mainly or exclusively for their fibres to make textiles, such as flax (grown widely in the Old World) and cotton (grown in the Indus Valley, Mesoamerica and Peru).

In some areas crop combinations were themselves the means of agricultural intensification. In the Mediterranean, where irrigation had little part to play, civilization was based on the Mediterranean triad of wheat, vine and olives. In Peru civilization depended on the exploitation of two different crop complexes: the maize/bean/squash combination of the coastal area and the potatoes and other root crops of the highland zone.

Animals

Accustomed as we are to a diet rich in animal foods, it is salutary to recall that many societies consume very little meat. In ancient Mesoamerica only the dog and the turkey were domesticated and there were no large mammals to hunt, although fish, birds and small game were caught. Naturally dairy products were not available, and there may have been a shortage of animal protein in the diet. It has even been suggested that the practice of human

American Assyriologist Thorkild Jacobsen showed how the citizens of the Diyala area responded to this problem by changing their crop from wheat, which can only tolerate 0.5 per cent salt in the soil, to barley, which can tolerate nearly 1 per cent. In the mid-third millennium BC wheat formed about 16 per cent of the total cereal crop; later in the millennium it had dropped to 2 per cent, and after 2000 BC it is not mentioned in the records at all.

Some crops were grown not for food but for the production of textiles. This Egyptian funerary papyrus of the Eighteenth Dynasty shows the harvesting of flax, used to make linen.

Rice and millet were the main cereal crops of ancient China. Rice was grown either on terraces or in paddy fields, as seen here in southern China today.

sacrifice may have been related to this possible deficiency. The theory has not gained much support, though it is true that Aztec victims were eaten – we have the accounts of horrified Spanish observers! In Peru the guinea pig and the muscovy duck were domesticated for food, and the llama and alpaca as pack animals and for wool. Deer and guanaco (a close relation of the domesticated llama) were sometimes hunted, though here too meat consumption was probably not high.

In the Old World the situation was different. Sheep, goats, cattle and pigs were kept in almost all the early civilizations, and other domesticated animals also occur: buffalo and elephants in the Indus, donkeys in Egypt and Mesopotamia, and camels in several parts of Western Asia. Together they provided not only meat, but dairy products, wool for textiles and traction power for ploughs and carts. Except in areas where annual flooding served to renew soil fertility, animal manure was also of great importance in ensuring good cereal crop yields.

The exploitation of animals for dairy products is much more economical than for meat – about six times more efficient in terms of output per hectare – though it is still far less productive than cereal agriculture. One possible disincentive to milk production is that a high proportion of the world's population (Europeans being the major exception) is intolerant of lactose after early childhood and unable to digest fresh milk easily. However, lactose is broken down by fermenting and souring, and lactose-intolerant individuals could certainly have eaten yoghourt and cheese, as they do today.

Hunting continued to be important in the Old World civilizations, and it is likely that meat was eaten on a considerable scale, at least by the better-off members of society. Indeed, in the civilizations of Egypt, Western Asia and Europe the diet was fundamentally very like ours today; of all our staple foods, only potatoes are real newcomers; the rest would seem quite familiar to any ancient Egyptian or Sumerian.

Manufacturing industries

Crafts

Early civilizations are characterized by a high degree of craft specialization compared with earlier prehistoric societies; they sometimes involve new technology and they frequently reach new levels of skill. None the less the crafts themselves are rooted in the prehistoric past, and most of the techniques were old when civilization began. Take stone, for example. One of the best documented crafts in the early civilizations is stone-working, and all its techniques – chipping, pressure-flaking, grinding, polishing, pecking, incision, drilling – were developed in the Neolithic or earlier. This is as true of large stone sculpture, like the Olmec basalt heads or Egyptian granite obelisks, as it is of smaller objects such as Chinese or Mesoamerican jades, Mesoamerican obsidian artefacts, jewellery of turquoise and lapis lazuli in Egypt and Mesopotamia, steatite seals and beads in the Indus Valley, or vases made of rock crystal and other stones in Minoan Crete.

Pottery manufacture, another well documented craft in the early civilizations, also has a long prehistoric ancestry. Technological innovations played a negligible role in the development of the industry in the early civilizations. In the Old World the potter's wheel appeared *before* the emergence of civilization, at least in Mesopotamia and China, while in the Americas it was never used at all. In the early civilizations improvements were made to the form of kilns and higher temperatures were achieved, but these were hardly revolutionary changes.

Metallurgy was well established in the Old World civilizations, and again it was clearly built on prehistoric achievement; this is true both of the cast bronze tradition of the Chinese and of the more diverse metal-working technology of the western civilizations, which includes lost-wax casting, beaten metal working, and a variety of surface decoration techniques, such as inlaying, engraving and embossing.

In the New World, metal was abundantly used in Peru: gold and silver working goes back to Chavín times, while in the later empires of Chimu and Inca copper and tin were also worked, alloys were made, and casting, gilding and inlaying were practised. In Mesoamerica metallurgy appears only after *c.* AD 900 – using mostly gold in Oaxaca, mostly copper in the Valley of Mexico.

Crafts based on perishable materials such as textiles are more often known through written records than through archaeology, so their prehistoric background is uncertain. However, there is evidence of wool-production in prehistoric times in several parts of Western Asia, ancestral to the very important woollen industry documented in clay tablets from the Mesopotamian and neighbouring civilizations and from the Aegean. In Egypt the use of linen cloth began in the prehistoric period, while cotton, known from cloth in the Indus civilization, has turned up (in seed form, so not certainly used for cloth) around 4000 BC on a site in Baluchistan. In both Mexico and Peru finds of cotton cloth predate civilization by a considerable period. In China, silk cloth was not certainly produced in prehistoric times, but there is a distinct possibility that it was, since the industry was highly developed by the Anyang period.

Some crafts did develop only after civilization was established. The turquoise-coloured glazed paste known as *faience* appears first in both Egypt and Sumer in Early Dynastic times, while true glass was developed a little later in Mesopotamia. In China the first use of lacquer – a natural varnish made from the juice of the lac tree (*Rhus vernicifera*) – occurs in the Shang period. There were also innovations that occurred later in the history of civilization, such as the development of iron technology in the second millennium BC in Anatolia and probably independently in the first millennium BC in China.

Technology

The early civilizations depended overwhelmingly on human energy for production: there was very little mechanization or use of animal, wind or water power. What mechanization there was included the use of the potter's wheel and rotary lathes and drills for stone work. These devices were not substitutes for human energy, though they certainly increased the efficiency with which it was exploited. The craft production of the early civilizations was really the

Opposite: This vase in the shape of a duck, carved out of a single piece of rock crystal, was found in Grave O of Shaft Grave Circle B at Mycenae and dates from the sixteenth century BC.

Opposite: Jade burial suit of the Han prince Liu Sheng, who died in 113 BC. Liu Sheng's suit and that of his consort Dou Wan each contained more than 2,000 pieces of jade, sewn together with gold thread.

Above: Faience bowl from Egypt, of the Eighteenth Dynasty. Faience was made with a core of quartz or quartz and soda lime, fired so that the surface fused into a glossy coating. The turquoise colour was achieved by adding copper salts.
Right: In the Americas the technique of casting metal in moulds was first developed in Colombia, where it was applied to gold and the copper-gold alloy, tumbaga. This gold pendant in the Darien style (*c.* AD 1200–1500) was cast by the lost-wax method.

craft production of prehistory writ large: what was new was the *scale* of production, in terms of both the number of objects produced and the amount of work invested in each one. Not only were larger and more elaborately decorated objects produced, but some production processes involved several different stages.

Lost-wax bronze casting, for instance, involves making a clay model of the object, coating it in wax, coating that again with clay, and baking it to fire the clay and melt the wax; then the bronze (an alloy of copper and tin which has already gone through several stages of production) has to be heated until it melts and poured into the mould; then, after cooling, the mould must be broken and the casting extracted; finally the bronze surface must be finished by abrasion and polishing; it may be decorated further by a variety of surface ornament techniques. Some objects required repeated applications of the same process: Chinese lacquer goods had many layers of varnish applied to the wood or fabric surface, each polished to a high finish. Other labour-intensive products are those involving a variety of different materials or many small pieces of the same material, such as the inlaid objects produced by Sumerian craftsmen or the mosaic masks made by the Aztecs.

The organization of craft production

In the early civilizations craftsmen were full-time specialists. The use of multi-stage techniques and the amount of labour involved would have been impossible for specialists working on a part-time basis. Moreover the objects they produced were for elite consumption only, and consisted in most early civilizations of three main classes of artefact: goods required for the glorification of the gods and the practice of religious ritual; the personal equipment of the royal family and the aristocracy in life and death; and the military equipment required by the army.

Craftsmen were, to begin with at least, supported directly by the state, and their products were commissioned by the elite. There is no evidence of freelance activity or of craftsmen producing goods for sale to possible buyers at a price not agreed in advance. Freelance craftsmen and mass-production are both associated with the market economy, which developed only at a later stage (see p. 111).

The approximately 25,000 cuneiform tablets found at Mari on the middle Euphrates give us particularly full information about the organization of crafts in the Mesopotamian palaces in the early second millennium BC, when Mari was the most important city in the area. The most important crafts documented are textile-working and metallurgy, but we also have information about workers in semi-precious stones, leather, wood and basketry. The work was controlled by workshop directors, two of whom have been identified in the Mari tablets, each responsible for several departments and answerable to the king himself, who took a direct interest in the organization of both supply and production. Large numbers of workers were involved: one tablet lists 58 men and 29 women in only one of five departments concerned with textiles at Mari. Many of the workers, both male and female, were slaves, often prisoners of war; others were freemen of local

origin, who were trained by palace staff. The workers were paid in clothes, wool and cereals; they seem to have been allowed some holidays. Working mothers sometimes brought their children to work with them and were given an extra ration for the child. This payment according to need rather than productivity is a good indication of the 'non-commercial' nature of economic organization.

Long-distance trade

One of the striking features of early civilizations is the very long distances over which both raw materials and finished goods were traded (using the word 'trade' in its widest possible sense to include any method by which goods changed hands). Lapis lazuli, the semi-precious blue stone favoured by elites in Egypt, Mesopotamia and the Indus Valley, came, as far as we know, from a single source in Badakshan, northern Afghanistan. The elite of the Shang civilization of northern China imported cowrie shells, tortoise shells, turquoise, jade and perhaps tin from south China. In Mesoamerica cacao, the plant from which chocolate is made (a favourite elite drink), was imported to the highland areas from the tropical lowlands where it grew, while jade and obsidian were also traded over considerable distances. Here we shall look at the purpose of such trade and how it was organized.

Necessities and luxuries

Although both necessities and luxuries were traded in the ancient civilizations, necessities were normally acquired either from the local area or from regions not far away. The difficulties and dangers of long-distance trade would have made it unwise for any society to become dependent on such trade for everyday needs. However, we should be wary of making too much of the distinction between necessities and luxuries, since necessities can only be defined as those things which are *felt* to be necessary. As the economist Karl Polanyi has said: 'What we term "luxuries" were no more than the necessities of the rich and powerful, whose import interest determined foreign economic policy.' And it is true that, just as craft specialization in the early civilizations was geared to elite consumption, so was long-distance trade, which provided the raw materials used by the craftsmen and sometimes manufactured goods as well.

Goods and materials chosen for prestige consumption should have certain characteristics: they should be absolutely rare and available only from a few restricted sources, preferably they should be susceptible to further elaboration at the craftsman's hands, and they should have good display value, that is they should be visually rich and dramatic. Modern valuables, such as gold and diamonds, have these qualities, and indeed many of the metals and stones that we label 'precious' today clearly had high prestige value in ancient times. However, we should not transfer our values wholesale to these earlier societies, who sometimes awarded high value to items we deem of little account. When Moctezuma told Cortés and his companions that the Aztecs valued quetzal feathers more than gold, the Spaniards were sceptical, but there is no need to doubt the truth of the statement: quetzal feathers fulfil the specifications of prestige goods just as well as gold.

The organization of trade

Until the emergence of a market economy, perhaps in the mid-first millennium BC in the Mediterranean (see pp. 112–13), trade was controlled directly by the state, that is either by the temple personnel or by the royal family and the nobles. This applies equally – as it must – to import and export trade, but the mechanisms involved in the two cases were quite different. Whereas the goods for export were collected through a system of taxes, rents and tributes paid in kind, the imports were acquired through expeditions to the sources of the materials. In some cases no trade was involved, since the expedition was to the source of the material itself, which was quarried directly. The Egyptians organized expeditions of this sort to Sinai to obtain turquoise, where no other party was involved. More often the goods were acquired through trade with another party. The kind of trade was not the market form familiar to us, but the type known as administered or treaty trade. It was always organized by government or government-controlled groups. All aspects of such trade – storage facilities, the actual physical method of exchange, checks on quality, control of the trading personnel and prices – were agreed in advance. Price was in no way dependent on supply and demand as it is in a market system.

A particularly well documented example of administered trade is known through the fortunate discovery of the records (consisting of some 16,000 tablets) of a Mesopotamian trading post at Kanesh in Anatolia, dating to the early second millennium BC. These tablets record the transactions of a group of Assyrian merchants who occupied a walled cantonment, known as a *karum*, on the outskirts of the native city. The merchants belonged to a series of family 'firms' all working directly for the king of Assur; the main exports from Mesopotamia were textiles and tin, while the main imports were gold, silver and copper. Each consignment of goods from Mesopotamia had to pass through the palace of the

Opposite top: Black-figure cup of the sixth century BC showing the king of Cyrene (a Greek city of north Africa, now in Libya) supervising the weighing and packing of wool for the export trade.

Opposite bottom: Vulture pendant from the tomb of Tutankhamun. It is made of gold, from Egypt's eastern desert, and lapis lazuli, imported from its distant source in northern Afghanistan.

Below: In China cowrie shells were used as money as early as Shang times and continued in use alongside metal coins in later periods. This bronze container from Southern China was used to hold cowries; it was made in the second or first century BC.

native ruler, who could exercise an option to buy or else levy taxes. The long overland journey was not always accomplished successfully. One tablet from Mari records a caravan that was detained on the way to Kanesh from Karana in the northern region of Mesopotamia.

Merchants

In the early civilizations merchants were direct employees of the state; they came from the upper class and enjoyed high status; frequently they were members of the royal family. In some cases, as among the Aztec *pochteca*, they were organized in guilds. Like the craftsmen, the merchants did not live by making profits out of their transactions; instead they acted for the king and were rewarded by status revenue, often in the form of landed property. We know from the tablets found at Mari that the Assyrian merchants at Kanesh lived very well: they often took local wives and ran comfortable households with slaves to do the menial work. They controlled the whole Assyrian trade network in Anatolia through their own officials, but they were subject to Anatolian laws and paid taxes to the Anatolian king.

Only with the development of the market economy do we find the emergence of freelance traders, who traded for profit. And when they did appear they were members of a lower class, like the *metics* in Athens, who sometimes became very rich, but who were debarred from owning land or houses and thus excluded from the privileges of the elite (see p. 112).

Types of economy

Any discussion of economy in the ancient civilizations has to take account of a debate between scholars on economy in primitive societies. The 'formalist' school takes the view that economic laws worked out in present-day conditions apply equally well to primitive and ancient societies. The alternative 'substantivist' position, developed by anthropologists, claims that in primitive societies economy cannot be separated from other aspects of life – that economic transactions take place within a framework of social interactions.

Substantivists argue that formal economics, with its emphasis on the profit motive and on supply and demand, can be applied only to the formal market economy. In primitive societies, by contrast, production, distribution and consumption are structured by the system of kinship relations; the main motivation is prestige (or its counterpart: obligation) rather than profit, and supply and demand have little to do with it. This view seems to us to offer more enlightenment on the early civilizations. Among the first of the substantivists was the American Karl Polanyi, who identified three main types of economic organization: reciprocity, redistribution and market exchange (better called the market economy).

Reciprocity

Reciprocity is the form of economy typical of a simple segmentary society with little hierarchy – the kind of society which has characterized most of our long prehistoric past. In this type of society goods change hands as *gifts*, but gifts which have to be reciprocated, in a system of obligations based mainly on kinship. Exchange can take many forms; examples include reciprocal feast-giving, dowries and bride prices, and arrangements often called 'trade partnerships', although they do not involve trade in the formal economic sense, since the types of goods that can be exchanged are strictly prescribed, the relative values are established by custom, and haggling is outlawed. In terms of the way goods move around in space, reciprocity is associated with symmetry and has no centralizing tendency.

Redistribution

Redistribution is the form of economy associated with chiefdoms, that is with societies which are markedly hierarchical in structure but still organized on a kinship basis. It also characterizes early state societies, in which it was only gradually replaced by a market economy. Reciprocity can be regarded as 'pooling': it involves the collection of goods from the members of a group and their redivision within it. Redistribution contrasts with reciprocity in its highly centralizing tendency: goods are first concentrated at a centre, whence they will be redistributed; the two-way symmetrical exchanges characteristic of reciprocity are lacking. (In fact the two economic modes are not mutually exclusive and can function within one society, but one mode will always be dominant.) One thing that redistribution has in common with reciprocity is that it too is 'uneconomic' as the term is used popularly today; that is, it is motivated by considerations of obligation and prestige rather than profit.

Redistribution is visible archaeologically: it is associated with central places, larger than the

Large pottery jars were used to store grain and oil in Minoan palaces which served as centres of redistributive economies. These are at Mallia in northern Crete.

average settlement and often displaying distinctive ceremonial architecture. Such sites are also likely to be rich in artefacts, especially if storage areas can be located. Where redistributive systems were associated with writing, archaeologists may find the administrative records themselves.

All the earliest civilizations described in this book had redistributive economies, but two cases are particularly well documented through written records. These are the 'Great Organizations' of Mesopotamia (the Temple and the Palace), and the palaces of the Minoans and Mycenaeans.

All the earliest Mesopotamian tablets, which came exclusively from the temples, and many of the later ones, often from palaces, are book-keeping documents – records of the state economy. The earliest examples are simple lists of types and quantities of commodities, whereas later on there are more elaborate records, including lists of incoming food and other products from the local population, lists of raw materials and manufactured goods from distant sources, and lists of outgoing rations of food and materials, allotments of parcels of land, etc.

The Mycenaean palace at Pylos in south-west Greece has provided a particularly useful group of Linear B tablets. The 1,200 or so tablets all refer to the last year in the life of the palace, some time around 1200 BC. They include lists of land grants (naming tenants-in-chief and sub-tenants), rations issued to slave women (mostly wheat and figs) and records of flocks of sheep. One particularly interesting series of these tablets relates to bronze working, listing the smiths at various places and the amounts of bronze issued to them.

The market economy

The true market economy is defined by the existence of the market itself: not the *market-place* (since similar places can occur in different economic systems), but the *institution* of the autonomous price-fixing market. Only in such a system are economic activities separated from social life. The American economist Walter Neale has expressed this succinctly: 'In a Self-Regulating Market System the whole complex of personal life is irrelevant. Religious faith, social status, political belief, family life, loving, hating, gossiping, do not decide what shall be done, except as they are part of the complex of motives and emotions creating demand for products.' In this world prices are related to supply and demand and the motivation is profit.

How can we recognize the market economy in the archaeological record? When did it emerge and how did it develop out of the very different system that preceded it? Market economies have the same centralizing tendency as redistributive systems, so they may appear similar in the archaeological record. Their existence may be indicated by the use of coinage where this was in general circulation and not used only for state purposes, but the best indications come from documents that record commercial transactions of a market type. True market economies seem to have developed remarkably late: few would claim them before fifth-century BC Athens and some would say much later. They seem to have developed gradually, starting with a fringe of private enterprise growing up around the redistributive state economy and increasing as time passed.

Above left: The development of the market economy saw the emergence of shops, bars and taverns of a kind familiar today. This Roman 'take-away' in Herculaneum had large jars set into the counter to hold cereals and vegetables, while a stove behind the counter kept dishes simmering.

Above right: Wall painting from Pompeii showing a bread shop. The baker is selling loaves that resemble carbonized examples found in an actual baker's shop at Pompeii.

The rise of commercialism

Of the types of economic organization that we have just outlined, only the market economy is readily familiar to the citizens of modern Western civilization. We can all identify without difficulty some of its more striking components:

> the seller
> the purchaser, or consumer
> the market-place
> the price
> money and coinage
> mass-produced and throw-away items
> shop sites
> the concept of 'supply and demand'
> the concept of 'scarcity'
> the 'profit' motive

In Chapter 1 we described a rise in the intensity of trade in the Mediterranean area in the first millennium BC, the advent of coinage, the first tentative establishment of a market economy in fifth- to fourth-century BC Greece and the coming of the throw-away container (amphora) in Rome (see pp. 24–7). However, trade in the ancient world differed in important ways from its modern counterpart. A thorough-going market economy, and a society dominated by the market-place, are phenomena that have developed since the Industrial Revolution, and in some respects only in the last twenty to thirty years.

Trade

Ancient society did not see 'the economy', as we tend to, as something separate. Even by the fourth century BC, there existed no conceptual tools for handling a formal economics. The economy was not perceived explicitly, and was still embedded in other state institutions, such as group relationships governed by honour and obligation. When the change to commercialism came, it was very gradual, fluctuating and (possibly until very recently)

Standard weights and measures were an important feature of the Roman economy. This bronze balance from Pompeii, which worked on the steelyard principle, carries an inscription giving the date AD 47 and certifying that the weights are in accordance with the specifications laid down in that year. The counterweight is in the form of the bust of a boy, perhaps a member of the imperial family.

incomplete – redistributional practices and ways of thinking persisted alongside the market economy, and on occasion regained their ascendancy. To the elite hierarchy of a redistributional state, the takeover by a new world of trading for profit was not at all welcome.

It is against such conceptual difficulties, and in the context of a transitional stage between the two systems, that the philosopher Aristotle (384–322 BC) attempted at various points in his *Ethics* and *Politics* to comment upon economic issues. He clearly reflects his class (upper) and his period, when he says that supplying necessary goods or practising a useful craft is something that the good citizen does for the benefit of the *community*: for honour and status, and never purely for personal gain. In Aristotle's Athens, such services were performed by Athenian citizens, assisted in most cases by their numerous slaves. Aristotle did not criticize this arrangement or the institution of slavery.

To begin with, trade for profit was tolerated on the fringe, carried on for the most part by 'metics' (a class of semi-resident aliens) and 'foreigners'. A similar resistance to participation in 'trade' on the part of Victorian gentry, together with the concept of the 'tradesman's entrance', forms a reasonable parallel. The idea that the price of goods could be so 'marked up' that gains could accumulate into the kind of wealth that would enable an individual to join the landed class, would probably have been anathema to Aristotle. There existed no really separate merchant middle class with social aspirations.

There was, however, a marked change from the Hellenistic period (third century BC) onwards, with the formation of a Greek merchant middle class. Ironically enough, it is now the elite Romans who despise them, as we can see in the satirist Juvenal's contempt for the 'lying Greek'.

Context

Clearly significant in the rise of commercialism is the advent of coinage, probably in the late seventh century BC. At least two centuries were to elapse before 'small change' was available in Athens; it was well into late Hellenistic and early Imperial times before the individual had anything like a range of 'shops' and 'bars' at which to spend his coins. It was perhaps only in Imperial Rome that a truly cheap coinage became freely available.

While some kind of trader's stall probably has a much greater antiquity, on permanent shop sites even Imperial Rome was to remain ambivalent. Consider, for example, the 'shopping precinct' and 'arcades' of the emperor Trajan's Market. The Market is situated next to Trajan's Forum. It is, however, the Forum that has pride of position and treatment, with its extravagant use of space and its peristyle. The Market is relegated to a difficult hill site nearby. Admittedly the architectural solution is ingenious (including the need to cut away the hillside), but there can be little doubt that the central state institutions have the better site.

Changes in the concept of property and ownership are also connected to the rise of commercialism. Most pervasive, as we saw in Chapter 1 (p. 25), were changes in systems of land tenure. The key concept is that of inalienable ownership. Whereas typically redistributive societies employ status and obligation to regulate land use, with 'lease' being provisional and on behalf of the group or state, the market economy operates on the principles of inalienable property, price and contract. Earlier societies placed a clear ban on the notion of profit from basic transactions, such as those in staple foods. In the 'free' market, however, everything – including people, services, and food supplies – can be bought up. To quote Juvenal again, *omnia sunt Romae venalia*: 'everything at Rome can be bought and sold'.

Morality

One important aspect of the market economy – and a reason perhaps why its original advent and its subsequent development have seen many troubled stages – is its essential amorality. The earlier state societies with their redistributive economies and 'administration' of group symmetries and interests, had certain principles built-in. These principles involved obligation and reciprocal ties, which by definition were moral. The elaboration of these principles in society was not necessarily admirable, and we do not wish to idealize such societies here. Antiquity soon recognized, however, that the new unbridled freedom of the 'free' market brought large problems into state management. The greater and more conscious range of choice enjoyed by the individual was also two-sided, since one man's free enterprise was another's exploitation. In the event, intervention and the renewed use of redistributive and 'administered' structures were practised, and by some remarkable agencies. Ptolemaic Egypt, for instance, in spite of the cosmopolitan nature, say, of Alexandria, kept a strict state control on the movement of goods such as beer, oil, metals, spices, perfumes, salt and textiles. Quality was monitored, and hefty customs imposed. In Imperial Rome the emperor Hadrian rescued certain craft trades from extinction, while Diocletian introduced a programme of 'consumerist' legislation to moderate abuses.

Above: While in redistributive economies craftsmen were employed by the state and their products were commissioned, in market economies they worked for themselves and sold their products in the market. This first century AD Roman relief shows a cutler at work. The seated man is holding an iron bar and working the bellows, while the other hammers on an anvil.

Left: Under the Romans not only craft products but also food came into the orbit of the market economy. As Roman control spread across Europe, farmers, who had previously farmed for themselves or within the framework of a redistributive local chiefdom, were incorporated into the Roman commercial system. This first century AD relief shows a Gallic peasant taking his produce to market.

6 Religion and Belief

Religion is a universal of human society. It involves belief in supernatural beings who can influence the lives of living men and women and who can themselves be approached and influenced through performance of the appropriate ritual. Religion consists of a system of *beliefs* (ideas) and a body of *ritual* (action). Approaches to the study of religion can be grouped into those that regard beliefs as basic (such an approach is sometimes described as 'intellectualist') and those that concentrate on the ritual (sometimes described as 'sociological' or 'symbolist'). In all societies before recent times religion was closely integrated with other aspects of social life. It is not surprising therefore to find that different types of religion are characteristic of different types of society.

Religion in band societies

The supernatural beings of band societies are individual spirits with distinctive personalities. Anyone can make contact with a spirit; there are no temples or shrines and no organized priesthood. The only specialist in the supernatural – usually a part-time specialist – is the *shaman*, who is concerned mainly with curing illness. His usual method of contacting the spirit world is through possession (like a medium). Illness and bad luck are thought to be caused by sorcery, and the job of the shaman is to identify the sorcerer and sometimes to remove the foreign object that the sorcerer has inserted in the body of the sick individual. By contrast with these activities relating to individuals, religious ceremonies involving groups of people or the whole society are presided over not by shamans, but by elders who are not religious specialists.

A widespread feature of religion in band societies is *totemism:* a totem is a species of plant or animal which enjoys a mystical relationship with the members of a group. Ceremonies associated with totemism, especially 'rites of increase', which are designed to ensure the well-being and continuity of the particular totemic species, can be seen (according to a sociological interpretation) as serving to promote group solidarity.

Tribal religion

The supernatural beings of tribes inhabit a more ordered cosmos than that of bands, arranged in a structure that mirrors the segmentary organization of society. There is sometimes a tribal supreme spirit,

Opposite: A figure, perhaps of the god Quetzalcoatl (or alternatively of a priest), from the Huasteca culture in north-east Mexico, of the Late Classic period (AD 600–900). He carries on his back a child symbolizing the sun and his body is tattooed with motifs of flowers, blades of corn, suns and other signs.

Below: In band societies the only religious specialist is the *shaman* or healer who has privileged access to the spirit world, often achieved through a state of religious ecstasy or trance. This modern shaman's rattle made of painted wood comes from Vancouver Island.

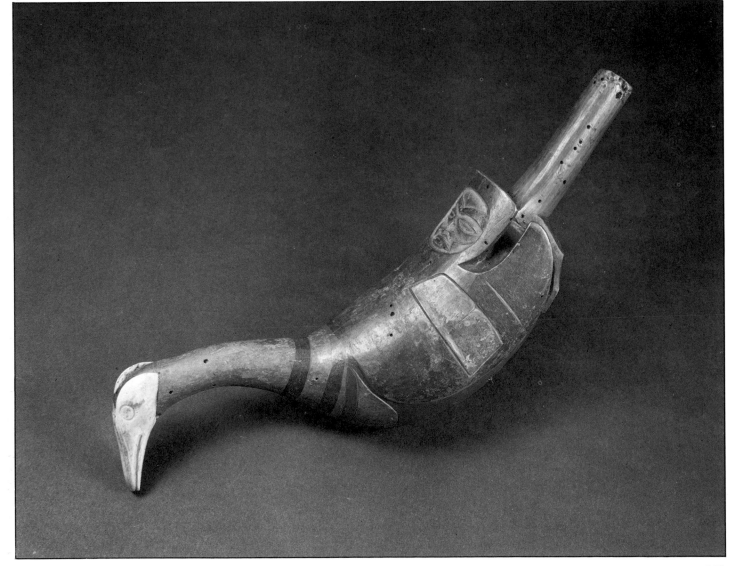

The Gateway of the Sun at Tiahuanaco in Bolivia (AD 300–600) bears a relief-carved frieze *c*.3.5 m long and 1 m high. In the centre is an anthropomorphic deity, often described as the 'Gateway God'. This was the chief deity of Tiahuanaco and probably represents the sun-god.

Little is known about the religion of the Indus civilization, where few religious remains have been found. This clay figure from Mohenjo-Daro is sometimes described as a Mother Goddess, but could as easily represent a priestess or a figure from mythology.

whom we could perhaps label a god, whose domain is as extensive as the tribe and who is often the original creator. Lower-level spirits have 'departmental' responsibilities for crops, rain, war and so on. Still lower levels of supernatural beings are totemic spirits, fetishes and ghosts. Tribal religion features a variety of cults, but is characterized by an interesting phenomenon: the amount of ritual devoted to a spirit is inversely related to its position in the cosmos – in other words, the lower down the spiritual scale the more ritual there is. This seems to be because the lower the spirit, the more influence it has on everyday affairs. The supreme spirit often has no associated ritual at all, but then, as Marshall Sahlins says, 'the Supreme Being often doesn't do much – or at least what has he done lately?' By contrast, the most prominent cults are associated with totemic spirits and even more with fetishes and domestic ghosts. These lesser spirits are concerned with everyday domestic activity; to quote Sahlins again, 'this is where the action is, and the problems'.

Associated with the lineage organization of tribal societies is ancestor worship; there are cults of both domestic (ancestral) ghosts and of collective clan ancestors. The lineage is seen as consisting of both dead and living members, and the dead are held responsible for the condition of the living. Sorcery and witchcraft also play an important role, as in band societies (see above).

Tribal societies often have permanent places of worship – shrines or cult houses – but they rarely have a permanent priesthood: as in bands, cult leaders are generally elders who, by virtue of their age and experience, have the deepest knowledge of the rituals, but they are not supernatural specialists. Healers and witch-doctors, by contrast, are specialists, like the shamans, but again they are rarely full-time specialists.

Religion in chiefdoms

In the cosmos of chiefdoms, the hierarchical ordering of supernatural beings is emphasized, reflecting the hierarchical structure of society. Cult activities at the domestic level continue, but collective cults are now more important. Cults quite often occur in tribal societies at village and regional level, but in chiefdoms we find 'national' cults, invoking great gods on behalf of the chief and the chiefdom. The ancestor-cult aspect is also emphasized: the great god of the chiefdom is the ancestor of the reigning chief and has a direct interest in his prosperity and the continuation of his line. Such national cults frequently become institutionalized and are associated not only with permanent places of worship, which may be elaborate temples, but also with a permanent specialist priesthood, frequently headed by the chief himself.

Religion in the early civilizations

Religion in the early civilizations is chiefdom religion writ large. The god of the chiefdom becomes the god of the city-state, the kingdom or the empire. He is still the ancestor of the monarch, however, and is therefore directly concerned with the prosperity and continuity of the reigning dynasty, which is thought to ensure the well-being of the whole people. This relationship is often reflected in the terms used in the literature. In Sumer, for instance, all citizens were members of a temple community and were consequently described as 'the people of the god Nannar' (or Enki, or Ningursu, or whoever). Ancestor worship is particularly well documented in Egypt, China and Peru, but was probably a feature of *all* the early civilizations. The institutionalization of religion progressed apace: the early states had vast and elaborate ceremonial architecture and a large, permanent priesthood which administered not only religious affairs but also the economic business of the state.

As we have seen, later civilizations, both in Europe and in Mesoamerica, became rather more secular in orientation. State religion continued to be important, but did not dominate society to quite the same extent as before, while some activities, such as craft practice and trade, were removed from the religious sphere altogether. Moreover, when civilizations entered an imperial phase, involving territorial expansion into regions with quite different local deities, state gods may have seemed remote and irrelevant to many citizens. This sometimes led to the resurgence of local cults or to the emergence of religions like Christianity and Mithraism in the Roman Empire, which, as we saw in Chapter 1, offered the individual a personal god and the chance of personal salvation.

Terracotta figure from Khorsabad, short-lived capital of Assyria under Sargon II (721–705 BC). It represents Gilgamesh, hero figure of Sumerian and Assyro-Babylonian epics, who was a real king of Uruk's First Dynasty.

Chinese ritual vessel from a tomb near Anyang, the last Shang capital (c. 1300–1030 BC). The vessel, of the *lei* type, served as a container for wine offered to royal ancestors. It is decorated with a large *taotie* mask and rows of dragon-like animals and birds.

Religion: the archaeological evidence

Sources of evidence for religion in ancient societies fall into four main categories: religious buildings, religious objects, burials, and religious texts. There may also be other, more peripheral, documentary sources.

Religious buildings

We have already described the temples of the ancient civilizations, but that was in the context of social organization. Here our concern is with the nature of religious beliefs and practices, so we focus attention on features and fittings, such as altars, platforms, baths or basins; on decoration, with particular attention to its symbolism, and on evidence for particular ritual practices, such as animal or human sacrifice. For instance, one of the shrines within the wall of Mycenae included a series of platforms. One, in the centre of the room, had a slightly concave surface and might have been used for libations. On another platform in the corner, the highest in the

room, stood a large female idol, thought to represent the goddess of the shrine, while in front of her was a low round table, perhaps used for offerings.

Religious objects

Various objects found on archaeological sites are regularly labelled 'ritual'; examples include models of people or animals, ranging from diminutive figurines to life-size or larger figures; human or animal bones given special treatment; and artefacts of all sorts which are unusually elaborate and found in 'ritual' contexts. The label 'ritual', however, disguises a degree of ambiguity about the status of these objects. Are they, in fact, the *objects* of worship, or are they *ex voto* offerings to a deity in thanks for favours received or in hope of those to come, or, finally, are they artefacts used in ritual practice? Often their status is unclear, but at times we may be able to choose between the options with some confidence. Although exceptions are certainly possible, large individual statues in prominent positions within temples can generally be regarded as the objects of worship, like the large female idol in the shrine at Mycenae mentioned above. Smaller figurines or other objects found in considerable numbers on religious sites are most likely to be *ex voto* offerings; they occur frequently in shrines of the Hellenistic and Roman periods. Examples of equipment used in religious ritual include items as diverse as the bronze ritual vessels of Shang China, which held offerings of food and wine for the ancestral deities; the stone knife used by the Aztec priest to cut open the chests of sacrificial victims; and the cup used in the Church of England communion service.

Burials

Burials can cast light not only on social organization, which we have already discussed, but also on religious beliefs and practices. One example is belief

Among the many religious monuments found at the Olmec ceremonial centre of La Venta were monumental carved stone objects: colossal heads, stelae and, as shown here, altars with figures carved in relief.

For some ancient civilizations we have evidence not only of public religion, in the shape of monumental state temples, but also of domestic ritual. The household shrine in the House of Menander at Pompeii displays crude wax and wood images of family ancestors in a recess behind an altar.

in an after-life, most delightfully demonstrated in the tomb paintings of Egypt's New Kingdom, which show the deceased nobles reaping bumper grain harvests, making wine, hunting, eating and drinking in style and generally enjoying all that was best of their life on earth. We may also find evidence of religious practices: human sacrifice has already been mentioned; it was practised excessively by the Aztecs, but is documented elsewhere in the New World and also in the Old World – in Mesopotamia, China and occasionally among the Mycenaeans. Other recorded practices include ritual purification by fire, often associated with the practice of cremation, in civilizations as diverse as the Greeks and the Aztecs; ritual feasting, found in almost all the ancient civilizations; and the deliberate breaking of grave goods: an example of this is a rapier from a Mycenaean tholos tomb near Pylos which was deliberately bent before deposition.

Religious texts

The ancient civilizations offer a wealth of documentary records on religion. These range from complete holy books like the Bible, through collections of myths, hymns and spells to records of divination, like the Chinese oracle bones. We also find sacred calendars, like the Etruscan version on the Zagreb mummy wrapping, and records of offerings made to gods and goddesses, such as those recorded on the Linear B tablets from Pylos. In later periods we may find incidental references to religion in literary works, and in the case of Mesoamerica we have the eye-witness accounts of the horrified Spanish observers of Aztec religious ritual. Finally, by the time of the classical civilizations we have conscious attempts to explain religion, beginning as early as the Presocratic philosophers in the sixth century BC and characteristic above all of the Stoic tradition. Cicero's *De Natura Deorum* (45–44 BC), which examines the views of three different philosophical schools (Epicurean, Stoic and Academic) on the nature of the gods and the existence of a Divine Providence, is an example of this tradition.

Interpretation

It is possible to assess the role played by religion in the life of a past society, and it may also be possible to reconstruct its constituent rituals. It is particularly difficult, however, to reach an understanding of the beliefs of past religions, even where an extensive religious literature is available. This is because religious belief is expressed through symbolism – including physical symbols, their images in language or pictures, and symbolic action in ritual – and archaeologists have yet to develop useful approaches to understanding the symbols of past societies. In general archaeological practice has veered between naive over-simplification (such as the tendency to label all female figurines 'mother goddesses') and a retreat into cynical rejection of the possibility of ever being able to interpret such symbols. And yet some of the approaches to symbolism developed by anthropologists may offer enlightenment. In the first place we should resist any temptation to search for specific meanings for religious symbols; certainly we should not expect one-to-one correlations of the type 'blood = life', or 'female sexual organs = fertility'. As the anthropologist Fredrik Barth has written,

'Just as no one would engage a symphony orchestra if the same could be said in words, so we can assume that rites say things that cannot be said in other ways'. Some anthropologists, like Victor Turner, claim that symbols have complex and multi-layered meanings; others, like Dan Sperber, argue that they do not have meanings at all. If symbols do have identifiable meanings, these are not particularly important: the value of symbols lies in their *emotional* force, their power to transport the individual onto a spiritual plane, apart from everyday life. And emotional resonance arises not at all from precise meaning, but rather from its opposite, that is from separation from normal language and activity and through association with other, equally disconnected, ritual symbols and activities. Ambiguity, imprecision, impressions of secrecy and exclusiveness all *add* to the emotional value of symbols. Thus in studying past religions we should be better advised to concentrate on identifying the symbolic themes that carry the emotional message, rather than on pointless attempts to determine specific meaning.

But what about those cases in which there are conscious attempts by participants to explain religious beliefs and practices, as in the classical world and, to a greater extent, in the continuing religions of Judaism, Christianity, Buddhism and Islam? These works are the equivalent of the native informants of ethnographic fieldwork, who 'explain' to anthropologists what symbols 'mean'. Should we not accept the explanations of those who are 'in' the religions and therefore, one might argue, ought to know what they mean? Dan Sperber has argued that in fact such explanations are not interpretations; rather they are extensions of the symbols and must themselves be interpreted. Such works therefore provide added emotional depth for participants in the religion, but they do not offer analysis or explanation.

Well-born Egyptians often had individual chapels associated with their tombs. This funerary papyrus of the Nineteenth Dynasty shows the tomb chapel of the Royal Scribe Ani. It is shown situated on the Western Mountain, close to the papyrus reeds of the Nile valley.

Religion and society

If we ask the question 'What purpose does religion serve?', we straight away face a dichotomy, because religion serves both purposes for the individual and purposes for society, and these may be quite different. The 'intellectualist' and 'sociological' approaches to religion can be seen as concentrating on belief and ritual respectively; in a different perspective, however, they may be regarded as concentrating in the one case on the function of religion for the individual and in the other on the role of religion in society. We shall look at some 'intellectualist' arguments later on, but here we shall concentrate on the 'sociological' views favoured by many anthropologists. Marshall Sahlins is quite clear about the primacy of the social role of religion: 'From this societal function, the individual "thumb-sucking" function of religion is clearly derivative.' It is likely that most anthropologists would agree with him on this, although they might well be more polite about the religious needs of individuals!

However, although most anthropologists agree that the social function of religion is primary, there is no such agreement between them as to what that function is. One of the main interpretations is that associated with the great French anthropologist, Emile Durkheim, according to whom 'God is another name for society'. What he meant by this is that the supernatural world represents the secular world: it stands for society, whose members constantly affirm the authority of society through repeated religious rituals. Thus religious beliefs are seen to mirror social structure, while ritual practices symbolize social values and relationships. The function of religion is to integrate society, to promote unity and to maintain continuity.

An alternative view is associated with another great anthropologist, this time a Briton, Bronislaw Malinowski; he developed it specifically in relation to *magic*, although it can be extended to cover religious beliefs and practices generally. Malinowski suggested that the function of magic was to take over where human competence and know-how left off. Man could control through ritual those aspects of his environment which he could not control through his technology and economic practices. To take one example, to produce a good harvest, man would prepare the ground, sow the seed, keep the fields weeded and the animals out of them; he would still need magic ritual, however, to bring the rains at the right time, to ensure the correct amount of sunshine and to ward off plagues of insects and crop diseases. In Malinowski's view, there is an inverse relationship between the amount of magic ritual practised and the degree of real (technical) control over any activity. His best-known example comes from the Trobriand Islands, where he did much of his fieldwork. The Trobriand Islanders are great fishermen, fishing both in the inner lagoon, where it is an easy, reliable and safe activity, and in the open sea, where it is dangerous and uncertain. Malinowski found that no magic was practised in connection with lagoon fishing, while there was an extensive body of magic ritual associated with fishing at sea.

Both Durkheim's and Malinowski's explanations are functionalist; they assume that religious beliefs and rituals (and they emphasize the rituals) serve the interests of society as a whole. Certainly some types of ritual are specific to particular groups in society. Among the rituals which anthropologists label 'rites of passage' or 'life crisis rites', those that mark the change from childhood to adulthood are sex-specific, with different rites for boys and girls. Other types of ritual may also be restricted to one sex or the other, or to particular age groups, or to special groups such as warriors. It is assumed, however, that these rituals are but part of the whole and contribute to the smooth functioning of the whole society.

In a Marxist interpretation, religion takes on a quite different aspect: it becomes an instrument of exploitation – Marx called it 'the opium of the

Creation stories and origin myths are found in all religions. This detail from the Aztec Codex Fejervary-Mayer shows the god of night, death and destruction, Tezcatlipoca. He is tempting the Earth Monster to come to the surface of the great waters by using his foot as bait. She swallowed up his foot but lost her lower jaw; the earth was created from her body.

people' – used by the ruling class to keep the working class in thrall. According to such an interpretation, religion serves both to justify the *status quo* (as exemplified by the phrase, 'the rich man in his castle, the poor man at his gate') and to console the dispossessed for their unenviable position in the present world by promise of compensation in the next ('the meek shall inherit the earth').

It is possible to combine the functionalist and Marxist views in an evolutionary interpretation. In egalitarian societies, as we have seen, religion clearly functions in the interests of society as a whole, but as society becomes increasingly hierarchical and divided vertically, so religion increasingly comes to serve the interests of elites alone. Indeed, as we saw in Chapter 4, religion may have been the means through which chiefdoms were converted into states. Religion is an excellent instrument of oppression, from the oppressors' point of view, simply because it is so difficult to challenge. If temporal power is seen as divine in origin and if it is constantly reinforced by the acting out of rituals which have been practised 'from time immemorial' (or so it seems, since that is the character of ritual), then it is completely invulnerable to criticisms of logical inconsistency, defiance of natural justice or any other argument based on rational analysis. The message that is thus conveyed is that the world is as God set it up and therefore cannot be altered. Only in the multi-cultural societies first encountered in the early empires did a way out become apparent, and this was through the availability of alternative religions. In the Roman world marginal religions, imported from far-flung corners of the Empire, appealed to minorities to whom the state religion had little to offer. Christianity started out as a religion of the oppressed, only to become in its turn, in the Christian state from the later Empire onwards, the religion of the oppressors and itself an instrument of oppression.

Above: Religious rituals serve a variety of purposes both for society and for the individual. 'Rites of passage' mark important transitions, such as the passage from childhood to adulthood. The photograph shows part of the first menstruation ritual of the !Xo Bushmen of the Kalahari. The older men hold branches to represent the horns of gemsbok whose mating behaviour they mimic.

Left: Some rituals are concerned with such matters as success in hunting or agriculture and human health and fertility. In this photograph of a !Xo healing ritual, the healers dance around the fire accompanied by the chanting and clapping of women.

121

Religion and the citizen

What we have said so far takes us some way towards a model of ancient religions. But what would Sumerian state religion have meant to the citizen of Sumer? What did early state Christianity mean to the citizen of the late Roman Empire? Do we assume a parallel – or a contrast? Traditionally many scholars, particularly of the 'intellectualist' persuasion, have seen an *explanatory* role for religion as self-evident and universal. For them, the religions of civilization offer the citizen an explanation of how the world came to be as it is, how it works, and where he stands in the order of things. In particular, early religious belief and literature tend to be seen as the primitive precursors both of the supposedly more sophisticated theology of later religions, and also of the modern moral, social and physical sciences. That some caution may be advisable, however, is indicated not only by the 'sociological' and 'symbolist' positions on religion, which emphasize the pitfalls of too literal an interpretation, but also by the ever-present danger of anachronism. The great world religions with which we are familiar today are generous with explanatory literature. Religions such as Christianity, Islam and Buddhism adopt an explicit and deliberate explanatory stance, a proselytizing attitude in which they package their beliefs and practices for the potential believer. However, we cannot take these later religions uncritically as a universal model. We need instead to distinguish between early state religion and later state religion.

State religion

Let us begin with what the citizen may find common to both. State religion, both early and more recent, has as its primary objective the reinforcement of the state's validity and identity. It tends to support power hierarchies (both priestly and secular), class and occupational differentiation, state administration and institutions, and it does this by the repetition of rituals which continually re-establish accepted priorities and values. Emphasis is upon the ceremonial act, upon services of renewal (e.g. for the king, although mostly conducted by the priesthood on his behalf), upon great communal feasts and festivals, and upon ritual assemblies. Liturgies supply the dialogue for the ceremonial, and 'religious' literature the wider context. Some aspects of state religion project a crude and direct symbolism for the citizen. In religious architecture, for instance, enormous equals important. The great ceremonial building, temple or tomb, located in a specially elevated or central position, decorated with expensive, elaborate or unusual finishing materials, achieves a splendour and dominance quite unknown to the ordinary buildings of the city. The dimension of timeless eternity is vital, and great effort was expended to produce buildings that would not deteriorate – an example of this can be seen in the widespread use of fine marbles for cladding purposes. Hence also the nervously active continual rebuilding of the major Mesopotamian temples, where rapid weathering and disintegration of the mud-brick structure produced particular problems of deterioration.

The approach of state religion is literally theatrical. It is difficult now to imagine, for instance, just how blindingly dazzling the Great Pyramid of Cheops would have been when its original surfacing of fine Tura limestone was still fresh and intact. This is theatre, not only because a great religious complex will act as a 'backdrop' to major processions and festivals, but also because the buildings are *always* there. It is permanent theatre. The citizen lives out his life with this same stage, and all the values it implies, standing as background. He is dwarfed not only by the gigantic scale of the buildings and their spatial setting, but also by a timescale of construction and use which reduces personal significance to the infinitesimal.

Most of what we have written applies to both ancient and more modern state religion. Just how closely this 'symbolism' is connected with the reinforcement of state values and institutions can be judged from the fact that a very similar architectural 'language' is used to spell out the importance of other power centres in the state – such as, for instance, the construction of palaces for royal families and, in our own day, of great buildings for giant commercial companies, banks and state institutions.

Top: The central structures of Toltec Chichén Itzá illustrate well the symbolism of state religious monuments. The large central pyramid is the temple of the god Kulkulkan, while in the foreground is a *chacmool*, a standardized reclining human figure, whose stomach was probably used to hold offerings, including the hearts of sacrificial victims.

Bottom: Wall painting from the tomb of Tutankhamun showing the pharaoh Ay, who succeeded Tutankhamun for a few years, performing the ritual of opening the eyes and mouth of the dead king's mummy.

Early state religion

Where early state religion differs markedly from its later counterpart is in the *content* and justification of its belief system, and in the degree of remoteness from the citizen, especially one who stands lower down the state hierarchy. Early state religion is unashamedly the religion of the king, the immediate upper aristocracy and the reigning priesthood. It makes no political apology. It is the state and its top control system writ large.

Early state religion informed the citizen from a remote height of his place in society, but offered very little in the way of pragmatic understanding that would help in his daily life. Although the religion might officially reckon him 'one of the people of the God', it did not regularly involve him in its processes, except at a distance. For the most part, the powerful colleges of priests kept all ceremonial to themselves. The more important the ritual, the fewer the priests that would participate, and the more secretive the processes. The complex of buildings itself would also not be generally open to the 'public', with progressive restriction of access to the inner areas and sancta. In many ways, the classical civilizations of Greece and Rome (before official Christianity) show an interestingly late version of this early state religion. The proverbial Olympian aloofness of the Greek gods is a linear descendant of this exclusive attitude.

Moreover there was little in the way of individual moral guidance. In a sense, early state religion is almost amoral, and not particularly 'religious'. Moral control was managed by the group, as it was in chiefdoms, with the rewards of acceptance, honour and preferment, and with the sanctions of their opposites. At this stage, God is not involved as a final and unchallengeable authority; nor is the promise of heaven and the threat of hell.

'Religious' literature, which would not for the most part have been directly accessible to the more lowly citizen, reflected the values and preoccupations of the aristocracy, and the ingenuity of the priests. Something like the Egyptian story of Osiris being murdered by Seth and cut into sixteen separate portions, and of his subsequent miraculous re-assembly, has more to do with the political unification of sixteen administrative areas of Egypt, than with any 'religious' motive. Creation myths glorified the state, and put it and its administrators into a suitably eternal context, but as for the average man, as in the Mesopotamian *Enuma Elish*, he was created not for the glory of God, but for the service of his betters.

Although early state religion as a type offered little personal identity, support or guidance to the individual citizen, it is probable that right from the beginning of the earliest city-states the individual had recourse to a whole range of minor deities, cults and magic for practical assistance with life's problems. As in tribes and chiefdoms, these lesser religious activities could exist alongside the main state religion, and need have little direct connection with it. As long as the beliefs and practices of these fringe cults were not politically and socially subversive, they could easily be tolerated. The deities involved were typically family or domestic, as in various forms of ancestor and group ancestor cults; local, as in strictly regional agricultural cults;

Above: The tumbled stone heads of Greek gods, Zeus and Apollo, executed in local style at Nemrud Dag in Turkey, show the wide geographical spread of Greek religion, and other aspects of Greek culture, in the Hellenistic period.

Left: Priests were powerful figures in the ancient civilizations. This polychrome wall painting from Teotihuacán shows a priest in elaborate gear.

123

This basalt carving of the Aztec god of creation, Tonacatacutli, shows a characteristic early state deity: impersonal and forbidding.

upon the later development of religion and thought.

Interesting too was the development of smallish groups of people of like mind living together in what were virtually religious communities: an outstanding example is the late sixth-century BC Pythagorean community of Croton in southern Italy. There are certain links with the mystery cults, but also distinct features. The religious community centred around a teacher figure who had many of the qualities and attributes of the earlier band and tribal shaman. The figure of Pythagoras himself is very shadowy. Characteristically the Master of such a community would write nothing down, but progressively a body of sayings would be attributed to him. As time passed, it would become very difficult to differentiate between what might have been part of the original teaching, and later additions and adaptations which were ascribed to him for authority. Pythagoreanism was very influential upon Plato and, probably through his writings, became one of the many components that eventually entered Christianity. Central to Pythagoreanism were the idea of the soul as a fallen divinity imprisoned within the body as in a tomb, sentenced to an almost unending cycle of reincarnation in varying life-forms, and the need for purification (Greek *katharsis*) and various abstinences.

Later state religion

The transition from early to later forms of state religion, at least for the future western world, began during the first millennium BC. This millennium, which was, as we have seen in Chapter 1, so strongly characterized by the rapid and turbulent changes stimulated by the spread of urbanization, the growth of literacy and the switch from a redistributive to a market economy, promoted changes of value and organization in the city-state itself. In religion, this period saw the fringe cults offering a much more direct political challenge to official state religion. In particular, fringe sects developed which often had a radical and fundamentalist outlook. Some of these were of zealot or fanatical persuasion and did pose a threat to the stability of the state. Others were content to limit their radicalism to matters of the soul and the after-life. Unlike the mystery cults, these groups were evangelistic by nature. Prominent among them were the 'saviour' cults, in which a saviour figure or deity – Mithras in Mithraism, and Christ in Christianity – promised personal and eternal salvation to the convert.

In these saviour cults we can see certain parallels with the initiatory stages of the mystery cults, such as the seven 'grades' of Mithraism: the Raven, Bride, Soldier, Lion, Persian, Runner of the Sun, and finally Father. In Christianity there are parallels with the purificatory rite of baptism and the participant sacraments. Ideas of asceticism and purification are common, together with 'mystic' imagery, such as darkness and light, sacrifice and blood, life through death and victory over evil.

The crucial transition that was to alter the *content* of state religion in western civilization was the popular spread of the mystery cults and saviour religions under the early Roman Empire. These cults drew very large numbers of adherents, Mithraism being popular with the successful merchant classes and Christianity with the non-commissioned officers and private soldiers of the

or specialized in some way – responsible for a particular aspect of daily life such as the weather, or for the protection of craft skills. Some of these cults might involve belonging to a small restricted 'brotherhood' with a closed membership, often organized from craftsmen with a particular skill.

The distribution pattern of central state religion and peripheral personal cults can be studied as late as the classical civilizations of Greece and Rome, although some care should be taken as by then things were beginning to change. Of special interest here are the 'mystery religions' or cults, the most notable being the Orphic and the Eleusinian. By mystery cult we mean properly a small closed society, admission to which was by a series of 'initiation' ceremonies. These stages of initiation were not intended to fail suitable applicants, but to ensure that they could only reach the heart of the group by a slow process of learning and acceptance, and that they were finally shown to be fit people to be trusted with the cult's ritual truths and secrets. These reserved truths were not necessarily especially 'mysterious' in a modern sense, but it was from them that such groups took their name. Some of these cults amounted to movements and possessed, as with Orphism, a long history and a developed body of religious myth. Orphism had close connections with the fine arts and music; while its imagery of primeval Chaos, the 'cosmic' egg and black-winged Night, and its belief in the transmigration of souls and punishment after death, all had a powerful influence

army. It is normally reckoned that the emperor Constantine took the decisive step at the Council of Nicaea in AD 325 of effectively establishing Christianity as the new state religion of Rome. This development, in many ways parallel to the earlier adoption of Buddhist ideas at state level in India, and to the later establishment of the Islamic state, brought to civilization a state religion that, officially at any rate, was now focussed upon the life and interests of the individual citizen. Cynically, we might credit Constantine with more political foresight than contemporary sources would suggest!

It is this later type of state religion with which we are now familiar. It is to its characteristics that we would tend to give the term 'religion'. It is to these crucial developments and to the particular ancestry of these fringe cults that we owe, for instance, the link between personal morality, public morality, and God and religion. The rulebook approach is characteristic, for example, of Pythagoreanism – which lists many do's and don't's – and of the extremist sects. The heavy preoccupation with moral failings or sin may go back to similar antecedents, or it may reflect the predominance of Judaeic sources underlying both Christianity and Islam. A nice contrast between the two types of state religion is pointed up by two versions of man's original fall from grace: in the Mesopotamian *Adapa* legend, Adapa is offered divine food at the table of the sky-god, Anu, which will bring immortality and eternal happiness to himself and the future of mankind; he fears

however that it is the food of death, and does not eat. He makes a mistake which is perhaps a comment on the wayward ill-luck that dogs man, but there is no idea of temptation and no hint of moral guilt or sin. It is just bad luck. In the Judaeic creation myth found in Genesis, on the other hand, Adam is morally culpable.

A fourth-century AD mosaic from Hinton St Mary, Dorset, England, shows a deity with a human face: Jesus Christ, a personal god, offering salvation to the individual.

125

7 Writing and Literacy

Writing is technology, a set of practical skills which, like so many of man's other invented technologies, has interacted with the structure of society to produce large and irreversible changes. Strangely enough, however, its importance is often overlooked. Whereas people are ready to concede the considerable impact on society of, say, the motor car or the aeroplane, the advent of writing is often seen as a mere detail – a low-level recording technique that is purely incidental to the main developmental trends in human society. In particular, the history of writing has been the Cinderella of serious academic study.

Writing is of central importance to civilization. The development from preliterate to literate society came early in the history of civilization (the earliest examples come from fourth-millennium BC Mesopotamia), and it is not fanciful to claim that without writing the city-state would never have exceeded a modest size, nor indeed ever have proved an enduring and stable form of social organization at all.

Virtually all the activities and relationships of a developed state society *assume* the existence and use of writing. Even a few atypical examples do not disprove this point. It is true, for instance, that the Incas appear at first sight to have run an empire of considerable extent without a writing system. However, their use of the *quipu* – a device consisting of cords on which information was conveyed by the position of knots of differing sizes – in fact represents a very primitive recording system. Writing does not necessarily increase man's intelligence and capacity for organization – any more than a hydraulically-assisted ram actually increases man's physical strength. A technology is an added enhancement. In the case of writing, that enhancement acted directly upon man's capacity for understanding, and for the appreciation of possibilities. The advent of writing marks the beginning of the long and gradual process that has continued ever since, in which language information of all kinds has become a commodity that can be processed, packaged, re-packaged, shifted and, above all, stored.

Opposite: Wood carving from the tomb of Hesire, an official of Egypt's Third Dynasty, at Saqqara (*c.* 2700 BC). Hesire holds in his left hand the long staff and club-like sceptre of his rank, while from his shoulder hang the tools of the scribe; a stone palette with two sections for holding ink cakes, a case to hold a rush brush and a container for water to moisten the brush.

Below: High on a rock face at Bisitun in north-west Iran the Persian king Darius I had an inscription carved, recording his military victories in 516 BC. The inscription is trilingual, in Old Persian, Elamite and Babylonian, all three written in the cuneiform script, and it provided the key to the decipherment of both the script and the languages.

Storage

Writing enables language items to be stored, divorced from their purely personal source, and transmitted through space (i.e. to spatially disconnected persons), or through time (i.e. preserved for posterity). This is particularly valuable to state society, since, as we have seen, such a society is distinguished by a shift from face-to-face relationships based upon locality and kinship, to interconnections of a more remote and institutionalized type. Storage across space and time permits the keeping of records, the systematization of administrative and legal instruments, and the growth of bureaucracy. It also favours the gradual accumulation of information, allows cross- and back-reference to 'look up' items, and provides the basis of subsequent formal educational systems. The transmission which is thus encouraged from generation to generation of an ever-increasing body of cultural information and knowledge, duly has a knock-on effect in favour of the further development of institutionalized society. Such development in turn intensifies the exploitation of the recording system, and the result is added incrementally to the transmitted culture. It is this central contribution of writing to developmental *cycles* that accounts for so much of its constructive influence.

Analysis

Storage by writing also facilitates all processes of analysis. The fact that cross-reference is possible from one stored item to another, frees the user from the ephemeral impermanence of speech, and is likely to suggest new possibilities of arrangement and co-ordination, such that the limited span of purely oral statements might never appreciate. In particular, the ease of cross-reference between documents, or 'files', favours analysis by categories and its subtler differentiation. The fact too that written records, especially bureaucratic documents, tend to be divorced from the immediate personal context, favours the growth of a more critical analysis, since there is less inhibition relating to difference of social status and respect for familiar elders.

Complexity and the visual

Further, writing systems in general encourage the storage of items of increasing length or complexity, or of items that have complex interconnections with other items – such as simultaneous membership of various different 'files'. Typically, the order of this complexity is beyond the 'oral' or 'aural' memory-span of any given individual or group of individuals. In the context of complexity, the *visual* aspect of writing is of crucial importance. Just think how difficult it is to memorize very long lists, long sentences with several subordinate clauses, parts of a legal document, or a mathematical computation. We need to *see* the visual items and review them before we can process the complexities involved. Writing is therefore a prerequisite for all cases that mount beyond a certain level of complexity, such as the development of law-codes, of numerical systems (a special case of writing), and of the symbolic languages used in mathematical and geometrical operations. Especially interesting here is the contribution of early writing systems to the analysis of language, and to their own evolution. The use of primitive writing systems, and the gradual

appreciation of their inadequacies, involves sooner or later a type of linguistic analysis, and this in turn enables writing systems to be further refined.

Personal and state identity

The freedom given by writing from purely inter-personal communication has effects upon the development of both individual and state identity. For individuals there is now, potentially at any rate, a medium for creative literature that offers greater permanence and individuality than the previous oral tradition. The individual writer can leave personal memorials and record individual attitudes and experiences that will reach a far greater readership than personal contact could ever have achieved. As the Roman poet Horace wrote of his own verse, *exegi monumentum aere perennius*: 'I have set up a memorial more lasting than bronze'.

Similarly writing provides the state with a medium through which a state 'persona' can be elaborated. This is a powerful instrument for moulding the attitudes of its own citizens, and for creating an external national identity. The king, the priests, or the administrative rulers, can ascribe to the state policies, hopes, intentions and values, as if to an individual; and they will have wide coverage and considerable permanence. The observer, depending on his viewpoint, can see the resulting development as an honest attempt to, say, recover and describe the nation's historical evolution, warts and all; or as a calculating and selective version of events that happens to favour the administration, i.e. propaganda. Either way, writing provides the vehicle for greater individualization on the one hand, and for clearer state and nation identity on the other.

Early writing

The beginning

It is difficult to say when man first began to experiment with recording language items on material objects. Such an initiative would be spasmodic at first, perhaps involving various independent trials with varying degrees of success. Candidate topics for these early efforts are bureaucratic on the one hand, and liturgical on the other. Bureaucratic processes would include counting, classifying and summarizing; planning the disposition of stored items, or the use of space; and recording ownership. Liturgical uses would arise from the need to store long and involved ritual texts, and pass them on within the priesthood; or from the enhancement of authority offered by the 'magic' powers of script. In a general way, therefore, attempts at writing would be associated with the development of more complex societies, and with the growing need for organizational instruments, such as records and plans.

We can really only recognize early writing for certain when we find a system of signs. Isolated possibilities from earlier periods, such as the *tectiforms* of Upper Palaeolithic cave art, and bones of the same period with incised notches and lines, may amount to some kind of writing, but there is no evidence of formalized use. The same has to be said of rock engravings, stones and other objects that have been claimed on occasion to portray script-like characters. The earliest systems of written signs are precisely that – systems – and they show some evidence of formalization from their first appearance.

Pictographic and ideographic writing

The earliest writing systems all occur in the context of, and early in the history of the 'primary' urban civilizations: Sumer, the Indus and Egypt. Of these the Sumerian examples are normally reckoned to be the earliest (fourth millennium BC). The first two stages of these early systems are usually described as 'pictographic' (picture-signs) and 'ideographic' (idea-signs) respectively. These are often seen as the first two terms in an evolutionary sequence which runs as follows: pictographic, ideographic, syllabary and alphabet. But analysis by such a series of discrete stages owes more to the compartmental nature of recent scholarship than to divisions in the evidence.

First, the term 'pictographic' is not satisfactory. It implies that the process is simply to draw pictures to represent objects. This, however, is not true of the scripts as we first find them. Just any old picture, for instance, would not do. Very often the symbols as first found are already clearly formalized. They would not be immediately recognizable as pictures to the untrained reader, and would mostly not be intended to be. A so-called pictographic script is stylized and closed. Both its execution and its interpretation would have to be learnt, and both would be closely reserved 'professional' matters. The signs have to be drawn within quite tight constraints of form and style, and there is no room for the scribe to indulge personal idiosyncrasies. New signs may not be added at whim.

Similar criticisms apply to the second stage in the supposed sequence, that of 'ideographic' signs. Taken literally, this term would imply the existence of signs which represent 'ideas' or concepts. Yet, in a strict sense, it is again difficult to find unambiguous examples in the evidence. It is difficult, too, to imagine how ideas *could* be represented directly in script in this way. While it is easy enough to concede, for example, that a sign for the sun might also on occasion imply a connection with such related concepts as 'shine, excel, day, shine upon, show favour toward, god, father, etc.', there is no simplistic way in which signs can stand as equalling, as it were, 'any related concept'. Semantic fields, i.e. language words and phrases related by meaning rather than by form, are notorious in linguistic analysis for their circular extensibility. A script that permitted such a variety of reading alternatives would be unusable.

Scripts based upon the purely pictorial representation of objects and ideas are implausible, even at the earliest stages in the development of

Early-third-millennium BC stone figure of Lamkimari, king of Mari, from the Temple of Ishtar. Signs of 'pictographic' type, normally considered to be antecedent to the cuneiform script, can be seen inscribed on the shoulder.

writing. The existence of signs that sometimes seem to have a manifest pictorial shape tells us nothing of their *use*. We should not confuse the source of a sign with its script value. Egyptian hieroglyphics are visually very pictorial, but they are strictly formalized and their use is phonological, i.e. they represent language sounds. Loose talk of 'primitive script' is reminiscent of other mythological approaches to the study of early man.

Were such a script to exist, it would in any case be unable to capture large and important areas of human language, and would be incapable of expansion. All human languages characteristically deal not only with what we users reckon to be persons and objects in the real world, but also (just to mention a few examples) with imputed states, processes, changes of status and role, changes of scene and time, and – worst of all – with relational and logical connections. To a certain extent the former may be drawable, but the latter certainly are not. Imagine the impossibility of drawing the 'if . . . then' relationship of a conditional clause!

Apart from the basic difficulties we have now outlined – the 'irrationality' of a semantically-based script, and the total 'undrawability' of the vast majority of objects and concepts – a true pictorial or semantic system would require, even at the crudest analysis, many hundreds of thousands of individual signs. Even for a determined priesthood, learning and using such a script would be quite beyond the realms of practicability!

However, beyond the implausibility of pure pictographic and ideographic signs, a further claim is made: that these early signs have no phonological component, i.e. no representation of language sounds. This distinction is then seen as an important point of demarcation from all later scripts. There seems, however, no good reason why we should believe that any ancient user of a script would make such a divorce between sign/picture on the one hand, and language-word or language-phrase on the other. On the contrary, it is likely that even the earliest scripts all incorporated some element of phonological representation. All spoken language uses articulated sound as the physical exponent of language form. It is plausible to imagine that scribes writing and reading these scripts would think of each sign as the 'sign for so-and-so', and 'so-and-so' would obviously be one language word or phrase, or at most one of a small number of possibilities. On the other hand, the divorce of picture from sound would seem to have more to do with the analytical processes of subsequent scholarship.

Left: Relief design of a messenger from the Olmec site of La Venta. The signs to the right of the figure are of the Maya type, and probably give a name and place of origin for the figure.

Below: Detail from an Egyptian king-list from the Temple of Ramesses II at Abydos. The script is Egyptian monumental hieroglyphic, and, as is conventional, the names of the kings are circled round in a 'cartouche'.

Below: Chinese oracle bone from the Shang dynasty. The ritual of oracular prediction involved drilling and heating the bone. Then the answer was read from the resulting fissures. The inscription, in an early form of the Chinese writing system, was inscribed after the ritual, possibly to serve as a sacred record, and to secure the validity of the prediction.

Sound and syllable

Sound versus meaning

A usable script requires signs to represent *sounds*, not meaning. This is a counter-intuitive requirement. Intuitively man thinks of language as a medium for meaningful communication. Paradoxically, however, it is the carrier – the sound of the language – that has to be represented, and not directly the message, if progress with script is to be achieved.

It is more helpful, therefore, to see the development of script as a progression of confused attempts at phonological representation. Would-be-literate man would not be thinking in such terms, and there would be confusions between sound and meaning. The constraint, however, remains. Only a phonologically-based system will yield a total number of symbols that is learnable and usable. A script that represents 'whole words' by individual symbols will need enough signs to accommodate the vocabulary in use: perhaps 1,000 to 10,000 for restricted purposes, and 30,000 to 50,000 for the vocabulary of a literate person. The first case is at the edge of learnability, while the second goes well beyond. At the level of the 'individual sound', however, and for any given human language, we only need some twenty to thirty symbols to represent its systematically distinctive sounds, its *phonemes*. The development of historical scripts may be seen as occurring between these two extremes. Interestingly this range may be used diagnostically to identify the developmental stage reached by a given script: the use of thousands of symbols indicates the presence of many word-based signs; the use of hundreds indicates a syllabary with determinatives; while a number in the range twenty to forty indicates an alphabet.

Word to syllable

Some early scripts were word-based. In such a system, each sign represents a phonologically different word or phrase. The symbol used may attempt a pictorial representation of the meaning of that word, where that is feasible. This accounts for the pictorial appearance of some early scripts. Such a

script is likely to be adopted for a language whose words are, or are felt by the users to be, monosyllabic and invariable. There are various reasons for this. For example, the total number of 'words' found in a monosyllabic system is much lower than in a polysyllabic language, and this helps to reduce the overall number of signs needed. There is no problem with the representation of words related to each other by word-variation, such as inflection, affixation or agglutination (e.g. English *man, men, manly*; or Latin *homo, homines, homunculus*, etc.), since such links are not typical of such a language. Chinese script exemplifies some of these points.

There are, however, difficulties even with a language that is predominantly monosyllabic. Theoretically, the total number of monosyllables available will be limited to those that the users feel are distinctive. In any language, not all possible articulatory differentiations are employed. The number of different syllables that are actually used and felt to be significantly distinctive, will be relatively limited in number (probably only in the lower hundreds at most). To provide enough variants to carry an adequate vocabulary, these will need to be further differentiated by other phonological devices. Chinese, for example, uses a system of 'tones' – different sequential patterns of spoken tonality. A decision will need to be taken as to whether such devices are to be represented in the script. In any case – whether or not they are – such a language will also typically contain many *homophones*: single phonological sequences, such as *nu, ka*, etc., but each with several different meanings. Because of these uncertainties of interpretation in the script, a second sign will be felt necessary to narrow down interpretations to the intended reading. These *determinatives* will add to the total number of signs in use, and thus to the already formidable learning problem.

For a language of polysyllabic structure, however, a word-based script poses greater difficulties. In this case, the number of phonologically distinctive words that can be formed from linear permutations of the available syllables is very high. A modern compact dictionary of English, for example, contains some three million separate entries. It is impossible for any significant proportion of these to be represented at word-level. The difficulty is compounded by the need to show inflectional and agglutinative variants as related forms.

It is interesting to note, for instance, that when Chinese characters were adopted for writing Japanese (which is by contrast of polysyllabic structure), these had subsequently to be supplemented by a syllable-based script. Again, it has often been noted with some surprise that even the earliest hieroglyphics found for written Egyptian (also of polysyllabic structure) appear already to be syllable-based. This has led to the speculation that a word-based 'ideographic' stage, written on perishable materials, has been lost; or even to the conclusion that this amounts to evidence that Egyptian writing is derived from Sumerian pre-cuneiform script. Since word-based scripts, however, are impracticable for polysyllabic languages, there would seem no reason to assume that such languages use a thoroughly developed

An early pre-cuneiform clay tablet from Jamdat Nasr. Dated late in the fourth millennium BC, it records areas of fields and crops. The pictorial appearance of the script at this stage is striking, with several symbols recognizably imitating human and animal shapes. Notice also the use of circular and semi-circular indentations to represent numerals.

word-based stage at all. It is true that in antiquity the limitations of word-based script may well have gone unnoticed – so long as the variety of topics, and therefore the range of vocabulary, was kept closely restricted. Such conditions would obtain, as we have already indicated, in the bureaucratic recording of stock, or the priestly recording of highly repetitive liturgies. In such a situation the potential application of writing is not realized, and there is no pent-up demand for its further exploitation. Any attempt, however, to move beyond these narrow confines would run up against the difficulties we have just outlined. To make further progress, a syllable-based script is required – the *syllabary*.

The syllabary

A script based upon syllables is a great improvement upon a word-based script. In a 'pure' syllabary, the number of symbols needed to represent the syllables of a given language would be quite modest, varying between about 80 and 120, depending on the level of sophistication. Among attested scripts, however, there are virtually no undisputed examples of the pure syllabary. Instead, what we find much more commonly is that ancient scripts, although

undergoing some development, tend to become stuck for very long periods of time in a kind of limbo somewhere between word-based and syllable-based systems – although much nearer the latter. These imperfect syllabaries tend to use larger numbers of symbols, somewhere between about 200 and 700. This is because they make some use of word-based symbols, either for a small range of common terms or, more commonly, as determinatives to resolve ambiguity.

Impression made by a Mesopotamian cylindrical seal of the Akkadian period (*c.* 2300 BC). The scene shows the sun-god, Shamash, climbing the mountain of the Underworld. He is greeted on the one side by his sister, winged Ishtar, and on the other by Ea, god of the waters. A lion, symbol of death and the underworld, attends Ninurta, the hero of the gods, who, with his bow, has just slain the bird of evil. Such elaborate mythological scenes, and the workmanship implied in their small-scale execution, give some idea of the status of the person to whom the seal belonged. His name is presumably that given by the syllabic signs in the box above the lion.

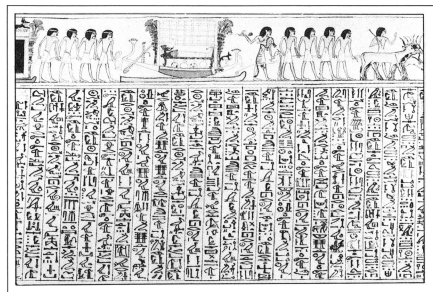

'Page' of Egyptian hieroglyphic text from the so-called Book of the Dead – a collection of religious and magical texts which has survived in several versions. This example comes from the version prepared for the scribe, Ani (*c.* 1250 BC). The scene at the top shows a second-stage funerary procession (i.e. after mummification of the deceased) in which the mummy, installed in a canopied ceremonial barque, is dragged upon a sledge. Just how difficult these syllabic writing-systems could be in use, even for scribes with long training, is well illustrated by this papyrus.

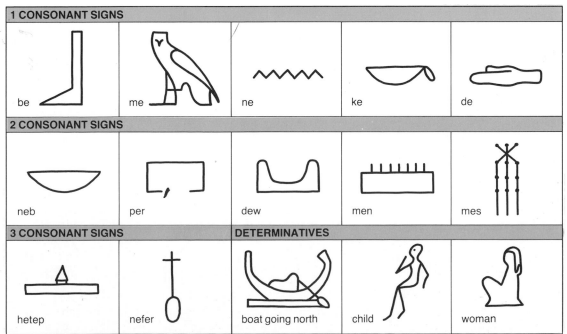

1 CONSONANT SIGNS				
be	me	ne	ke	de
2 CONSONANT SIGNS				
neb	per	dew	men	mes
3 CONSONANT SIGNS		**DETERMINATIVES**		
hetep	nefer	boat going north	child	woman

Left: Table showing four classes of Egyptian hieroglyphic symbols. Of these the first three shown are truly syllabic. Vowels were not represented, but traditionally an 'e' is added in modern transliterations to aid reading. The fourth class are signs based upon words or phrases, and are often called 'determinatives'. These would be added to a syllabic sequence, to make clear the area of reference, and to resolve some of the many ambiguities caused by the inconsistencies of the syllabic script.

Three scripts

Cuneiform

The Mesopotamian script, known as cuneiform from the Latin *cuneus*: wedge, is characterized by wedge-shaped marks made by stylus upon moist clay tablets. After an early word-based phase (fourth millennium BC) in which some signs show a pictorial origin, the characteristic cuneiform symbol is a composite and formalized sign, made up of an array of wedge-shaped impressions.

The script was first used to record Sumerian. The syllables are of three types:

> single vowel only, e.g. *a*: water.
> consonant plus vowel, e.g. *ka*: mouth.
> consonant plus vowel plus consonant, e.g. *sag*: head.

For simple monosyllabic roots of this kind, a word-based script would in any case amount to a type of syllabary. A syllabary proper, however, is additionally necessary, because Sumerian is also *agglutinative*: it combines the monosyllabic roots into what are then perceived as other words. Beyond these syllabic signs proper, extensive use is still made of word-based signs and 'class' determinatives, such as the 'god'-sign for the name of a deity, and the 'man'-determinative for a profession.

An early tendency to multiple and inconsistent equivalencies (*polyvalency*) in the script has caused problems to modern interpreters, and must also have troubled ancient users. Complications are compounded by the 'popularity' of the script. In the mid-third millennium BC the script was adapted for the writing of Akkadian, the language of a Semitic people. Sumerian itself went out of everyday use, but was preserved as a 'classical' written language. Akkadian cuneiform led on during the second millennium BC to a somewhat 'streamlined' version of the script (down from some 2,000 to some 700 characters) which endured throughout the history of the Assyrian and Babylonian kingdoms. A version of cuneiform was used by the Hittites in the later second millennium BC, and other forms became 'general currency' throughout the Near East. Each change of language tended, as is commonly the case with borrowed scripts, to bring not only alterations in symbol-value but also shifts in structure. Interesting are cases such as that of the Elamites, who 'slimmed down' Akkadian cuneiform to something near a pure syllabary, and the late 'pre-alphabetic' cuneiform derivatives of the mid-second millennium BC.

Egyptian hieroglyphs

Greek writers called the characters of the ancient script used upon Egyptian monuments *hieroglyphs* (holy engravings). Like cuneiform, this monumental script settled down to some 700 signs, and remained in use for some three millennia. Unlike cuneiform, however, its symbols retained their pictorial and naturalistic appearance throughout this period almost unchanged. This conservatism is the more remarkable when one considers first the difficulty of cutting these curviform signs on stone with a copper chisel, and secondly the odd fact that the Egyptians also developed two cursive (flowing) forms of script – *hieratic* (priestly) and *demotic* (public) – for non-monumental sacred and secular writing.

Despite the pictorial appearance of the stylized drawings of creatures such as vulture, owl and quail-chick, the script represents an established syllabary from its earliest examples. Syllables are represented on a different basis from the one employed by cuneiform. Vowels are not represented, and the symbols fall into three classes:

> one-letter signs representing a single consonant, used for a monosyllable, such as *r*, e.g. *ro*: mouth.
> two-letter signs representing a succession of two consonants separated by an unrepresented vowel, such as *mr*, e.g. *mer*: pyramid.
> three-letter signs representing a succession of three consonants separated by two unrepresented vowels, such as *htp*, e.g. *hetep*: rest.

Opposite top: Relief panel from the great temple of Amun at Karnak, Egypt. Two cartouches to the right above the forehead of king Tuthmosis III contain his official titles; the right-hand one is the royal title, Menkheper-re, and the left-hand one his name, Tuthmosis. As is usual in Egyptian, the inscription uses a mixture of word symbols, syllabic symbols (both simple and complex) and ideographic symbols to reinforce the reading.

Opposite bottom: Linear B clay tablet from the palace storeroom records at Knossos, Crete. The script contains symbols for five different values of vowel, usually transliterated as *a, e, i, o* and *u*; and correspondingly five versions for each consonant, e.g. *ka, ke, ki, ko* and *ku*. Interestingly, however, such groups of symbols are not associated by any shared sets of visual features, and what we would now feel as related values would have had to be learnt as arbitrary shapes.

Cuneiform tablets from Tell-el Amarna, Egypt – two of a group called the 'Amarna letters'. This collection, dating from the fourteenth century BC, consists of correspondence from various Western Asian rulers addressed to the pharaohs of Egypt. The tablet on the left is from Shawardata, prince of Hebron. It conveys the urgent message that he 'stands alone, and needs a large force to rescue him'!

Besides these consonantal series, the script also contains a large number of determinatives. Although this pattern of distribution is familiar from cuneiform, the background may be different. First, because of the polysyllabic nature of Egyptian, it is unlikely that the determinatives are simple relics of a word-sign script. Secondly, the ambiguities they resolve stem largely from uncertainties created by the non-representation of vowels. Unlike cuneiform, Egyptian script did not enjoy a 'cosmopolitan' vogue, and its influence upon other scripts is uncertain. It is tempting to see in the uni-consonantal (one-letter) signs a proto-alphabet, which may possibly have had some impact upon the development of actual proto-alphabets in the Levant. There is no evidence, however, that the ancient Egyptians themselves ever shared such a perception.

Mycenaean Linear B

Linear B is the third and latest of three scripts – one of 'hieroglyphic' appearance and two of 'linear' arrangement – distinguished by Sir Arthur Evans. Linear B is found principally on a large number of clay tablets discovered at a range of sites, foremost among which are Knossos in Crete, and Pylos and Mycenae in Greece. The successful decipherment of Linear B by Michael Ventris in 1952 showed the script to be a syllabary which had been adapted to write what we may call Mycenaean Greek. The texts are bureaucratic records, cataloguing matters such as personnel, livestock, land use, equipment and religious ritual. Beside the 87 or so syllabic symbols proper, Linear B uses some 100 to 150 'ideographic' word-signs. The script also uses a numeral system, and separate systems for dry measures, for liquid measures, and for weight.

Greek is singularly ill-fitted for writing by syllabary. Not only does the language tend to be polysyllabic, but it also contains consonant clusters, as in a*nthr*opos: man. Linear B includes the representation of vowels, but opts for an unwise solution in not allowing for consonants that are not followed by vowels. Thus, to write a word such as *dendron*: tree, the sequence -*ndr*- would have to be rendered *no-do-ro*. In fact, however, Linear B has a further rule: that at the end of a syllable or word, -*l*, -*m*, -*n*, -*r* and -*s* are omitted. Accordingly the rendering of *dendron* would be more like *de-do-ro*. Since final -*s* and -*n* are very common in Greek, as for instance in nominative and accusative terminations, many ambiguities are introduced. For example, the two signs *pa-te* could be either *pater*: father, or *pantes*: all. Initial *s*- is also omitted, so that *sperma*: seed, becomes *pe-ma*, while *stathmos*: sheep-pen, becomes *ta-to-mo*.

Linear B shows an interesting pre-alphabetic attempt to write down the words of a polysyllabic language with frequent consonant clusters. Rules for the use of the script seem to have been worked out carefully, and there is surprising consistency between widely separated sites. Possibly because of these difficulties of use, and because literacy in the script was limited to internal palace scribes, Linear B did not survive the breakdown of the Mycenaean regime. Following its disappearance, we have no evidence for a writing system for Greek until the advent of the Phoenician alphabet several centuries later.

The alphabet

The transition from syllabary to alphabet marks the final stage in the development of writing, both because later alphabets still follow the same principles and are derived from the early examples, and because an alphabet as commonly found is near to peak values of efficiency. Modern alphabets still contain inconsistencies and redundancies, but the critical order of difference between existing examples and a phonemic script (see p. 132) is not great, and replacing the former with the latter would not strikingly reduce the number of symbols. The major gains in ease of learning and ease of use are achieved by the switch from syllabary to alphabet, and do not depend on the exact merits of any particular alphabet.

The move from syllabary to alphabet depended upon linguistic analysis. A separation had to be made between consonants and vowels, which, as speech is a continuum of sound, involved some degree of abstract categorization. How conscious this might be, is an issue for which we shall find little evidence. That the virtues of an alphabetic script are not intuitively obvious may be seen from the fact that the Egyptians long had one-letter symbols, which amounted to a consonantal alphabet; but far from exploiting this potential, they actually made less use of these symbols in the later phases of their script.

An alphabet reduces the number of symbols needed for phonological representation from the syllabary's range of about 80 to 120, to a range of around 20 to 30. To take one example, whereas a syllabary needs separate signs for *pa, pe, pi, po, pu; ba, be, bi, bo, bu;* and *ma, me, mi, mo, mu;* an alphabet needs only *p, b, m,* and *a, e, i, o, u:* a reduction which will be repeated for all the other consonants. Alphabets are able to drop the library of 'ideographic' signs that encumber most syllabaries, because redundancy and ambiguity are greatly reduced.

As to the actual switch from syllabary to alphabet, the situation is confused. Groupings of 'alphabetic' texts have been found from the Ugarit area in the north of the Levant, through the Byblos area, and eventually to the Red Sea. The texts are found on various artefacts and monuments, and vary widely in date from early second millennium to early first millennium BC. Parentage cannot be demonstrated either from cuneiform or from Egyptian antecedents. We seem to find along the Levant seaboard a series of experimental adaptations of script, some of which are definitely alphabetic in nature, and some only dubiously so.

Two sets of examples stand out. First we have a large number of clay tablets from Ugarit in what is

Top: Simplified table showing some possible phases of adaptation of the alphabet, from Early Semitic forms through to classical Roman script.

Below left: Phoenician inscription from Idalion, Cyprus, dated by its historical reference to 391 BC. The king of Idalion dedicates a decorative gold panel to the deity, Reshef-Mikal. This is a later version of the script, and the cursive quality of the letters, ill-suited to monumental use, can be clearly seen.

Below right: This sixth century BC Greek inscription from Ephesus is concerned with the practice of augury from the flight of birds. The penultimate line of the illustration contains the word *euonumos* (of good report, favourable), which is used euphemistically in such texts of the left (i.e. bad) side, and of bad omens. This word shows the Greek invented letters, E (*epsilon*, 'light e'), and Ω (*omega*, 'big o').

NORTH SEMATIC			GREEK		ETRUSCAN	LATIN	
EARLY PHOENICIAN	EARLY HEBREW	PHOENICIAN	EARLY	CLASSICAL	EARLY	EARLY	CLASSICAL
K	K	X	Δ	A	A	A	A
9	9	9	8	B	8		B
1	1	1	1	Γ	Γ		C
Δ	9	9	Δ	Δ	Π	Π	D

known as the Ugaritic Cuneiform Alphabet, including some 'textbook' ABCs, and dating from the middle of the second millennium BC. The language is Ugaritic, of the West Semitic group, and the script is alphabetic. There are 30+ symbols, and the script experiments with the representation of vowels. The script runs from left to right. Although the individual signs are made up, as in cuneiform proper, from wedge-shaped impressions, it is not clear that they derive from previous cuneiform signs.

Our second case comes from Byblos. Monumental stone inscriptions show an alphabetic script. Two of the earliest examples belong to king Ahiram and date to the eleventh or twelfth century BC. The symbols of this alphabet do not derive easily from any known syllabaries. The shapes of the letters have a cursive (flowing) appearance, which suggests that they were not developed for monumental purposes, but had a previous use over a lengthy period, probably on papyrus. This alphabet, sometimes called North Semitic or Canaanite, has only 22 symbols, since vowels are not represented. Writing is from right to left. The script is directly antecedent to later and modern alphabets.

Ugaritic and Byblos scripts are, however, linked indirectly by the Ugaritic ABCs. Significantly, the first 22 symbols shown on these ABCs have similar phonetic values to the Byblos script, and are given in the Byblos order. The values which the two scripts do not share are then added. Though there is little surface similarity between the two sets of symbols, this coincidence is strong enough to suggest the existence of an earlier 'proto-Levantine' alphabet, with which both Ugaritic and Byblos scripts are associated. It also means that the basis of the Byblos alphabet, which is itself source for subsequent alphabets, can be located as early as the sixteenth or seventeenth century BC.

Phoenician and Greek

The Phoenician alphabet borrowed by Greeks in the eighth century BC was a direct descendant of the Byblos script. The Greeks kept the same order of letters, and also took over their names, which are preserved fairly faithfully in modern Hebrew: *aleph, beth, gimel, daleth, he, waw, zayin, heth, teth, yod, kaph, lamed, mem, nun, samekh, ayin, pe, sade, qoph, resh, shin* and *taw*. These were names of objects in Semitic, e.g. *beth*: house, and *daleth*: door (Greek *beta* and *delta*), but must have seemed technical terms to the Greek borrowers. Following the example of the earlier Ugaritic script, the Greeks added signs for vowels. They did this by redeploying symbols for which Greek had no equivalent. For example, Phoenician *aleph*, a smooth breathing, was used for *a*, or *alpha*; Phoenician *heth*, a guttural fricative, was taken over as *e*, or *eta*, initially both long and short; Phoenician *ayin*, another guttural, was employed as *o*. Extra signs were invented for Greek sounds unrepresented in Phoenician, and these were placed at the end of the alphabet after *tau*, e.g. *phi* and *psi*. Subsequently extra vowel signs were added to differentiate vowel quality and length, such as *epsilon*, short *e*; and *o* was differentiated into *omicron*, 'small *o*', and *omega* 'big *o*'. Possibly these were formed directly from the original signs, i.e. *epsilon* from *eta*, and *omega* from *omicron*. The addition of vowels much improved the flexibility of the alphabet for application to other languages.

Etruscan and Roman

From its earliest examples, the Greek alphabet assumes two versions, roughly eastern and western, which adopt different solutions to the adaptations just outlined. The alphabet taken up by the Etruscans, probably in the seventh century BC, not surprisingly has affinities with western Greek. It is likely, however, that the Etruscans also made direct use of Phoenician models, because, for instance, the Etruscan alphabet retains an extra Phoenician sibilant and some guttural distinctions which had been discarded by Greek models.

The Romans took over the Etruscan script. Etruscan ancestry can be seen in such values as *x* for the sequence *ks* (=*ch* in eastern Greek alphabets), in the non-differentiation of *c* and *g* (Etruscan did not differentiate unvoiced and voiced stops), and in the retention of the Phoenician trio of unvoiced gutturals, *c*, *k* and *q*, which were originally used differentially before vowel qualities, as *ci-, ce-, ka-* and *qu-*. Thus, *c* was used before 'front' vowels *i* and *e*; *k* before 'medial' vowels such as *a*; and *q* only before the vowel *u*. This last restriction we still retain in our own script, e.g. we write *q*uite and not *c*uite or *k*uite.

The Cippus of Perugia, an Etruscan inscription of some 130 words, which is normally interpreted as discussing boundaries and land measurement, and was possibly itself a boundary marker. Running from left to right, the text seems to record an agreement between the Velthina and Afuna families. It uses single points apparently as word dividers. Dating from the second to first century BC, it shows marked convergence with Roman script.

Literacy and education

The technology of writing has widespread and reciprocal repercussions upon the structure of society. The higher the index of literacy, the greater and more thoroughgoing its potential effect.

Open versus closed society

If we follow the model proposed by the philosopher Karl Popper, of seeing social and political institutions and ideas as tending either to an 'open' (good) or 'closed' (bad) society, a technology such as writing is in itself neutral. On the good side, literacy gives the individual access to a new level of participation within the state. The choices open to a literate person will be greater, since with access to better and fuller information, he will be more aware of the opportunities potentially available to him, and better able to estimate the strength of obstacles or the danger of sanctions. In a word, he is better informed.

In such ways, literacy permits the growth of criticism, and eventually the accumulation of scepticism. This trend is well documented from first-millennium BC Mediterranean countries, where the adoption of the alphabet in itself aided the spread of literacy and stimulated radical debate on social and political systems. Writing, by changing the *type* of cognitive and mental operation that people are able to perform, e.g. by the promotion of analysis by alternative categories, produces a change in modes of thought. 'Either . . .or' dichotomies are the product of a literacy that turns columns into categories, and categories into tables. By changing the type of data that is selected, and by developing methods for its storage, writing offers a different set of binary choices to the individual. The potential divorce that writing brings between words, ideas and reality, may free the writer and reader from canalized thinking, suggest a separation between idea and occasion, and encourage abstraction and analysis. The general effect of all this can be to increase awareness, and to stimulate the development of 'meta'-thinking, by which we mean the ability to stand outside the writing and analytical process and critically review its operation.

On the bad or 'closed' side, however, the greater complexity introduced into the state by the technology of writing permits the state closer control of the individual, and offers to one individual, official, or group, an enhanced opportunity to exploit another by manipulation of the 'system'. The 'fine print' of regulations and laws is a product of writing sytems, but its written distinctions increase the likelihood of abuse. Modes of dissemination of information that follow the spread of literacy can also be used to spread disinformation and propaganda.

In a strange sense, literacy is a new game, the word-game and the 'paper' chase. There is evidence that man loved games of one kind or another long before the advent of urban civilization. These earlier games could be played simply for their entertainment value, they could be associated with religious ritual, they could reflect social status and perhaps even momentarily laugh at it, or they could even, on occasion, have deadly consequences for the loser. Permission to play could be granted or withheld, sometimes with serious consequences. All these possibilities apply equally to written word-games. To prosper in the new urban societies, you need to know the rules, and at least on occasion you, or someone acting on your behalf, has to play.

Writing requires formal training, not only for the basic learning of the script, but also to give familiarity with the areas of social life that are structured and administered by written instruments. From the early states, for instance, we find not only exercise documents which rehearse the mechanics of the script and of keeping files, but also training texts which demonstrate the applications of categories. The alphabet itself, unlike the earlier scripts which are not so easily systematized for the learner, has an established order of symbols, that can be used both to ease the task of initial learning, and to give an obvious filing sequence for all kinds of organization. Perhaps above all, an alphabetic order is a practicable basis for listing and analysing the

This relief from the Maya site of Palenque appears to depict a scribe, perhaps seated at a writing 'desk', and holding a writing instrument. Mayan-type 'pictographic' signs are visible in the top left-hand corner.

language itself, which will stimulate the elaboration of dictionaries and grammars, and have a significant effect on the use of language in society – i.e. society will increasingly become language-oriented.

Evidence from the early urban societies shows the development of writing working in the ways we have just described. To begin with, writing is a skill which functions as one of the new specializations in society. If you need writing, you employ a writer, a scribe. Because of the association of writing with administration, the scribe always has from the beginning the status, not of a craftsman, but of a professional person. Besides having the status of a separate profession, the ability to read and write also became progressively associated with certain other high-status walks of life; one of these was the profession of priest, where writing would encourage the elaboration of increasingly lengthy and repetitious ritual texts, liturgies and sacrificial prescriptions. An important priestly special case was the growing use of sacred calendars. The advent of writing meant that ritual could insist not only upon the exactly prescribed actions being duly performed, but also upon the virtue of the precise words and verbal formulae. Sacred calendars become sacred annals, and offer, as they stretch back centuries into the past, a satisfying timeless perspective and an unchallenged basis for authority. Similar considerations apply to the keeping of king-lists, which led to the office of royal annalist. Another high-status area of public administration lies with the law and the legal profession. In this case the written document is indispensable, both in making and refining the law, and in its day-to-day administration.

In the ancient states, training for the literate professions was largely synonymous with the training of a civil service. The candidates selected for such training tended to be the sons (not the daughters) of those who already held high status and office. The candidature and with it literacy only spread as the demand for specialized literate personnel grew. The state initially had no interest in overall education or mass literacy. The gaining of literate status would not be a passport to upward class mobility in a state where there is virtually no class mobility, and the literate professions form a segregated and closely guarded area. The code of Hammurabi of the early second millennium BC, for instance, lists three classes: those of gentlemen (*awilum*), commoners (*mushkenum*) and slaves (*wardum*). At this stage, literacy only equals opportunity in a limited sense within the first class.

As the complexity of state organization grew, however, two trends became apparent: first, as writing and the use of documents permeated more and more of the areas of community life, the status of literacy in itself slowly diminished; and secondly, the state began to show a wider, less class-restricted interest in the training of its literate manpower. We can see the beginnings of this official trend in late Republican and Imperial Rome. Even there, however, literacy was still clearly limited to a modest percentage of the population (see Chapter 1, p. 28).

Right: Red-figure cup by the 'Eretria painter', *c.* 430 BC, showing what may be a music lesson. The standing boy, labelled Musaeos (a mythical singer) is reading from waxed wood tablets, while the seated man, labelled Linos (sometimes described as the music teacher of Heracles) unrolls a scroll.

Left: A selection of stamp seals from the Indus Valley. The Indus Valley script remains undeciphered. The signs are generally of a 'pictographic' appearance, and some 400 symbols have been isolated.

Below: The Aztec Calendar Stone from Tenochtitlán. The Aztecs believed that they were living in the fifth of a cycle of successive worlds. This is personified by the deity Tonatuih, seen here encircled by the four previous worlds or suns.

139

8 Building, Technology and Transport

Planned and conscious change

Since at least Palaeolithic times man has been building, and often changing the structure of the physical and natural world in the process.

Palaeolithic man built huts, as for instance at Pincevent in central France and on the Russian steppes. Neolithic man extended construction to more ambitious projects such as the central and northern European Long House. Neolithic man probably also on occasion built separate accommodation for his cattle, as suggested, for instance, by the distributional patterns of sheep and goat dung and fly pupae at Egolzwil in Switzerland. By the time the first cities began to take shape in the Near East, the local technique of mud-brick building was established.

Unplanned change

However, the construction of buildings is only one aspect of man's environment. Since possibly the same period, man has had an effect upon the natural world around him, and upon the landscape. Unlike the built environment, man could be largely unaware of these effects until alerted by economic collapse, or most recently by environmentalist lobbies. The cultivation of specific crops and the domestication of animals impose changes upon the ecological structure of the terrain which are directly reflected in its appearance. For example, what modern urban man sees as the rolling landscape of a beautiful pastoral countryside is almost totally the result of man's previous activities. In particular, the practice of grazing animals may radically change local flora in favour of those types that are less easily edible. The omnivorous goat, an extreme case, may denude an area of vegetation, thus offering an easy prospect for soil erosion. Similarly, the clearing of areas of forest may be undertaken for a number of conscious motives, such as collecting timber for building or for fuel, but the consequent erosion is no respecter of motive.

Civilization: an artificial environment

The contribution of urbanization seems to have been, as so often, to raise activity to a higher level of organization and elaboration. From the first cities onwards we can speak of man as constructing his own artificial environment. Urban civilization is man's supreme artefact. It is the one inside which he

Opposite: Monumental public buildings are characteristic of civilization. This great ziggurat is the central building of the city of Choga Zanbil (ancient Dur-Untash) in south-west Iran, founded as a second capital of Elam in the thirteenth century BC.

Below: Neolithic man sometimes built substantial houses. The village of Skara Brae on Orkney, constructed in the third millennium BC, consists of six or seven houses and a separate workshop. The buildings and internal fittings were all made of stone and survive in remarkably good condition.

lives. Oddly enough, however, this separation from natural habitat may itself be an unplanned result, a side-effect. Moves towards urbanization must have been undertaken first with an eye to short-term gains from co-ordination, and without any conscious model of a new type of society. Once established as a normal way of living, however, civilization presented man with a separate constructed home, both physically, mentally and psychologically. The depersonalizing and alienating institutions of urbanized society were chiefly responsible for this. Specialization of craft and profession meant that each group, sometimes even each individual, tended to see this environment from a different perspective. Life as a farmer and life as a high priest were totally divorced, both literally and conceptually.

Nowadays, however, we tend to use the word *environment* to describe the general 'cityscape' or 'countryscape' in which people live out their lives. This is our sense when we complain, for instance, of the inability of architects to produce an 'environment fit for people to live in'.

Town planning

How far so conscious a concern with the management of the environment existed in antiquity, and if so, how early, are questions we cannot answer. We might conclude when we find an orderly arrangement of streets and open areas, as for instance at Mohenjo-Daro in the Indus Valley, that the city was laid out to a plan. The converse, however, does not follow. The apparent randomness shown by the streets of a typical Mesopotamian city may include areas or phases of order, or may overlie earlier more obviously planned phases; and in any case we know from later historical examples, such as the medieval period in Europe, that multi-angle building often requires more rather than less planning. A grid plan is therefore not so much

Although many ancient cities show clear evidence of town planning, it is unusual to find actual plans. This plan of the Mesopotamian city of Nippur, *c.* 1500 BC, is a rare exception. It is an accurate scale map showing walls, city gates, rivers, canals, temples, shrines and a central park.

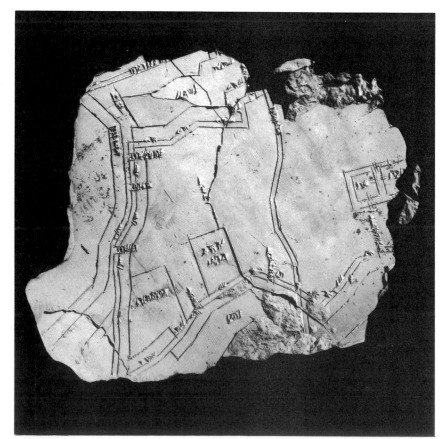

evidence of planning, as indicative of speedier one-phase development.

We may reasonably assume some degree of planning in all ancient cities. States that developed writing as an organizing instrument would also tend to be familiar with its near relative (and possibly in some cases predecessor), the plan. It is likely too that states with strong centralized governments also planned and controlled the use of land. However, to assume the existence of state planning is not to assume a contemporary-style concern with the environment. On the contrary, it is likely that motives and criteria in the ancient civilizations were quite different.

We should expect the 'environmental' policy of an ancient state to mirror its own symbolic and conceptual preoccupations. Priority would be given to the reservation of suitably elevated and spacious sites for the erection of important state buildings, such as temples, special tombs and royal palaces. The lay-out of other areas might then reflect either class structure or profession and craft specialization, or the need for storage. The provision of services, such as water supply, drains and roads, would reflect the priorities felt by the particular society. The importance, for instance, accorded to public health, the provision of sewers and care over their discharge varied enormously from state to state in antiquity, and from period to period. The Indus Valley cities

The Classic Maya site of Palenque, situated in the forest on the edge of the Chiapas mountains, was laid out with an attention to the natural topography unusual in ancient city planning. The many temple-pyramids and the central Palace Complex shown here were constructed with only minimal alteration of the original land surface.

went to considerable trouble over their services: water was available from a number of wells, some of them inside houses; clay pipes and gulleys collected waste water from the houses and discharged it into brick-built drains running along the streets; properly built manholes were provided at regular intervals for the clearance of blockages. By contrast, Mesopotamian cities never seem to have achieved more than rudimentary standards in this area.

As to unplanned side-effects, ancient states even as late as the Greek and Roman period seem to have had little perception of them. Even where we may charitably assume some perception, ancient states for the most part lacked the technology to reverse deleterious trends. In Sumer, for instance, intensive irrigation by river-water combined with a lack of rain-water led gradually to higher levels of soil salinity. The initial reaction was to switch from wheat to barley (which is more salt-resistant), but ultimately the whole pattern of major settlements was shifted further upstream. From Roman civilization we have the example of the attempted drainage of water-logged areas; this was normally done in order to reclaim land for cultivation or building, without much perception of the changed ecology or of ultimate benefit or harm. Interestingly, the link between such marshy areas and the mosquito, and hence malaria, was not appreciated. The only solution was evacuation, as at Roman Ostia.

The settlements of pre-civilized societies rarely include monumental structures or show signs of large-scale planning. An exception is Jericho, which already in the eighth millennium BC, or even earlier, was surrounded by a monumental stone wall and a deep rock-cut ditch, seen in this view of the excavations.

143

Building and engineering

Short-term to long-term building

Palaeolithic man built huts; Neolithic man built villages by erecting a group of huts, large and small, and probably an animal compound. The basis of these constructions was mostly timber where available, e.g. logs, branches and twigs, surfaced and weatherproofed variously by hides, mud, daub, and different types of grass thatch. These constructions were mostly of modest scale and had few technical problems to solve, except perhaps that of wind-resistance – as, for instance, in the numerous villages on the windswept plain of the southern Italian Tavoliere. More important, however, was the short building time and life expectancy of such constructions. Small Neolithic villages such as these would probably have 'migrated' locally from site to site, and re-established themselves at quite short intervals.

If we look instead at the large pre-urban settlements of central Anatolia (Çatal Hüyük) and the Near East (Jericho) we find a different pattern. Here the use of mud-brick and stone for building was well established. One reason for this may have been shortage of timber, especially in the Near East, but the policy of the community was also important. The use of mud-brick and stone involves much longer stages of preparation, the building time is longer, and life expectancy is much greater.

The outlook of the urban state is definitely long-term. The use of mud-brick is particularly significant, as it is possibly the first use of a modular element. The buildings of the urban state, both small and large, are characterized universally by being constructed out of a large number of prepared and standardized modular units, be they mud-bricks, fired bricks, stone cut to size, etc. These buildings imply the pre-existence of a specialist production system for the modular units. They also imply the existence of a planning stage for the construction of the building, which is now an elaborate jig-saw

Opposite top: To bridge a gap with a stone lintel, as in the Inca fortress of Sacsahuaman, requires a massive supporting structure.

Egyptian wall painting from the tomb of Rekhmire, vizier under the pharaohs Tuthmosis III and Amenophis II (fifteenth century BC), showing a team of labourers making bricks. The workers are foreigners, identified as Syrians and Nubians.

puzzle. And they imply long-term intentions on the part of the builder and user. All these implications are typical of the building and engineering of the urban state.

Building the walls

The first stage of urban building is building the walls. Unlike huts, for which the simplest shape is circular, most modular constructions, from the early civilizations onwards, are roughly rectangular and essentially composed of one or more 'boxes'. This probably gave greater ease of planning, laying out and roofing. Circular structures are inconvenient because they often require curviform modular units of pre-calculated radius, they do not make good use of limited space, and they are awkward to modify and extend. Most early constructions were low-rise with modest if any foundations. Mud-brick is easily laid using more of the same, i.e. liquid mud, as mortar; weakening of the structure due to large and numerous apertures (often a problem in more modern structures) would be unlikely, since 'windows', i.e. holes, would be small and high up to give light and ventilation only.

Building with stone is more difficult. Most ancient stone buildings were erected without mortar, and depended on the accuracy of cut of the block. Mostly, it seems, ancient builders relied upon goodness of fit and sheer mass to hold the building together; some types of stone will actually fuse between blocks over a long period of time. Other strategies, as used by the Greeks in temple building, involved the concave rebating of block ends so that only the visible edges needed to be in accurate contact, and the use of linking 'straps' of metal or hardwood to keep the blocks from wandering out of registration.

Awareness of problems of stress in buildings, and especially in the supporting walls, seems to have arrived late, and experience of collapse seems to have been the teacher. The Babylonian Code of Hammurabi provided for damages caused by the collapse of buildings, and it looks as if collapses in the early states were mostly due to lack of awareness and technique. By Roman times, engineers were aware to some extent of the problems, especially of high-rise and grand-scale buildings, although still very unclear as to theory and remedy. In prestigious buildings Roman designers incorporated excessive numbers of failsafe structures, as, for instance, in the use of relieving arches in the Pantheon. In cheap housing, such as the Roman *insulae* (tenement blocks), commercial pressures towards economy meant that there were many collapses.

Bridging the gap

Most taxing of building technique is the bridging of large gaps (perhaps created in a wall for a ceremonial doorway), and above all the roofing of the structure. Wooden beams offer a satisfactory solution, but with certain disadvantages. The length of span is limited not only by the size of timber available, but also by the beam's own weight and the loading that can be placed upon it. Also all roof structures transmit stresses to the walls, notably outward forces. Antiquity seems to have been slow to recognize the value of trussed structures (integrated fixed triangular shapes), and Greek temples played safe by

propping up the middle of the span with separate structural walls and pillars.

Stone beams are structurally disastrous. Even if it is possible to cut a sufficiently long piece and raise it into position, its structural reliability once in place is almost nil. The pressures exerted upon a structural beam are those of compression (downward on top) and tension (tendency to split open at the bottom under strain). Timber, with its fibrous construction, resists both of these well. Most types of stone have very little resistance to the second force, and once a crack starts the strength of the beam is destroyed. Most forms of limestone, the commonest building stone in the Mediterranean, are particularly weak. This means that stone beams must be short and very thick. This mundane limitation has as much to do with the distances between pillars of the Greek classical temple as any fancy claims of sophisticated proportioning.

Some pre-urban megalithic buildings already show another solution – the *corbelled* arch or vault. A good example is seen at Maes Howe, a large passage-grave in the Orkneys. A corbelled structure bridges the gap by a serial process: each course of masonry is stepped out by a small amount until the courses finally join up in the middle. This is usually a stable solution, but has no great development potential. The structure can only be assembled with fairly large pieces of stone, and considerable cantilever forces must be maintained on the inner surfaces of the stones.

The 'true' arch is assembled from 'voussoirs' – specially angled pieces of stone which lock against each other to counteract any collapse, and are themselves locked by the 'keystone'. Unlike the beam and corbelled structures, the arch is ingenious in its exploitation of destructive forces to strengthen the structure. It also transmits load and stress diagonally into the side supporting walls. The principle of the arch underlies the barrel vault (essentially a longitudinal integrated series of arches)

and the dome (a kind of rotated arch). Given an alternative to the method of interlocking shaped stones (which is less practicable for large multiple structures), the potential for roofing extensive spaces was now present. What freed the use of the arch, the vault and the dome, was the advent of concrete.

Concrete

How conscious the Roman discovery of concrete was, is debatable. What seems clear, however, is that progressively from the late Republic into the early

Below left: A fragmentary Roman ruin at Baalbek in the Lebanon shows the first few segments of an ornamental arch; this example is probably *not* structural.

Below right: Facade of the Palace of the Governor at Uxmal, showing the Maya form of the corbelled 'arch'.

Above: Roman tombs in the Isola Sacra cemetery outside Ostia are rectangular in shape and roofed with barrel vaults. The cemetery was used mostly by small traders and craftsmen.

A characteristically Roman structure, found throughout the Empire, is the amphitheatre, built to stage complex and spectacular events in front of an audience of thousands. This example is at Nyssa in Turkey.

The significant transition enabled by the new material was that modular construction gave way to plastic construction. The properties of the shape itself, be it the arch, vault or dome, were appreciated for their own characteristics, rather than the individual or combined properties of building blocks, beams, and their linking mortars, if any. The freedom given to design, especially of the new imperial extravaganzas, is hard to overstate. Concrete solved the problem of the extension of the arch, just as in more recent times the reinforced concrete beam and the pre-stressed beam have solved the old weaknesses of the beam.

The new concrete structures had to be cast on site in wooden moulds made of suitable timber shuttering. With the more complicated shapes, this must have involved considerable expertise in carpentry, not only to realize the complex forms, but also to support the weight of the aggregate until cured. When the shuttering was removed, the concrete surface revealed was naturally not very attractive, and the practice arose of surfacing it in some further way, perhaps by plaster or tiles. Possibly because these after-treatments meant one further stage in the building process, and no doubt another 'wet trade' on site, two particular treatments grew up which gave a more economical finish and were more integrated with the construction process. In one, cubes of stone were incorporated into the surface to give a decorative 'network' effect (*opus reticulatum*). This procedure seems to have been associated with weaker cores, and gained a reputation for instability. In the second treatment, courses of slim triangular bricks were inserted into the concrete to give a simulated appearance of fine brickwork (*opus testaceum*). These two surfaces are now very familiar to modern visitors to surviving Roman buildings.

Empire, Roman builders were experimenting with various types of mortars, particularly mixes that showed hydraulic and waterproof qualities. Central to this experimentation seems to have been one particular material, *pulvis puteolanus* (dust from Puteolum, modern Pozzuoli, on the northern edge of the bay of Naples), which had waterproof qualities and yielded a mix with good structural properties. Even so, this potential seems to have been slowly realized, and it is only in the redevelopment of Rome following Nero's great fire in AD 64, that we find Roman engineers expressing themselves more freely in the new shapes.

The barrel vault proved versatile. Once it had been realized that such a structure could be pierced by side arches and other barrel vaults, the design possibility had arrived of light and airy structures, which gave relatively unimpeded internal space, and provided lightweight support for the superimposition of storey upon storey. A good contrast between the pre-concrete technique of multiple pillars (which could lead to forests of internal pillars) and the free space permitted by the new plasticity, is shown by the Thersilion at Megalopolis (fourth century BC), and the Basilica of Maxentius at Rome (fourth century AD), respectively. In the Thersilion, a large assembly hall, pillars were ingeniously arranged in radiating lines to minimize visual interference between speaker and audience. In the Basilica, the huge area of some 80 by 50 m was covered by intersecting vaults in such a way that only four pillars intruded into the internal space. A good example of the vault used as support for the superimposition of storeys is seen in the Flavian Amphitheatre (the Colosseum), where the structure is used to advantage as spectator access corridors, and as support for banks of seating.

Services

Urban civilization is characterized not only by its buildings, but also by the provision and administration of services for the city's inhabitants, such as the organization of food supplies, the construction of recreational facilities, sports grounds, assembly halls, distribution and administrative buildings, and the provision and maintenance of water supply, drains, sewers, internal roads, and so on. In the later civilizations, citizens began to expect and demand further services, as at Rome, where the notion of state amusement seems first to have been added. All these functions were reflected in the design and use of buildings and the engineering of facilities. Of all these services, perhaps the most fundamental is that of water supply.

The early civilizations seem to have used wells to provide water. The feasibility of successful well-digging would therefore have been a factor in the selection of the original sites. The use of specific engineering techniques to divert water sources for city use probably dates from late in the second millennium BC, and examples are documented from the Levant and from Greece. A remarkable early Greek example (sixth century BC), where evidence still remains, was described by the historian Herodotus. This is an aqueduct on the island of Samos, off the coast of Asia Minor. Here a tunnel was driven more than a kilometre under a hill to connect an upper water-source with the city. The tunnel was apparently driven from both ends simultaneously, but a sharp bend and a change of level had to be incorporated before the two ends met up successfully. The portion between the exit of the tunnel and the city itself was completely buried, possibly for defensive reasons.

By far the best known engineering systems for the transport of city water supplies come from the Roman period. Roman aqueducts commenced under the Republic, the earliest construction being fourth-century BC. This, however, was almost wholly in the ground or subterranean. The characteristic arcaded structures of the Mediterranean landscape,

which carry watercourses on their upper tiers, mostly date from the Imperial period. The prevalence of the stone-built arch in these structures is remarkable, with considerable heights being achieved by their reduplicated superimposition. Contrary to the popular image, these prominent constructions were only used for linking across river valleys, as at Pont du Gard in Provence in the south of France; or for crossing open areas of low-lying countryside without losing too much height. In spite of the elaboration of the arcaded bridge itself, in all other respects the Roman engineers seem to have taken great trouble to avoid major engineering. For example, the Aqua Marcia, whose early stage historically forms the third of Rome's aqueducts, connected a source 52 km away with the city. The length of the entire system, however, which meanders around hills and minor outcrops, measures some 91 km in all, of which only some 11 km are carried on the familiar arches.

With rare exceptions, Roman engineers seem to have preferred non-pressurized systems. Wherever possible the water was carried in culverts. These were covered to prevent contamination but not atmospherically sealed. The water does not seem to have been filtered and must have carried along with it considerable amounts of sludge. To combat this problem, some aqueducts incorporated settling and clarifying chambers, such as the *piscina mirabilis* at Baiae.

Roman engineers used superimposed arcades of stone-built arches to take aqueducts across some river valleys. Here, at the Pont du Gard in southern France, the water course was carried on top of three tiers of arches, the first level doubling as a road bridge, which is still in use.

147

Transport

The ancient civilizations needed to transport goods and materials in large quantities, both within their internal redistributive economies and for long-distance trade. Transport could be overland, in which case it was dependent on the muscle power of men and animals, or it could be by water, where it was possible, sometimes at least, to harness the power of the wind.

Overland transport

Porterage. Human porterage must have been an important method of transport in the ancient civilizations. It probably dominated in the domestic economy, being the means by which the farmer conveyed his produce to the redistributive centre or market, but it also had a role in state trade. The largest handling operation in the ancient world, the annual import of grain to Rome from Egypt, Sicily and Africa, was managed by porters without the use of wheeled vehicles or mechanical aids. Some 500,000 tonnes (about 17 million sack-loads) were off-loaded from sea-going ships at Ostia, then reloaded onto river barges for the final stage of the journey up the Tiber to Rome.

Pack animals. For long-distance trade overland the normal method throughout the ancient world was by pack animal. The main animals employed were donkeys and mules (used in Egypt, Western Asia and the Mediterranean), camels, both the Arabian single-humped dromedary and the two-humped Bactrian camel (used throughout most of Asia and later also north Africa) and the llama (used in South America). A llama can carry a weight of *c.* 60 kg, a donkey 70–90 kg, a mule 90–140 kg, and a camel up to 270 kg (compared to up to 40 kg for a human porter on easy ground, considerably less over difficult terrain). Both oxen and horses were sometimes used as pack animals, but more commonly to draw vehicles. The size of caravans varied widely, from a few animals to many hundreds. On exceptional occasions thousands might be used. When Alexander the Great sacked the Persian capital of Persepolis in 331 BC he is said to have used 5,000 camels as well as other animals to carry away the loot.

Wheeled vehicles. The wheel had been invented by the fourth millennium BC (when it figures on the early clay tablets from Uruk), and most of the ancient civilizations made use of wheeled vehicles. The exceptions are the New World civilizations; even the Incas, who, curiously, had children's toys with wheels, made no use of wheeled vehicles. The animals usually employed to pull vehicles were oxen, horses and mules. Oxen pull from their powerful shoulders and are best harnessed by a yoke resting on the neck connected to the vehicle by a central pole, while horses and mules pull mostly from their hind legs and are best harnessed by a collar resting on the shoulders. However, it seems that efficient collars were not developed in the ancient world and consequently the load-pulling capacity of horses was so restricted as to make them unsuitable for commercial transport. It is in any case unlikely that any civilization before the Romans made much use of wheeled vehicles for this purpose, perhaps because of the inadequacy of their roads. Certainly most of the vehicles known from the Mesopotamian, Chinese, Mycenaean and Greek civilizations are light two-wheeled chariots, used for military and display purposes.

Egyptian New Kingdom tomb painting from the tomb of Amenemtrab Ramesside at Thebes portraying the pilgrimage to Abydos, using the characteristic papyrus boats of the Nile.

Right: Bronze model of a horse-drawn carriage and attendant from a tomb of the Eastern Han (second century AD) at Wu-wei, Kansu, China. The carriage has spoked wheels, and the horse has a harness greatly superior in efficiency to the throat-and-girth harness used in the west and inferior only to the hard collar of modern times. With this harness one horse could pull a carriage holding several people.

Fourth-century AD Roman mosaic from the villa at Piazza Armerina in south central Sicily. This fragment of the Great Hunt mosaic shows an ox-drawn cart in side view, with two of its four wheels visible. The wheels are of the primitive solid type, made in segments, which continued in use alongside more sophisticated spoked wheels throughout the classical period. Solid wheels were usually fixed to rotating axles, which explains why Roman carts were often described as *stridens* ('screeching').

The Romans *did* make considerable commercial use of four-wheeled vehicles, and several different types are known; opinion is divided as to whether they had pivoted front axles or were restricted to fixed ones. We know from literary sources that they had considerable difficulties with harnessing, traction, braking, coping with cambers and even turning corners (which would have been particularly difficult if they did not have pivoted front axles). That these difficulties gave rise to real problems is indicated by the Theodosian Code of AD 438, which imposed severe loading restrictions on vehicles: *c.* 90–270 kg for light carts, and 450–680 kg for heavy carts used by the Imperial Post.

Water transport

For the early riverine civilizations of Egypt, Mesopotamia, the Indus and north China, the great waterways provided the most obvious and easiest method of transporting both people and goods within the civilizations. In Egypt the characteristic boat form was the papyrus or reed boat, made from bundles of reeds lashed together and equipped with a sail from the prehistoric period onwards. Such boats were made rigid by the technique of bending the aftermost reed bundle as far forward as possible and lashing it to the hull. The mast usually had a forked foot to distribute the thrust on either side of a reed bundle. The Mesopotamians also used boats made of reeds, but achieved the necessary rigidity by covering the reed framework inside and out with a layer of bitumen, producing a hard waterproof surface. Reed boats were probably used on the Indus too, and, as recent experiments have demonstrated that such boats are seaworthy, it is likely that they were used in trade throughout the Persian Gulf and the Indian Ocean.

The Egyptians also built wooden boats from an early period, as the ship found in a grave close to the Great Pyramid at Giza bears witness: this was a flat-bottomed vessel built of 1,224 separate parts, mostly of cedar; it was 43.4 m long and 5.9 m wide, with a displacement of some 40 tonnes. Wooden boats were also used in the Indus area, and even in treeless Mesopotamia. The Egyptians imported timber mostly from Lebanon, while the Mesopotamians probably acquired theirs from the Indus.

In China wooden boats were in use from at least the Shang period: the *sampan*, a broad-beamed, flat-bottomed boat with an open horned stern, seems to be represented in the sign for 'boat' on the Anyang oracle bones, while the sign for 'sail' indicates an almost square sail set between two upright spars. From the Han period onwards (AD 25–221) the Chinese developed the highly aerodynamic lattice sail with battens and multiple sheets, exploiting the qualities of two local materials, matting and bamboo.

Water transport does not seem to have played a significant role in the civilizations of Mesoamerica, but in South America the Incas used great sailing rafts made of balsa wood and equipped with cotton sails; they could carry 60 or 70 tonnes of goods on long journeys up and down the Pacific coast.

The later civilizations of the Mediterranean employed more sophisticated wooden ships. There were major technical improvements, including the development of vessels with keels and the use of wood-working devices (pegs, cleats and mortices and tenons) to join strakes (the side-planks of the vessel), instead of lashing them together. As well as the round merchant ships, which continued to be propelled by sails, the later Mediterranean civilizations also developed long fighting ships which were usually propelled by large numbers of oarsmen. The cargo ships could be of considerable size: from the fourth century BC onwards ships of 150 tonnes were common, while some were in the 350–500 tonne range, and we learn of a few 'super ships' (like that built for King Hiero of Syracuse around 240 BC) of 1,700–1,900 tonnes.

Even in Roman times commercial travel was still slow, not simply because the merchant vessels were not built for speed, but because sailing ships are naturally at the mercy of the winds: for instance, the annual grain run from Alexandria to Ostia, mostly against the wind, took between one and two months, while the return trip, downwind all the way, took only two or three weeks.

Production

The technology of production in the ancient civilizations was influenced by two trends, pulling in opposite directions. First there was *production for elite consumption*, particularly marked in the earliest civilizations but present in them all. This kind of production aimed to create the most splendid objects possible for the glory of the gods, the king or the nobles. It was largely free of normal 'commercial' constraints, such as the need to meet competition, to provide 'value for money', or to conform to strict production schedules. Moreover, the artefacts were frequently unique pieces and did not have to be reproduced. In these circumstances the main constraints on the craftsmen were the characteristics of the raw materials, the available technology and their own skills. These circumstances encouraged the development of complex techniques, multi-stage processes and combinations of different raw materials.

In contrast there was *production for everyday use*, which also occurs in all the early civilizations but is particularly well-developed in the later ones, especially Rome. The aim in this case was the rapid and efficient production of goods of standard quality for mass consumption. The emphasis was on the development of techniques that simplified manufacture and allowed the speedy production of large numbers of more or less identical objects. Mass production was encouraged by the development of the market economy in the second half of the first millennium BC, when for the first time market forces began to control production (although state intervention was still a common occurrence: see pp. 112–13).

Fine art production

Some of the finest objects produced for the elites of the early civilizations were of metal and, of these, the bronzes in particular demonstrate the use of complex and multi-phase techniques. Apart from the initial processes of smelting and alloying, the smiths employed elaborate casting techniques (either section moulds or the lost-wax method) to produce the objects, which might then be decorated with a variety of surface ornament techniques such as engraving, embossing or inlaying. The lost-wax method (see p. 107) was widely used in the western civilizations of the Old World and was also employed in Mesoamerica and Peru. Well-known examples of fine lost-wax castings from the ancient civilizations include the head of Sargon from third-millennium BC Nineveh and the Etruscan statue of the Roman wolf suckling Romulus and Remus, now in the Capitoline Museum in Rome. The Chinese did not employ the lost-wax technique, but they produced enormous and elaborately decorated ritual vessels by section moulding: one vessel, the *si mu wu fang ding* from the royal cemetery at Anyang, weighs 875 kg and is the largest bronze casting known from antiquity.

Other examples of status goods, which must have taken months, if not years, to produce, are the textiles found at Paracas in southern Peru, dating from the last few centuries BC. These textiles, found wrapped around seated mummies, were sometimes of enormous size and elaborately decorated. The largest textile associated with Mummy 49 – an undecorated piece, produced on a single loom – measures 26.7 m by 3.4 m and contains an estimated 160 km of two-ply yarn. Characteristic forms were rectangular mantles made of three separately woven textiles joined together: the wide central section was usually made of alpaca wool, while the narrower side panels were of cotton. All were decorated with embroidered polychrome motifs, often in their hundreds; favourite motifs include human figures, serpents, birds and fish.

Chinese lacquer goods are another example of production for elite consumption. The juice of the lac tree, *Rhus vernicifera*, is a natural varnish which hardens on exposure to air. It was applied in many coats to objects of wood or fabric and polished after each application to produce an extraordinarily high finish. The finest lacquers of the Eastern Zhou and Han dynasties (spanning the period *c.* 770 BC to AD 220) include not only vessels and boxes, but furniture, musical instruments and even coffins. They were decorated with delicate polychrome painted designs and occasionally also inlaid with shell or precious metals. Han texts make it clear that lacquer goods were more costly than bronze.

Mass production

The technological developments associated with mass production, in strong contrast to those of fine art production, worked in favour of simplification and speed. Good examples can be found in the pottery industry, where we find both fine art items and mass-produced goods. The first development to speed up production was the potter's wheel, which appeared in the fourth millennium BC in Mesopotamia and was employed in all the Old World civilizations, although it is not found at all in the Americas. The wheel, operated by hand or, more effectively, by a treadle, could produce pots of more regular shape and faster than the techniques of ring or coil building used to make pots by hand.

A further development that assisted mass production was the use of moulds to form the decoration. A thick-walled mould with the design cut on the inner side was fastened to the potter's wheel; a bowl or dish was spun inside it, while pressure applied by the hand from inside ensured that the clay adhered to the mould. To make closed forms such as jugs two or more different moulds would be used. The technique was developed by the Etruscans to produce relief-decorated black *bucchero* ware, and subsequently used by the Romans to produce the glossy red Arretine ware and its

Textiles found wrapped around mummies at Paracas in southern Peru provide good examples of fine art objects, produced for elites at enormous expense of time and energy. The larger mantles were decorated with hundreds of intricately embroidered polychrome motifs.

successor, *terra sigillata* (widely but inaccurately known as Samian ware). This ware was produced in vast quantities in the factories of Gaul and distributed throughout the Empire.

Techniques of mass production were also used in the metal industry. In contrast to the elaborate lost-wax castings made for elite consumption, everyday tools such as knives or axes were made in section moulds, usually simple two-piece moulds, which could be re-used many times. Coins, another mass-produced item, were normally made by casting blank disks in simple open moulds. The blank was placed on a block of metal with an engraved device on it, a punch was placed on top and struck sharply with a hammer, impressing the decoration onto the underside of the blank. If the end of the punch was also engraved, a two-sided coin would be produced. Experiments suggest that one obverse die (the metal block) could produce some 16,000 coins before wearing out, while two or three reverse dies (the punches) would be consumed in the process.

Another example of technical development related to mass production occurred in the manufacture of glass. Before the first century BC, glass vessels were made either by using a sand core or by pressing in a mould, sometimes combined with cold cutting. Some very fine objects were produced, but the methods were inefficient and time-consuming. In the later first century BC, the technique of blowing glass was developed and very rapidly led to a whole range of new products, including many new types of vessel and the first window glass. By the mid-first century AD glass factories were established in many parts of the Roman Empire and glass, previously rare and used mainly for luxuries, became a common material used for all kinds of domestic purposes.

The development of the technique of blowing glass turned glass manufacture from a luxury craft into a mass production industry. This Roman blown glass vessel comes from Bacbouck, near Tyre.

The Etruscans developed the technique of producing relief decoration on pottery by the use of moulds, as in the black *bucchero* vessels shown here. The Romans subsequently developed the technique further, in the mass-produced Arretine and *terra sigillata* wares.

9 The Individual in Society

In this chapter we shall look at the role of the individual in society. In particular we shall try to assess in what ways life for the individual in the early civilizations was different from that of his or her predecessor in simpler societies. This exercise is very speculative – even more so than the other speculative exercises we have undertaken in this book – because we rarely have any record of individual experiences from early societies. As we have seen, in most of the early civilizations writing was used exclusively for state purposes. Where literary works exist, they too take a public form, such as myths, epics or wisdom literature; we find no personal writing at all, no diaries or autobiographies, no novels, stories or poems concerned with personal experience. At best we may get an occasional glimpse of daily life from letters, but these refer exclusively to the upper levels of society. We first find personal experience in the writings of classical authors, and we can learn something of the lives of particular individuals in Greek and Roman society. However, these individuals were exceptional, outstanding members of society; we still know nothing of the lives of people of lower social status. It is only the advent of widespread literacy that has given us access to the daily lives of suburban housewives, commercial travellers, criminals and school-children, to name but a few of those who write diaries and autobiographies – real or fictional – today.

Archaeology is of little help when we wish to study the lives of individuals. Indeed, the individual is hard to identify in the archaeological record except in death. And in death people tend to appear in their social *personae*, identified by age, sex, occupation, social class and religion, rather than by their individual characteristics – although one finds the occasional eccentric exception. To reconstruct the life of the individual in early societies, we must turn again to analogy – to the work of anthropologists for simpler societies and to the records of later

Opposite: Colima-style ceramic model of a seated hunchback, from western Mexico, *c.* AD 500. The figure is depicted with great individuality and is probably an actual portrait.

Below: Tombstone from Trier in Roman Germany depicting a typical family scene. The stone was set up by Gaius Julius Maternus, a legionary veteran, during his lifetime and dedicated to himself and his deceased wife, who is described as most sweet and virtuous.

The family

Right: In small-scale societies, whether of hunter-gatherers or farmers, social organization is based on the family. The Yanomamo people of the forests along the border between Brazil and Venezuela live by hunting and cultivating plantains, bananas and other crops. They live in large family huts clustered together in villages of 100–200 people.

Below: A Yanomamo family in their hut.

civilizations for more complex ones. In no society is the individual a free agent, able to spend his time exactly as he would like. There is the need to earn a living, to fulfil obligations to other people, and to conform to the law or to custom. The individual's behaviour is constrained, and indeed to a large extent defined, by the different groups in society to which he belongs – the family, the age-group, the trade or profession, the social class – as well as the culture of the whole society. This is not to take a deterministic view, or to deny the existence of free will, but only to point out the contexts in which the individual's pattern of behaviour is formed, and the forces which contribute to its formation.

In all societies, simple or complex, one of the groups that influences the individual most strongly is the family. All societies practise marriage and have families, though these institutions may not take the form familiar to us, that is monogamous marriage and the nuclear family; indeed an enormous variety of different systems has been recognized by anthropologists. We do not need to discuss these here, but we should emphasize their dominant role in small-scale societies, which are based entirely on kinship (i.e. family) relations.

In such societies every individual is related to every other, and these family relationships regulate their behaviour to one another. Because it is not actually possible for all inter-personal behaviour to be dictated by individual blood relationships, even in a very small-scale society, the kinship principle is followed through what anthropologists call 'classificatory kinship systems', in which all members of society are classified into categories in relation to the individual. For instance, a man may address several different women as 'mother' – a phenomenon that has often puzzled observers. It is not that he does not really know who his natural mother is, but rather that there is a group of women (often his own mother and her sisters) who all stand in the same social relationship to him.

The simplest and probably the most widespread type of classificatory kinship system is found in most bands and many tribes. In societies of this kind there is a division into two main groups, who practise 'reciprocal exogamy' (which means that men from one group take wives from the other) and usually 'virilocality' (meaning that wives live in their husband's village after marriage). For any individual

in such a society, most other people fall into four main groups: (1) own group (i.e. own village, father's family), own generation; (2) other group (i.e. other village, mother's family), own generation; (3) own group, adjacent generation (i.e. either parents or offspring, depending on whether one is an adult or a child); (4) other group, adjacent generation. Each of these four groups is subdivided into males and females, making eight main categories altogether, towards whom particular types of behaviour are appropriate. Grandparents or grandchildren may form additional groups.

Many kinship systems are more complicated than this and contain more groups, but the principle is the same: all members of society are slotted into some kinship category in relation to any individual, and most social behaviour is regulated by these relationships. So pervasive is this principle that when a total stranger, such as an anthropologist, appears on the scene, it is often necessary for a kinship tie, however fictitious, to be discovered before he or she can be accepted.

Thus in simple societies kinship relations provide one of the most important forces influencing the behaviour of individuals. But to what extent was this still the case in the more complex societies of the early civilizations? Clearly the role of the family in social organization was reduced. In a community numbered in thousands or more, it is impossible for any one individual to know everyone else, or for everyone to be incorporated into even the most theoretical of kinship systems. Instead, some relationships at least had to be organized in other ways. Some people may have been largely removed from kinship influence altogether: the behaviour of

groups such as the army, or priests, or, at the other end of the social scale, slaves, would have been based on different principles, such as service to king, god or master. For the majority of people, however, family relationships would have continued to be important for many purposes, including relations with the people they worked with every day: many occupations, including both crafts and professions, were organized by kinship groups; agriculture too was normally based on family organization. The main difference for the individual, as compared to earlier societies, was that he was now involved in other roles in society, as well as those dictated by kinship principles.

The individual and work

Top: In all societies much work is invested in the subsistence economy. This scene showing a cow being milked, her calf tied to her front leg, is depicted on the sarcophagus of Queen Kawit, wife of King Mentuhotep (2060–2010 BC) of Egypt's Eleventh Dynasty.

Bottom: Ceramic model from Jaina showing Maya women preparing tortillas, round flat cakes made from maize flour.

One of the factors that most strongly influence the lives of individuals is their work. In our own society the question 'What do you do?' is one of the first that we ask when making someone's acquaintance; what people do for a living is felt to be an integral and major part of their personality. There are good reasons for this. In the first place, a job takes up a high proportion of one's waking time; on this basis alone it is bound to be an important part of one's life. Secondly, work is closely associated with social status, whether judged by income and standard of living, style of clothes and belongings, or by respect in which one is held by others. Thirdly, work has a lot to do with one's feelings about life: if the job is enjoyable and one identifies with it, one feels good; if the job is unpleasant or, worse still, if one is unemployed, it can make life a misery. To what extent would all this have been true of earlier societies?

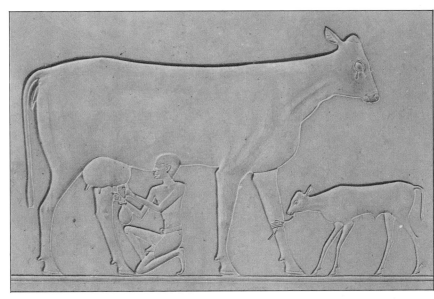

Work in simple societies

In simple societies studied by anthropologists, whether of hunters and gatherers or of farmers, most work is concerned with subsistence, there is little division of labour beyond that based on age and sex, and very few tasks are carried out by specialists. What any individual does in the way of work is dictated by the nature of the subsistence economy, by the season of the year and other fluctuations in natural conditions, and by the sex and age of the individual. In these circumstances, what attitudes do people have to work?

The studies made by anthropologists in the last thirty years have been very enlightening in this respect. It seems that the concept of 'work' as we know it does not exist in these societies: the idea that work is something one *ought* to do on a regular basis, for a high proportion of one's time, and should feel guilty about *not* doing – the 'Protestant work ethic' – is a product of at least relatively modern society. In primitive societies people may work hard, but they do so only for restricted periods of time and for specific purposes, such as gathering in a harvest; work of this kind is interspersed with periods when little is done except rest and play, as well as periods devoted to ritual activities. This kind of life-style gave rise to typical imperialist prejudices about the 'laziness' and 'fecklessness' of natives. The reality is somewhat different: members of these societies work simply as much as is necessary to produce food for their subsistence needs and see no reason to work more. They pursue what Marshall Sahlins called the 'Zen road to affluence', based on the assumption that human needs are few and easily satisfied.

Clearly, within such a conceptual world the role of work in the life of an individual is unlike our own. Work is not a major source of personal satisfaction and pride (although no doubt there *is* both satisfaction and pride in skill as a hunter or in a good harvest safely gathered in), for it is not an area of life in which there are great differences between individuals. Nor is it closely connected with social status; instead high status is associated with such attributes as generosity in gift-giving, wisdom and special links with the supernatural. On the other hand, work is rarely a source of misery in these societies either; what is done is seen to be necessary and is shared among the group, while emotional and intellectual energies are concentrated on other areas of social life. The only compulsion to work is imposed by the need to provide food for the family, and by social pressure within the kin group; there is no forced labour like that imposed on slaves, serfs or the urban proletariat of later societies.

Work in the ancient civilizations

Work must have become increasingly important in the individual's life as society became more complex. Two separate processes contributed to this. On the one hand there was the increasing specialization of labour. As technological processes became more complicated and social organization more hierarchical, more and more crafts became the preserve of specialists. For these craftsmen – potters, metal-smiths, stone-workers, glass-makers, jewellers, textile-workers, etc. – their work must have dominated their lives, occupying most of their time, influencing the people they moved among and dictating their status in society. As we have seen, these crafts were often organized by kinship groups, and kin relations may have governed the *internal* organization of the craft; nevertheless in terms of society as a whole the individual would be defined by the job and not by kinship categories. In other words, in the potters' quarter an individual might be known as 'John's son' and his role among the potters would be related to John's status and to the family ties between the members of the group. In the outside world, however, he would be known as a potter and his status would depend on the status of that craft in society and his own skill at it.

There were other specialists too, as well as artisans: there were the civil servants, the priests, the soldiers, the merchants, the teachers, the lawyers, the doctors, and so on. For all of these, work must have been thc among the most important parts of their lives. We know something about the status of these various specialists in different ancient civilizations. The professions just listed were high status jobs, as they generally are today, and they were normally restricted to the upper echelons of society. The status of craftsmen varied; they were rarely rated very highly, though usually above the peasant farmers. Some types of work had particularly low status and were thought suitable only for slaves, such as mining in the classical civilizations; other crafts were carried out predominantly by slaves, such as textile manufacture in both Mesopotamia and Mycenaean Greece.

This leads us on to the other process contributing to the growing importance of 'work' in society: the increasing proportion of the population that was economically dependent and therefore obliged to work for others. Different civilizations had different social systems, but all had at least some slaves; in the classical civilizations a large part of the work-force consisted of slaves. Subject populations,

obliged to work the land of others, often labelled serfs, also occur in many early civilizations. And then there were the urban poor, often refugees from the countryside, deprived not only of land, but of family too, obliged to seek employment on almost any terms. For all these people the reality of work was often what it has been for so many workers since: unremitting drudgery for the benefit of others. This is the unacceptable face, not of capitalism, which was yet to emerge, but of civilization itself.

Interestingly enough, many simple societies do not have a word that corresponds at all precisely to our term 'work'. The Tikopians and Fijians, for instance, use a single term for activities that the anthropologist would label 'work' and 'ritual'; perhaps even stranger to our way of thinking are the Australian Yir Yiront, who do not discriminate between 'work' and 'play'. These distinctions are the products of particular social systems.

Civilizations support many new types of work not known in simpler societies. This Chinese painted pottery tray of the Western Han period (second to first century BC) from Tsinan, Shantung, depicts acrobats, dancers and musicians – all probably professional entertainers – as well as spectators or attendants.

Many crafts became full-time specialisms in the early civilizations. This Egyptian wall painting from the Tomb of Nebamun and Ipuky, *c.* 1300 BC, shows goldsmiths and joiners at work.

157

The individual and the state

The rule of law

In societies organized on a kinship basis, all relationships are in a sense inter-personal. Even in hierarchical chiefdoms, people have obligations to the chief in his own person, not to a theoretical abstract body, the state, of which he is the embodiment. In true states, by contrast, a new type of relationship has been created between two abstract entities: the citizen and the state. In reality the distinction is *not* clear-cut, and the authority of high-level chiefdoms merges into that of true states. However, there *is* a real distinction and it relates to the rule of *law*. The citizen has both rights and obligations in relation to the state, not sanctioned by custom and the authority of the chief as in earlier societies, but encoded in law. And we need to be in no doubt that in at least some ancient civilizations the law played an important part in people's lives. We have monumental law codes inscribed in stone from some civilizations, notably Mesopotamia and Greece, and a wealth of legal documents: law text books, court records and records of a variety of legal transactions, both between individuals (modern equivalents would be sales receipts, rent contracts, hire purchase agreements) and between individuals and the state (modern equivalents would be tax returns, licences for televisions, cars or dogs, pension books). A particularly rich body of legal documents comes from Mesopotamia, and we also have good evidence from classical Greece and Rome. For the other civilizations we do not have a systematic body of written law, but we often learn of the formal relationship between the individual and the state through records of taxes and so on.

Though the rule of law confers on the citizen both rights and obligations, the obligations are often more apparent than the rights in the historical record. This may reflect their role in the life of the individual, since rights are frequently appreciated only in their absence. Thus in our own society it is difficult to avoid feeling the burden of taxation, whereas freedom of speech is taken for granted and becomes a matter of discussion only if it is threatened in some way. Of the various duties of the early citizen, those most frequently documented are taxation, labour service and military service.

Taxation

All state societies finance state activities through taxation, and the ancient civilizations were no exception. However, it was not until a late stage that taxes were paid in money. Generally they were paid in kind, either as proportions of a harvest, or of a flock or herd of animals, or according to abstract units of value that were usually based on one or more valuable traded items, such as silver in Mesopotamia or cacao beans in Mesoamerica. For the individual, taxation was a burden. We can all identify with the sentiment expressed in the Sumerian proverb: 'You can have a king and you can have a lord, but the man to fear is the tax-collector'! Sometimes the burden was clearly unreasonable. The so-called 'Urukagina reform document' relates to the Sumerian city of Lagash in the second half of the third millennium BC and records a list of abuses, including the fact that 'from the borders of Ningursu [the patron deity of Lagash] to the sea there was the tax-collector'; it is followed by a list of reforms carried out by Urukagina. We also have records of crippling and unfair taxation from the Roman Empire, especially under some of the greedier emperors such as Nero.

Labour service (the corvée)

Labour service was important in most, possibly all, the early civilizations and was the main way in which public construction and maintenance works were organized: in Egypt, for instance, canal-digging and the building of pyramids or other royal tombs were carried out in this way; in Mesopotamia irrigation works, city walls and temples were built with corvée labour. It is assumed that major construction works in the other early civilizations were also organized like this, although we have little direct evidence. In particular we lack evidence as to who was liable for labour service and what proportion of their time was spent on it. We are better informed than usual in the case of the Incas, where every able-bodied male head of household was required to contribute labour to state projects every year. The labour included both work on state-owned farmlands and the *mita*, which was service on public works projects such as construction of public buildings, engineering works and agricultural projects. While working, citizens were fed, sheltered, equipped and entertained by the state. We may imagine that labour service in the early civilizations was no more popular with the citizens than taxation. One version of the Mesopotamian Gilgamesh epic begins with the citizens complaining about their forced labour on the city walls.

Military service

Another duty of citizens in all the early civilizations was military service. Professional standing armies were the exception (although most rulers supported a small professional 'praetorian guard') and the sizeable armies needed in times of military threat were raised by conscription. In Shang China the oracle-bone records suggest conscripted numbers in

All civilizations finance state activities through taxation. On this Romano-German sandstone relief from Trier a tax-collector is counting the money paid by a peasant.

the range 1,000 to 30,000. Sometimes conscription applied to every adult male citizen; sometimes there was a property-owning qualification or it was restricted to certain social classes. In both classical Greece and Rome the citizen was expected to provide his own weapons and armour, which would have effectively restricted participation to the better-off members of society.

If it was through taxation, labour and military service that the state most obviously impinged on the life of the individual, the relationship was not one-sided. From the state the citizen gained benefits from the use of the state-organized agricultural schemes, roads, city walls, etc.; also protection against attack from outside (through state armies) and the assurance of justice in transactions between individuals (through civil law). The extent to which the state affected the lives of individuals varied with location and social status. For the peasant farmer living in a rural village the role of the state would have been secondary to the traditional claims of kinship, while for the city-dweller, particularly the well-off member of the upper class, the role of the state would have been more important.

In the early stages of civilization major construction works were often carried out by compulsory labour service, though at later stages slave labour was more widely used. This relief from the palace of Sennacherib at Nineveh (*c.* 700 BC) shows workers, probably slaves or prisoners, dragging a huge statue of a human-headed winged bull across country.

The armed forces of the early civilizations, such as those shown here in a sea-battle scene on a marble sarcophagus from Greece, were recruited from the body of citizens by conscription. Professional paid soldiers did not appear in significant numbers before the Hellenistic period in Europe.

159

Personal choice

Among the values most appreciated in our society is the freedom we have over major choices in life: what sort of career to pursue; who to marry (or not); how to spend our spare time; what sort of style of living to pursue. Of course no one would deny that there are severe restrictions – especially of an economic kind – on the exercise of such choice, but the desirability of the maximum possible freedom is rarely questioned. Indeed the right of the individual to choose his or her life-style has been elevated to the status of a major moral principle: 'doing one's own thing' is applauded, sometimes even when the 'thing' in question is demonstrably anti-social or downright subversive.

This attitude seems to be a recent development; it is not found in the writings of the ancient civilizations. The emphasis there is on the behaviour of the individual in society, in terms of a series of obligations. The idea of owing anything to *oneself*, in the way of personal satisfaction or self-knowledge, does not appear in this literature. For instance, the Chinese thinker Confucius (531–479 BC) was concerned with the correct behaviour appropriate to each person's position in society, and the Buddha, also teaching in the sixth century BC, was equally concerned with ethical precepts about the appropriate behaviour between husbands and wives, parents and children, pupils and teachers, employers and employees. The nature of these writings makes it difficult to assess the actual degree of personal choice in these civilizations, so once again we have to turn to the careful use of analogy, model and theory.

Simple societies

We must emphasize that we are concerned here with personal choice in *major* matters, not with individual taste in food, clothes and ornament. In all societies there is variation in personal behaviour and the individual can choose between degrees of flamboyance, say, or the extent of his participation in group activities. The extent of real choice about important matters, however, is very restricted in simple societies. For instance, where a society practises a subsistence economy, there is little choice of work: what the individual does is dictated by the nature of the economy, by the season of the year and by age and sex. Social position is largely fixed too, determined mainly by genealogy, since society is organized by kinship and one cannot choose one's relations. The exception would appear to be the 'Big Men', discussed in Chapter 4, who can build up a position by generosity in feast-giving and the like. In many societies, however, the opportunity to become wealthy (necessary for a Big Man, even though he only collects wealth in order to give it away) is not readily available. The potential for increased productivity is normally present, but it requires group rather than individual activity and the motivation is frequently lacking.

There may be little choice of marriage partner either. Rules of marriage may mean that in small-

Above: Thinkers and teachers of the early civilizations, such as the Buddha, shown here in a colossal statue carved out of the rock at Leshan, Sichuan province, China, were concerned primarily with social ethics: the behaviour appropriate to individuals in society.

Right: Members of rural communities in the ancient civilizations probably had little choice of work, which was dictated by the demands of the agricultural calendar. This sixth-century BC Attic black-figure cup shows scenes of ploughing and sowing, which would have been familiar to earlier and simpler societies.

scale societies there are few eligible individuals available to start with. And often enough the choice is not made by the individuals themselves, but by older members of their families. And if men have little choice in this matter, women often have no choice at all – an issue that we shall look at again later. Freedom in personal behaviour is also severely limited, in this case by the force of public opinion. Characteristically, simple societies tolerate little deviance from their norms, and the social pressures on those who do not conform are considerable. This is not to suggest that primitive societies are full of individuals seething with frustration through lack of personal choice in their lives. On the contrary, 'what you never know, you never miss', and in the main people seem happy to act out their lives within the limits laid down by society.

The early civilizations

It seems likely that the growing complexity of society and the advent of city life increased the personal choice of some members of society at least. In terms of *jobs*, for instance, clearly there were more types of work to choose from; the extent to which individuals were free to choose, however, is unclear. At the top of the social scale, the son of a well-born family might have been able to choose between a career in the army, the temple, the civil service, or perhaps as a diviner, a doctor or a lawyer. At lower levels of society, however, there may have been little choice. As we have seen, crafts were often organized by kinship groups, and members of these groups might have had few alternatives to following the family profession. Where there may have been more choice, paradoxically enough, is among the really poor. Whereas in simple agricultural communities there is virtually no opportunity outside the village, in urban societies poor farmers or those deprived of land do not have to depend on the bounty of relatives, but can move to the city, where a variety of employment is available, albeit usually of a menial kind.

Although the ancient civilizations were class societies, sometimes very rigid ones, there was nevertheless always some social mobility. Slavery, for instance, was never confined to an unchanging group: free men and women could be sold into slavery (or even sell themselves) and slaves could be

freed. And among free men, individuals could lose or gain status by a variety of means, including cowardice or bravery in warfare, performance in athletics, or the loss or accumulation of wealth. Marriage alliances also provided opportunities for improving status, though it is unclear whether there was much more personal choice over marriage partners than in simpler societies.

There would have been greater choice in such areas as recreation and personal belongings, simply because a wider range of alternatives was available. There was almost certainly more freedom in personal behaviour also; in the city an individual could be anonymous and behave much as he wished, without fear of being seen and censured by his relatives. Many aspects of behaviour were no longer controlled by the family, yet did not come within the purview of law. We may conclude that by comparison with our own society, personal choice in the early civilizations was still very restricted; by comparison with simpler societies, however, it had considerably increased.

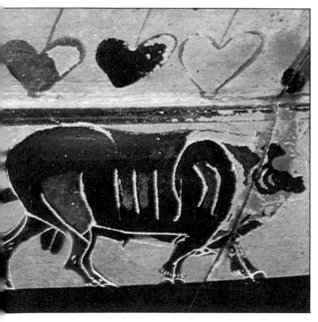

As society became more complex, the range of professional occupations, ritual activities and recreations all increased. This Jalisco-style pottery figure from western Mexico (AD 300–1000) shows a ball-player. Ball games served both ritual and recreational purposes throughout Mesoamerica.

Women in society

The evidence

Almost everything we have written so far in this chapter applies to men, but not necessarily to women. The role of women in society, and women's experiences, are prime concerns of modern scholarship, but they are particularly difficult to reconstruct for ancient societies.

The written sources are often either silent or ambiguous about women, and furthermore the vast majority were written by men – not a good starting point for assessing women's experience. On the other hand, administrative and legal documents can provide reasonably objective information about the economic and legal position of women in society, while histories give us some clues about their role in public life, though from a male point of view. More difficult to interpret are the literary works, and especially mythology, where women figure in a range of roles from goddess to whore, loving wife and mother to murderess. The extent to which these reflect real life is debatable. Various different interpretations see them as either true pictures of society; or as survivals from an earlier age with a different type of society; or as symbols of relations and tensions in society; or as the products of male fantasy, either hopeful or fearful.

The archaeological evidence is equally difficult to interpret; it includes burials of women, with associated tomb types, burial practices and grave goods; women's equipment; and depictions of women in art. In the past impressive theories have been constructed on flimsy bases: for instance, a predominance of female figurines, traditionally interpreted as 'mother goddesses' in spite of all the other possible explanations, is often thought to be an indication of female dominance in society. However, such an interpretation cannot possibly be accepted without some kind of corroboration from other sources.

In classical art idealized womanhood appears in portraits of goddesses by male artists. This statue by Praxiteles (later fourth century BC) represents either Aphrodite or Artemis.

The myth of the Amazons, a race of female warriors, is thought by some to indicate the real existence of matriarchal societies. Alternatively the myth can be explained as a typical 'traveller's tale' or, in psychological terms, as the product of fearful male fantasy. This Etruscan figure of an Amazon archer on a horse is a detail from the top of a bronze *cista* (a box).

162

The myth of primitive matriarchy

There is a widespread view that many prehistoric societies were characterized by *matriarchy*, that is a social system in which power rests with women. This view can be traced back to the nineteenth-century German scholar, Johann B. Bachofen, who published a book entitled *Das Mutterrecht (Mother Right)* in 1861, in which he argued that human society everywhere went through a matriarchal stage. The evidence included myths figuring female dominance, like the Greek myth of the Amazons, as well as the occurrence in ethnography and history of the practice of reckoning descent through the mother, known as *matrilineality*. The occurrence of matrilineality is not in doubt, but anthropologists since Bachofen's day have emphasized that it is not the same as matriarchy. In most, perhaps all, matrilineal societies power still belongs with the men, though the locus of family authority is not the father, but the mother's brother. In fact anthropologists have not yet found *any* society in which women dominate men, in spite of efforts by feminist anthropologists to search out such societies. In this light it seems extremely unwise to interpret the ambiguous archaeological remains of prehistoric societies as evidence of matriarchy.

Although women were never equal, let alone dominant, their position in past civilizations was far from uniform. In some cases they had considerable legal rights and degrees of freedom, while in others they had virtually none. Nor was the role of women uniform throughout society, but varied according to social class. In many societies both aristocratic and working-class women enjoyed a degree of freedom, while the least free were slaves, followed by middle-class women, to whom the canons of 'respectability' applied most stringently.

We know little or nothing about the role of women in the civilizations where written records are lacking, such as the Olmecs or Teotihuacán, or where the writing is undeciphered, like the Indus civilization, or not well understood, as in the case of the Maya. The best information comes from those societies where there is abundant written documentation, including legal records, especially Mesopotamia, Greece and Rome.

Child-bearing

Frequently women were regarded primarily as child-bearers and all other roles were secondary. In state societies child-bearing is the concern not only of the family, but of the state itself. We know something about this concern in both Greece and Rome. In Sparta, a regime attributed to the law-giver Lycurgus ensured the physical fitness of well-born women and spared them housework and clothes-making, so that they could produce healthy children for the state (which was constantly at war and required a continuous supply of new warriors). The Spartan women were relatively free compared to those of other Greek cities, especially Athens. Here too the principal duty of citizen women was the production of legitimate heirs for the families that constituted the citizenry, but at Athens this role was associated with a secluded life, domestic duties, modest clothing and complete subordination to husbands, comparable to the situation of women in strict Muslim societies today. The Roman state was also concerned with the rearing of children, and under the legislation of Augustus women who had borne children were rewarded. According to the *jus liberorum* ('right of children'), a free-born woman who bore three children or a freed woman who bore four was exempted from formal supervision by a male guardian.

Above: Roman women had no choice in marriage, but had to marry as their guardians wished. In this scene from a wall painting in a Roman mansion, the bride is being consoled by the goddess Aphrodite.

Right: Citizen women of Sparta fared relatively well compared with those of other Greek cities. They were spared domestic work and followed a regime of physical exercise, in order to produce healthy children for the state. This sixth-century BC bronze figure from the lid of a vase found in Yugoslavia is thought to represent a young Spartan girl athlete.

Female infanticide

Apparently contradicting the state's concern with the production of new citizens is the practice of female infanticide. This occurs commonly in band and tribal societies and is well documented in the civilizations of Greece and Rome; it may well have been practised in the other civilizations also. The apparent contradiction is explained by the fact that the state was concerned with the production of *male* citizens to supply its armies and ensure its continuity. But it was also necessary to limit overall population growth, at least in peacetime, so, in the absence of efficient contraception, both abortion and infanticide (mostly of females) were practised. In Greece and Rome exposure (abandonment of the infant in the countryside) was the usual method. Abhorrent as the idea is to us, selective female infanticide should not necessarily be equated with a low regard for women; in societies where population growth is controlled almost exclusively by the number of women who reach child-bearing age, it is the most effective means of population control available (since abortion involves an even chance of killing a male child, as well as being potentially dangerous for the mother).

Marriage

In most societies up to recent times marriage was not primarily a relationship between two individuals, but a social institution, concerned with child-rearing, the inheritance and transfer of property and alliances between different groups in society. Thus many different people were involved and individuals were not usually free to follow their own inclinations. A good proportion of surviving legal documentation concerns marriage, divorce, dowries and inheritance. There is considerable variety in these laws and it is clear that in some cases, Egypt and Mesopotamia for example, women got a far better deal than in others. However, the claim made frequently that 'women had equal rights under the law' is not true for *any* ancient society for which we have documentation. Women were treated as the property of their male kinsfolk; marriages were arranged by men, and involved transfers of property between men. Women were frequently married at a very early age, sometimes even before puberty.

The law code of Hammurabi, from early-second-millennium BC Mesopotamia, provides an example of 'liberal' laws on marriage and women's rights. For instance, a woman's dowry could never be taken by her husband; it remained hers for life, but on her death it either went to her sons or reverted to her father's family. She could leave a husband who ill-treated her and take her dowry with her. A widow could not be driven out penniless and an orphaned girl had to be provided with a dowry by her brothers out of their father's estate. Clearly such regulations offered considerable protection to women, but in no sense do they represent equal treatment of the sexes. However, they compare favourably with the law of Rome, which in theory at least invested the *pater familias* (the eldest male of the family) with absolute power, including the power of life and death and the power to sell into slavery, over all members of his household. Whereas adult males were emancipated by the death of the pater familias, women passed into the custody of the nearest male relative or another male guardian named in the father's will. Two main types of marriage existed: one transferred a woman from the power of her father to that of her husband; the other retained her in the power of her father. The decision as to which type of marriage should be undergone was taken by the father.

There was also no equality in the expected behaviour of men and women in marriage. The sexual double standard was normal, with adultery by the wife being more serious than by the husband. There was, however, considerable variation in the attitudes to female adultery. In Rome the pater familias was allowed to kill an adulterous daughter if she was still under his power; her husband was merely obliged to divorce her and bring her to trial. A woman was allowed to divorce her husband for adultery, but was not obliged to. In archaic and classical Sparta, by contrast, adultery was less

strictly defined and there are records of Spartan women having extra-marital relations, apparently unpunished and perhaps condoned, including at one stage in the eighth century BC with unfree men of the helot class while their husbands were away at war.

Slaves, of course, were worse off than free women. Under Roman law, for instance, slaves could not marry, though frequently they entered an arrangement known as *contubernium* (cohabitation). This was regarded by the slaves themselves as a valid marriage, but it had no legal basis and the children of the union were illegitimate. The children were automatically slaves and belonged to the master of their mother.

Property and inheritance

The extent to which women could own and control property, especially land, varied considerably. In Old Babylonian Mesopotamia, we know that some women were able to own land, but they may have been a restricted group. In the city of Sippar a group of women living in a cloister attached to the temple of Shamash are recorded as inheriting and buying large amounts of land and owning many personal possessions. In the Mycenaean Linear B tablets some women are recorded as owning land in the Sphagianes district of the kingdom of Pylos. All the women named had religious titles and it is possible that only women in the religious hierarchy could own land. In archaic and classical Greece there were differences between cities. Whereas the women of Sparta and the Cretan city of Gortyn were able to control their own property, in Athens women's property was managed by male guardians. In the Hellenistic period women in Greece generally participated more in economic affairs, and women are recorded as owning both land and slaves. However, in theory at least, men still organized economic affairs for women in most parts of the Hellenistic world. In the Roman Republic upper-class women sometimes disposed of large amounts of

Images of marriage from the ancient civilizations: *above*, Etruscan terracotta sarcophagus; *above left and left*, terracotta figurines in Nayarit style from western Mexico (AD 300–1000).

wealth, in spite of legislation restricting the amount they could inherit. On the other hand, until the second century AD Roman women could only make wills by a very complicated procedure and were prevented from leaving any property to their daughters.

In spite of the legislative differences documented for different areas and periods, it is clear that women were never on an equal footing with men over property ownership in the ancient world. If women were not formally in the hands of male guardians in financial matters, they were always restricted in the ways they could act. In particular, inheritance laws usually ensured that property returned to men on a woman's death, either to her father's family or to her husband's.

165

Work

The work available to women seems to have been very similar in all the civilizations for which we have evidence. Well-born women did not work outside the home, but were responsible for housework, often managing a household of slaves or other domestic servants. They were also responsible for making clothes, and even aristocratic women were themselves expected to spin and weave. The only alternative to a domestic life for well-born women was normally a religious one. Priestesses are known from all areas, and their positions were sometimes powerful ones; religion may have been the only route to independence and high status for women.

Slaves and lower-class women worked for others, but their work was generally still of the same 'domestic' type. In particular textile manufacture was usually in the hands of women, as were parts of the food industry. Another area of employment was as midwives, wet-nurses and child nurses. Occasionally we find references to female doctors – including one Babylonian example from Mari and one from Pompeii – but these are rare. Women singers and actresses are recorded in some civilizations; in general they would have performed for male audiences. Prostitutes occur in all areas, and occasionally prostitution could provide a route to wealth, independence and the company of high-ranking men (not just for sexual purposes). A famous example from the fifth century BC is Aspasia, who lived with the Athenian leader Pericles and is said to have wielded considerable influence over him. More frequently prostitution would have involved poorly paid and despised work in brothels or in the open.

Occasionally we find evidence of women working in what were normally male preserves. Tablets from Mari record nine women working as scribes early in the second millennium BC: a high-status profession usually practised by men. By Roman times we find women in a range of 'male' trades, including brick-laying and stone-cutting, as well as practising commerce; at Pompeii we find a landlady and a female money-lender. However, women were never more than a tiny minority in jobs of this kind.

Education

In most early civilizations there is no evidence that women in general received formal education; it is probable that they were taught domestic skills at home by female relatives. The normally early age at marriage would have precluded higher education, even if it had been available in theory. An exception is provided by women trained as priestesses, who received an education in civilizations as diverse as Mesopotamia, Rome and the Aztecs. There were other exceptions too: the female scribes at Mari had obviously learnt to read and write, as had the Greek female poets of the archaic age (eighth to sixth centuries BC), of whom the most famous is Sappho.

Opportunities for education for women increased with the passing of time. During the Hellenistic period women were increasingly learning to read and write: Egyptian papyri of this time show that some women were able to sign their names to contracts. We also find the re-emergence of women poets at this period, and we know that the philosopher Epicurus admitted women to the school in his garden on the same terms as men. By the Roman period education for women was more widespread, and upper-class women were sufficiently cultivated to participate in male intellectual life. Lower-class women could receive some education too, and even some slaves might be educated if they belonged to a wealthy household where they might be required to read to their masters or mistresses.

Public life

It was extremely rare for women to be rulers in the ancient civilizations, although there were three or four female pharaohs in Dynastic Egypt, including Queen Hatshepsut of the Eighteenth Dynasty. In the Ptolemaic period there were a number of famous

Above: In Greek society well-born women were generally restricted to domestic activities. This mid-fifth-century BC terracotta relief from Locri in southern Italy shows a woman pressing linen.

Right: Prostitution – 'the oldest profession' – is well documented in classical antiquity. This red-figure cup of the early fifth century BC, attributed to the painter Onesimos, shows a reveller with a prostitute.

Egyptian queens, culminating with Cleopatra who came to the throne in 51 BC. Elsewhere, in Mesopotamia for instance, and in the Hellenistic world outside Egypt, and in Rome, the wives of kings exercised considerable power, but though their husbands and sons, not in their own right.

It was rare too for women to hold high office outside the religious sphere. From China we know that Shang kings granted benefices (grants of land in return for military obligations) to women as well as men: these benefices carried obligations to help defend frontiers, and the oracle archives record two queens mounting military expeditions for this purpose. In Greece in the Hellenistic period women were occasionally granted political rights or held public office: we know of a female magistrate in Histria in the second century BC and another in Priene in the following century. In Rome women had no official right to participate in government, but upper-class women, by virtue of their education and their knowledge of political matters, were often able to exert influence through their husbands and sons. In no ancient civilization did women have political rights remotely comparable to those of men, whether in the traditional theocracies or in the experimental 'democracy' of classical Athens.

Private life

We know even less about women's private lives in the ancient civilizations than about other aspects of their existence. In general women would have spent much of their time with other women, and their relationships with their mothers, daughters, other relatives, friends and sometimes their female lovers, would have been very important to them. We know little about these relationships or about how women felt about men. To study women's experience we cannot turn to the writings of men, but must confine ourselves to those few occasions where we have the words of women themselves.

The letters written (or rather dictated) by women in the Mesopotamian cities of Mari and Karana in the early second millennium BC, relate only to women of royal or aristocratic families, but they reveal authentic human experiences, perfectly familiar today. For instance, we find Queen Iltani of Karana complaining to her husband that she had celebrated a festival at which nobody took any notice of her. And a woman called Lassani, who may have been Iltani's younger sister, wrote to her from Assur

explaining that she was still looking for a lapis lazuli necklace which Iltani had asked for.

The most moving accounts of women's experiences come from the Greek female poets. In the sixth century BC Sappho wrote lyrically not only of homosexual love, but of her daughter:

> I have a lovely child, whose form is like
> Gold flowers, my heart's own pleasure, Cleis . . .

Nearly three centuries later Erinna wrote a poem called 'The Distaff', a poignant tribute to her dead friend Baucis, recalling their shared childhood.

On a less elevated plane are the graffiti scribbled on the walls of Pompeii by women to their lovers, not always on a very loving note: 'You are too ugly', or 'What do I care if your health is good or bad? Do you think I would mind if you dropped down dead?'

Top: In the ancient civilizations it was extremely rare for women to hold high office, but the consorts of kings could sometimes wield power indirectly. Queen Nefertiti, wife of the heretic pharaoh Akhenaten, seems to have enjoyed considerable authority at Akhetaten (Tell el-Amarna) during the Amarna period.

Bottom: Later fifth-century BC painted frieze from Athens showing well-born Athenian ladies in the *gynaikon* or women's quarters, where they spent most of their time secluded from the male members of the household.

10 Beginnings and Ends

The idea of the decline and fall of civilizations has been made familiar by Edward Gibbon's great work; and, as we have seen in this book, the Roman Empire was by no means the only civilization to come to grief. For all its dominance in the world today, in historical perspective civilization does not stand out as a particularly robust social form. Several of the civilizations we have described underwent complete collapse; even those that survived for long periods went through phases of near collapse, when traits such as urban life and literacy barely survived. In geographical perspective, civilization has been slow to spread. For instance, civilized life was introduced to Britain by the Romans some 3,000 years after the first civilization emerged in Mesopotamia – a time lag as long as that taken by the spread of farming some three millennia earlier. Moreover, the spread of civilization has waxed and waned over time. Under the Roman Empire a single civilization dominated most of temperate Europe, the Mediterranean, north Africa and Asia as far as the Middle East, while further east other civilizations flourished in India (the Ganges civilization) and China (extending into South-East Asia). With the fall of the Roman Empire, the civilized area contracted sharply: in most of Europe and north Africa civilization more or less disappeared. Even in Mediterranean Europe, the homeland of classical civilization, urban life survived only precariously in a few centres. In fact, civilization in full, flourishing form was restricted once again to the Asian centres, where it had a longer history and a firmer base.

Why should the elaborate and complex achievement that is civilization be vulnerable in this way? In the most dramatic situations civilizations collapse totally and are followed by 'Dark Ages' lacking urban life, literacy and high achievements in art, literature, science and technology. Social organization reverts to tribal level, with settlement in villages, subsistence farming and little specialized manufacture or external trade. Even the memory of civilization disappears or survives only as 'folk memory' in mythology, passed down as oral tradition until such time as writing is reintroduced. The clearest examples of this are the Indus and Mycenaean civilizations in the Old World and the Classic Maya civilization in Mesoamerica. In all these cases the collapse was complete and apparently sudden and, naturally enough, archaeologists have been inclined to favour apocalyptic explanations of one kind or another. Three main sorts of disaster are regularly invoked: natural catastrophes, attack from outside and social revolution.

Natural disasters

Climatic change, volcanic eruptions, earthquakes, flooding and epidemic diseases have all been suggested as possible causes of the collapse of civilizations. In particular, flooding has been given prominence in the Indus, in view of the evidence for periodic inundations at Mohenjo-Daro and other southern Indus cities, while earthquakes and volcanic activity have been favoured in the Aegean, although the one well documented volcanic eruption – of the island of Thera – occurred too early to explain even the end of Minoan civilization, let alone that of Mycenae. Climatic change has been suggested for all the areas in question. A variant of this explanation, which involves human agency, is the suggestion that environmental conditions deteriorated as a result of over-farming. Epidemic diseases present another possibility. The inhabitants of ancient cities may have lived in conditions as over-crowded and insanitary as those of medieval Europe, where the Black Death killed at least a quarter of the population between AD 1348 and 1350. It is difficult, however, to find evidence of epidemic diseases in the archaeological record. References do occur in the written sources, for instance Thucydides' record of an outbreak of plague in fifth-century BC Athens, but there is little to suggest that such epidemics were threats to the survival of civilization itself.

Opposite: Some ruins present a powerful image of past civilization. This view is of a street in Timgad (Thamugadi) in Algeria, a Roman military colony founded by the emperor Trajan in AD 100.

Below: Little now survives of the eastern harbour of Corinth, Cenchreae, on the Saronic Gulf, but in the heyday of the city it must have been a flourishing port. This panel of *opus sectile* shows buildings along the harbour, including a possible temple on the left.

Right: View of Jiaohe, an ancient settlement in the Turpan depression, Chinese Turkestan. Once on the Silk Route, along which silk was conveyed from China to the West from the second century BC to about the ninth century AD, it now lies abandoned in the desert.

Below: Tholos tombs like the 'Treasury of Atreus' at Mycenae are among the surviving monuments of Mycenaean civilization. Although this civilization is described in Homer's epic poems, many scholars believed it to be mythology until Heinrich Schliemann excavated the cities of Troy, Mycenae and Tiryns in the 1870s and 1880s.

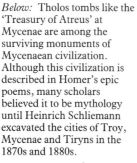

Attack from outside

Invasion and attack from outside are popular explanations, not least because where we have written records, there is usually evidence of such attacks. Indo-European-speaking Aryans may have invaded the Indus Valley; Dorian Greeks may have over-run Mycenae; while the Roman Empire succumbed to waves of barbarian invaders – Goths, Huns and Vandals. There is a problem with accepting this evidence at face value, however, since it is difficult to establish whether such attacks were cause or effect. Clearly a weakened state would be a prime target for predatory neighbours.

Internal revolution

The early states, after the initial stages when there was still a free peasantry, had at their base either serfs or slaves, in bondage to the ruling class. In such a structure lie the seeds of revolt, and if power was abused by the rulers – and power always *is* abused sooner or later – dormant unrest might explode into actual revolution. From classical writers we know of helot revolts in Greece (helots were a subject population, but not privately owned slaves) and slave

revolts under the Roman Republic. These were troublesome enough to the rulers of the time, but they did not bring down whole civilizations. Whether social revolution *could* lead to the collapse of civilization, as has been suggested at various times for the Indus, the Mycenaean and the Maya civilizations, remains an open question.

Multiple causes

Many authorities reject the notion of single causes for the collapse of civilizations, let alone one single cause for the decline of *all* civilizations. Instead they invoke combinations of circumstances contributing to final collapse. Colin Renfrew has attempted to apply mathematical Catastrophe Theory to the fall of civilizations (especially Mycenae). This allows us to see that even sudden collapse need not be the result of factors acting in the short term only, such as natural or man-made disasters. Instead long-term trends, often different trends in combination, can culminate in the sudden collapse of the whole system.

Cities were vulnerable not only to natural disasters and attack from outside, but also to social unrest. In AD 59 a riot, illustrated here in a wall-painting from Pompeii, broke out between the Pompeians and visitors from neighbouring Nuceria, in town for the gladiatorial games. Many people died in this incident – reminiscent of modern football hooliganism – and afterwards the amphitheatre was closed for ten years.

Ancient civilizations frequently came under attack from less developed peoples on their peripheries, and such attacks may sometimes have brought about or hastened the decline of the civilization. The Ludovici Battle Sarcophagus in Rome (*c.* AD 250) shows a fierce battle between Romans and barbarians, probably Dacians.

The fragility of the created environment

We have argued that civilization is the complex artificial environment created by man to insulate himself from nature. The world man built was elaborate and often beautiful, and it gave nourishment to the struggling human intellect and spirit, but it was also vulnerable in a way that was not true of earlier and simpler societies.

One reason for this is simply the concentration of population found in cities. If a disaster hits a city, it does far more damage than if the population is dispersed in small settlements through the countryside. Natural disasters may not have brought whole civilizations to an end, but they certainly killed individual cities: ancient towns destroyed by volcanic eruptions include Akrotiri on the island of Thera, Pompeii and Herculaneum in south-west Italy and Cuicuilco in the Basin of Mexico. Other cities died more slowly as the result of environmental changes. Some were abandoned when a river changed course, like Shahr-i Sokhta in eastern Iran in the second millennium BC. Some coastal towns were deserted after estuaries silted up, leaving ports high and dry; several Roman examples are known, including Salapia and Sipontum in south-east Italy, as well as the port of Rome itself at Ostia.

Crowded cities would also have been breeding-houses for disease, and during epidemics it might have been hard to sustain city life. Endemic diseases may have posed equally serious problems. Ostia was finally abandoned partly because of the prevalence of malaria; and several other cases are known from classical antiquity.

Technological failure, miscalculation and ignorance also posed threats to civilization. Of course men of all periods have sometimes made tools that broke, boats that leaked or houses that fell down, but in simple societies these create problems on a domestic level only. In cities, by contrast, the effects of technological failure can be profound. It is easy to find examples in the modern world: in 1984 a gas explosion in Mexico City killed hundreds of people, while an industrial disaster in the Indian city of Bhopal left 2,500 dead and thousands more injured. Even minor technical failures can pose major problems for city administrators: in December 1985 a burst in a 100-year-old water main in the city of Leeds left 300,000 people without piped water for several days and required the use of troops to distribute water from trucks. Similar problems may have affected ancient cities: although the archaeological record gives us little information, where we have written sources we sometimes learn of such troubles. For instance, we know of Roman towns that were abandoned because of polluted water supplies. There were sometimes longer-term problems too. The Romans, ignorant of the toxic effects of lead, made widespread use of it for water pipes – and may thereby have poisoned much of the population. Examination of some 450 Romano-British skeletons from Cirencester has revealed high levels of lead, so high in some children's bones that lead poisoning may have been the actual cause of death.

Beyond the problems created by population concentration and technological failure, civilization is vulnerable at other levels. In particular there are potential problems of *organization* and of *social unrest*.

As we have seen, the early states required complex bureaucracies, which, under the empires, had to sustain an organization over huge areas embracing diverse groups of different cultural origins. The demands made on such an organization were colossal and the possibilities of breakdown correspondingly great. By way of example we shall look at two aspects of organization: communication and transport.

For the functioning of a state system, it is essential that citizens know what is expected of them. How much tax should they pay and in what kind? Are they liable for military or other public service? What penalty would they incur if they got involved in a public brawl? In what way could they sell surplus produce and at what price? All these types of information and many others have to be conveyed. This is difficult enough in our own society, where almost everyone can read and we have multiple methods of communication. Imagine the problem in a society where literacy is restricted to a tiny minority and there are no aural methods of communication beyond face-to-face contact. Ancient civilizations had to devise systems to cope with this and then, under the empires, extend them into new areas where different languages were spoken. Lapses in communication could lead to failure of supplies, inefficient services, military mistakes and the breakdown of law and order.

More than 1,500 years before the eruption of Vesuvius that destroyed Pompeii, a volcanic eruption blew apart the southern Cycladic island of Thera (modern Santorini), burying the Bronze Age settlement at Akrotiri. This is one of the many beautiful frescoes preserved by the deep deposit of volcanic ash.

Left: The eruption of Vesuvius in AD 79 buried the nearby cities of Pompeii and Herculaneum on the Bay of Naples. This painting of a garden with trellis and birds adorns the wall of one house buried under the lava at Pompeii.

Below: During the third millennium BC the settlement of Shahr-i Sokhta in eastern Iran was a flourishing city with a population of perhaps 20,000 people, involved in the trade in lapis lazuli from northern Afghanistan to the cities of Mesopotamia and beyond. Some time early in the second millennium BC the Helmand river, on which Shahr-i Sokhta stood, changed course and the city was deserted. The ancient city is in the foreground, with the excavated part clearly visible; all around is desert.

Transport provides a set of related problems. Centralized economies, whether redistributive or market-based, require efficient systems for transporting goods and materials, as well as information, into and out from the centres. Both roads and waterways need constant maintenance, while caravans must be protected from bandits and ships from pirates. A few years' neglect could leave roads impassable from rock-falls and land-slips, ports silted up and unusable and journeys too dangerous for merchants to undertake.

Civilization is vulnerable also to social upheaval. In strongly stratified social systems, the workforce engaged in primary production consists of slaves, serfs or, at best, an exploited peasantry, all of whom would have good reason to feel dissatisfied with their lot. And cities provide a seed-bed for unrest of a type not found in villages. One reason is the nature of city populations, which contain a proportion of free-floating citizens, liberated from their predefined roles in rural communities and with a measure of freedom of thought and action. Secondly, the city presents alternative life-styles at close quarters; the manual worker can see the noble, the priest, the merchant and the civil servant and may question their right to a standard of living so much better than his own. Finally, cities contain the institutions of education, the schools and colleges. Education is essential for the transmission of information, but it also teaches students to think and opens up their minds to the possibility of other ways of organizing society. This is a problem that has faced many a modern despot wishing to train students to read technical manuals, but not Marx; to program computers, but not to think for themselves. However, it is impossible to have one without the other: all education has a subversive potential. Man has built into his complex artificial environment the tools with which, if he chooses, he can destroy civilization and possibly himself.

Civilization did not spring up independently in every corner of the globe. Although few people today would accept the extreme diffusionist notions of Sir Grafton Elliot Smith and Lord Raglan, who believed that all civilizations stemmed from a single source (believed to be Egypt by Elliot Smith, Mesopotamia by Lord Raglan), it is clear that civilization did sometimes spread from one area to another. But when we talk about civilization 'spreading', what do we mean exactly? It seems that we use the term to cover at least four different processes: direct imperial expansion; foreign settlement; the development of secondary civilizations; and the transmission of individual elements of civilization.

Imperial expansion

This process is perhaps the easiest to understand; it is certainly the most familiar to us with our recent imperial past. It involves the establishment in conquered areas of a system as nearly as possible identical to that of the homeland. Cities, buildings, institutions, laws, life-styles, all closely resemble those 'back home', with only the minimum modifications made necessary by different conditions. The language of the conquerors is usually spread throughout the empire for administrative purposes and as the language of education. The cities of the provinces frequently remain dependent on the homeland for supplies as well as for personnel for all important administrative posts; power is handed over only in limited degree, if at all, to the indigenous population. Such a model is familiar to us from the British Empire. In the ancient civilizations that we have looked at, the Romans provide the best Old World example, while in the Americas both the Chimu and the Incas of Peru and the Aztecs of Mesoamerica established true empires.

Foreign settlement

Foreign settlement can be distinguished from imperialism by the fact that the new cities are independent of the homeland. They may retain close commercial and cultural links with their mother cities and have treaty arrangements with them, but they are not structurally linked in an imperial organization, and they pay neither tribute nor tax. The cities themselves will, as in the case of imperial towns, closely resemble those of the homeland in their lay-out, buildings and institutions; however, there is usually little attempt to dominate the natives or to impose the life-style of the immigrants. Relationships with the natives may range from active hostility, through almost total separation to friendly commercial contact. Through such contact the indigenous population may acquire elements of civilization or indeed develop as secondary centres of civilization in their own right. In the ancient world the best-known examples come from the first half of the first millennium BC, when both Phoenicians, from the east Mediterranean coast, and Greeks, from mainland Greece and Asia Minor, established 'colonies' in the central and west Mediterranean, and in the case of the Greeks on the Black Sea also.

The development of secondary civilizations

Sometimes secondary civilizations emerge as a result of contact with pre-existing ones. In these cases, unlike imperial towns and those established by foreign settlers, the secondary centres are *not* close imitations of the original cities; they may share some traits, but they are fundamentally new creations and most of their features are original. When communities in areas adjacent to existing civilizations have access to raw materials such as precious stones or metal ores which are in demand in the primary centres, they have the opportunity to exploit this demand and, as Gordon Childe put it, to tap the accumulated surplus (the capital) of the original civilizations. If the peripheral communities can increase agricultural production, they can free a proportion of the population to work the desirable raw material. This can then be traded to the primary civilizations, in return for the fine products of their skilled craftsmen. Desire for such imported goods will stimulate further intensification in the subsistence economy, greater production of the raw material and a search for other potential exports, which may include both other raw materials and

Long-distance trade, which supplied the early civilizations with precious stones and other valued materials, allowed the establishment of secondary centres of civilization near the sources of the raw materials and on trade routes from them. Lapis lazuli from northern Afghanistan reached Mesopotamia where it was used for decorative purposes, as in the inlay work on the sound-box of this lyre from the Royal Cemetery at Ur. The city of Shahr-i Sokhta in eastern Iran probably developed as a result of this trade; an industrial area of the city has produced thousands of unfinished lapis lazuli beads as well as tools used in their manufacture.

Trade with the earlier civilizations of Egypt and Western Asia may have contributed to the development of Minoan civilization in the second millennium BC. Middle Minoan polychrome pottery, Kamares ware, was traded as far as Qatna in the upper Orontes valley and Abydos in Upper Egypt.

Imperial expansion spread Roman civilization throughout a large area of Europe, Western Asia and north Africa. Throughout the empire Roman buildings such as amphitheatres (*left*, the amphitheatre at Petronell in Austria) and theatres (*below*, the theatre at Ammam in Jordan) were built to a standard basic design.

manufactured goods such as textiles. In time the secondary centres may grow wealthy, become great manufacturing centres in their own right and serve in their turn to stimulate development in further, tertiary, centres.

Good examples of urban centres that grew up in this way can be found in Iran in the third millennium BC: Tepe Yahya in south-west Iran depended on the exploitation of a type of soapstone which was very popular in Mesopotamia, while further east Shahr-i Sokhta exploited the trade in lapis lazuli from Afghanistan to Mesopotamia and beyond, providing a point *en route* where the blue semi-precious stone was worked. In the case of individual cities that arose in this way, the stituation may be fairly clear; where whole civilizations were involved, it is much more complex. Because secondary civilizations are in a real sense original creations, built on a local base, and not simple derivatives, it is not always easy to assess whether a particular civilization arose truly independently or was secondary in the sense described above. The Minoan civilization, for instance, is regarded by some as a totally independent development, whereas others believe that it arose as a result of contact with the earlier civilizations of Western Asia and Egypt.

The transmission of elements of civilization

Civilization as a whole does not spread all that easily. It requires a subsistence base capable of intensification and a political and social system sufficiently hierarchical and centralized to support a complex administration. Individual elements of civilization, however, can be transposed much more easily. A writing system, for instance, may be adopted by groups at a lower level of organizational complexity than the civilization that developed it. The same is true of art and architectural styles, craft techniques and the use of coinage. At the time that the Roman Empire was expanding across Europe, many communities north of the moving frontier adopted aspects of Mediterranean civilization – the practice of wine drinking, the use of the potter's wheel, coinage, some limited use of the Latin language and writing system, to name but a few – though in organizational complexity they fell short of the level we would label civilization. Clearly, traits created by civilization can survive in contexts of different kinds.

Beyond the frontier of the expanding Roman Empire in Europe, people living in less complex societies adopted some of the elements of civilization. The Roman practice of wine-drinking – illustrated here in a wall painting from a wine shop at Herculaneum – was adopted by the elites of the Celtic- and Germanic-speaking peoples of central and northern Europe.

All societies have mechanisms by which traditions and practices are passed on from one generation to the next, since this is the way in which the continuity of society is ensured. This is as true of simple societies as it is of complex ones, only complex societies have a much greater body of accumulated knowledge to pass on and have developed a number of additional mechanisms for doing so.

The transmission of knowledge in simple societies

In simple societies learning usually takes place through face-to-face instruction and normally within the family. In civilized societies too, including our own, most teaching of *young* children takes place in the family. This is where children learn basic social skills and knowledge: what foods to eat and how to eat them; how to deal with their bodily wastes; how to behave with different people; the elements of religion, and so on. In simple societies other skills are normally taught by older members of the same sex, not always within the family: how to hunt and fish, tend cattle, build canoes, fight battles, cultivate fields, cook, look after babies; also a fuller understanding of religion and in particular the rites to be undergone at puberty, childbirth, etc. There may be a small number of specialist skills restricted to a few – healing, for instance – which are usually passed on from father to son or mother to daughter.

The transmission of knowledge in complex societies

In civilized societies there are many specialized skills and branches of knowledge that have to be taught, as well as the general social skills required by all citizens. There are the craft skills, now sufficiently complex to require full-time specialists and therefore to develop as 'trades'. There are also the new professions, such as civil servants, priests, lawyers, doctors and diviners. Between these two types is a gulf which has not been fully bridged even today.

Craft skills, exclusively in the ancient world and largely today, are not taught by 'book learning', but by precept and example. There may be more than one reason for this. The main reason is the social organization of the early civilizations: reading and writing were skills available to the upper classes only, while artisans usually occupied lower positions on the social scale and were excluded from formal education. Another reason, however, may be that writing is not a very good medium for conveying practical information. Think how difficult it is to follow manufacturers' instructions for your new washing machine or video equipment, and how easy it is when someone shows you how it works! Be that as it may, in the ancient civilizations craft skills were handed down not through the written word, but rather by word of mouth. Crafts of particular kinds were often restricted to particular groups, frequently hereditary organizations, who lived in special quarters of the city and guarded their trade secrets.

Craft skills were passed down from master to apprentice, within restricted specialist organizations, often organized on a hereditary basis. The Egyptian tomb painting, *above*, shows craftsmen making funerary objects, while the Greek terracotta, *right*, represents a carpenter at work.

The skills required by the professions, by contrast, were learned through formal education in schools. In theory the advent of the written word allowed a much more open system of education than was possible previously: through books, learning can be acquired by almost anyone in any place, without the physical presence of the teacher. In practice it did not work like that in the ancient civilizations, where school education was restricted to the elite, while the majority of the population, including in most cases all women, were excluded from it. And those who never learnt to read were deprived of access to written sources of enlightenment or pleasure. The manifest difficulties of early writing systems, hard enough to learn even with a lengthy formal training, would certainly have made 'teach yourself' attempts impractical. The development of the alphabet broadened the base of literacy, but it nevertheless remained accessible only to a privileged minority. Moreover, education was usually restricted in scope: most schools were attached to institutions and frequently offered a rather narrow vocational training. Religious and military schools occurred commonly in the early civilizations, while at later stages there were sometimes schools for specialists such as lawyers and doctors. The *methods* of education in schools were generally restricted too, involving much rote learning and repetitive copying of ancient texts. The kind of probing, questioning approach we associate with Socrates must have been rare in the ancient world, even in Greece; and indeed Socrates was too subversive even for the Athenians, who put him to death for it.

Breaks in transmission

Thus knowledge, skills and values were passed on mainly through the institutions of the family, craft organizations and formal educational establishments. Between them they provided a strong strand of institutional continuity, ensuring, one would have thought, the continuity of civilization. Yet civilizations sometimes came to an end, writing systems went out of use, knowledge and skills were lost. How could this happen? Clearly, if natural disasters or large-scale invasions occurred, there could have been a complete break in social life, with consequent loss of continuity. This might also occur if there were a catastrophic collapse as a result of long-term destructive trends. Often, however, there was no sudden collapse, but a slow decline. In these cases, the institutions would not all have collapsed together, but in order of strength, the most vulnerable first. The least robust would have been the schools, requiring the greatest complexity of organization to survive. At the level of the individual, many may have felt that in times of decline and insecurity a lengthy traditional education was a luxury they could not afford. The craft organizations would be vulnerable too, as a decline in demand for goods threatened the livelihood of their members. Whether technical know-how survived depended on the craft in question: where it was geared to elite consumption it might be lost, while more everyday crafts would probably survive. Craft knowledge would continue to be passed from father to son, master to apprentice, but probably within a less formal structure than before.

The institution of the family was undoubtedly the most secure and may well have survived even in the cases of dramatic civilization collapse, thus preserving continuity in the spoken language, in many aspects of subsistence practice and domestic organization, and in religious beliefs. A good example is provided by the 'Dark Age' of Greece after the fall of the Mycenaeans. The writing system disappeared completely, as did some crafts (e.g. seal-making), while more humdrum skills continued with little interruption (especially pottery manufacture). At the domestic level there was considerable continuity: the Greek language remained in use; subsistence practices continued little changed, and many of the gods and goddesses of the Mycenaeans continued to be venerated, although the buildings in which they were worshipped and the organization of religion in society changed completely.

Professional skills requiring mastery of reading and writing were taught through formal education, often in schools. The Romano-German relief sculpture from Trier, *below*, shows a teacher with his pupil. In Egypt officials and kings were educated people; the young pharaoh Tutankhamun took to his grave a writing kit, *below bottom*, consisting of an ivory scribe's palette and a case for reed brushes made of wood plated with gold and inlaid with faience.

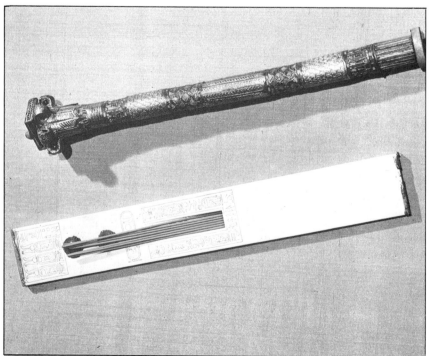

The past in the present

William Faulkner wrote of the American South: 'The past is not dead – it is not even past.' There is a sense in which this is true of all societies, including our own: our past plays an active continuing role in our present existence. By this we do not mean to state the obvious – that we depend on knowledge, practices and traditions developed in the past – which is true, but not particularly enlightening. What we are concerned with here is our *view* of the past and the *use* we make of it.

The origin myths of Western society

We employ different terms for the way societies describe their past. Primitive societies have *origin myths*; we have *history*. But we could put this another way and say that history is the name we give to our own origin myths. This statement would certainly give rise to protest in some quarters. Origin myths, it would be argued, are just stories, preserved in ancient texts or passed on through oral tradition by wise men, whereas history is fact, documented by evidence and verified by the methods of science. Two comments can be made on this. First, it may be

true that professional historians and archaeologists study the past in this way, but the majority of people learn their history from school books, without a thought for the primary evidence. In this sense, history teachers are the wise men of our society. Secondly, we believe that our history is factual because it has been studied in a rational scientific way; but then other people believe their histories are true because they have them from the mouth of god himself. We all know that we are right, but for different reasons. The scientific approach does not make history less of an origin myth; rather the scientific method is itself *part* of the myth. With or without science, we make for ourselves the past we want.

Choosing our ancestors

Societies often feel free to choose the ancestors they want. This can involve wholesale manipulation of recorded history, or simply judicious choice from it. Of the societies we have looked at in this book, the Romans chose to ignore their Etruscan roots in favour of a spiritual ancestry in Greece, while the Aztecs rewrote their history to claim a Toltec origin. Examples from recent times include Hitler's invention of a pure Nordic race, ancestral to the modern Germans, and the late Shah of Iran's decision to ignore much of Persian history, including the entire Islamic era, and to look to Cyrus the Great, who founded the Achaemenid Empire in the sixth century BC, for an ancestor with whom he could feel properly at ease.

Self-admiration

People commonly feel that they live in a society which, while not perfect, is definitely better than all other societies, both contemporary and earlier. Such an attitude provides a slant to the way we view the past, which is interpreted in terms of *progress*. We assume that earlier societies were inferior to us and that history will demonstrate a more or less steady progression towards the present. This view was particularly prevalent in the nineteenth century in Western Europe, where intellectuals at least tended to regard their own society as the pinnacle of human achievement. This was the era in which many of the scholarly disciplines were first established, and the attitudes of their Victorian pioneers remain deeply embedded in academic studies to this day. As a result, scholars have consistently underestimated the achievements of past societies and regularly express surprise when it is discovered that their ancestors had mastered a particular craft technique, for instance, or made accurate astronomical observations, or developed an elaborate legal system.

Self-denigration

There is, however, a contrary tendency – to regard one's own society as decadent and in decline – which colours the past in the opposite way. Earlier societies are seen through the proverbial rose-coloured spectacles as superior to one's own, not necessarily in technology and standard of living, but with superior values, closer to nature, perhaps closer to god, and untainted by the sins and vices of more modern times. In Western thought this view is associated particularly with the eighteenth-century French philosophical writer Jean Jacques Rousseau,

Above: The pyramids at Giza – and especially the Great Pyramid, seen here in the centre of the group – have provided the focus of many fanciful interpretations of the past. A special unit of measurement labelled the 'pyramid inch' was once claimed for the monument, while another writer believes that its builders required assistance from agents from outer space.

Right: The accuracy of the astronomical observations and calendrical calculations of the Mesoamerican civilizations surprised many modern scholars. This is the Caracol (the Observatory) at the site of Chichén Itzá.

but it is in fact a widespread attitude. It is found, for instance, in classical Greek, Roman and Chinese traditions, all of which extolled earlier 'Golden Ages', superior to those of the time of writing, and which some politicians actively aimed to recreate. A more modern version of this view is less concerned with moral values, but ascribes remarkable scientific achievements to earlier societies: monuments such as Stonehenge and the Great Pyramid are described as giant calculating machines or even computers. In its least academically respectable, but widely popular, form, agents from outer space are invoked to provide our ancestors with the necessary know-how for these achievements.

Predicting the future

Among those with the greatest interest in sustaining particular views of the past are those people who have specific hopes for the future – the politicians. These include those who wish to maintain the status quo and those inspired by reforming zeal, both on the right and on the left. Whatever their aspirations, all can find comfort and justification in the past. Those in favour of maintaining the status quo tend to emphasize the value of tradition, arguing that long usage is proof of viability and virtue. Of those who wish to alter society, right-wingers tend to choose some particular past era as model: Mussolini wanted to restore the Roman Empire, while Margaret Thatcher praises Victorian values. Those on the left, by contrast, tend to point out the faults of *all* past societies and aim instead to build an entirely new community free from these drawbacks; they often favour Marxist interpretations of history, based on concepts of class and class conflict. All have vested interests in seeing the past in their particular way.

In this perspective we can see too that there are histories still to be written, from viewpoints that have only recently come to prominence. Groups such as women, or the descendants of African slaves in America, find little of relevance to them in the conventional history of our society. These groups are beginning to find their own recent history; they will come in time, we may be sure, to search for their early history and prehistory too.

Why study the past?

We have been arguing that people choose the past they want, their views coloured by their politics and their religion, as well as their age, sex and general attitude to life. It might seem that in putting this case we are arguing ourselves out of our jobs as professional students of the past. For, if everyone interprets the past in their own terms, what point can there be in attempting to study it in a scientific way? Our answer to this must be that although no interpretation can be proved to be true, not all suggested interpretations are equally valid. Many views can be rejected on the grounds of logical inconsistency or untestability; new discoveries may *disprove* old theories altogether; some theories may fit the data better than others, or offer explanations for patterns that were previously unexplained. Thus new work on the past – both new *finds* and new *theories* – will alter the range of available interpretations: some old views will become untenable, while new theories will rise to the fore. What you make of them, of course, is up to you: your past is your own.

Above: The Romans adopted many aspects of Greek culture. Orpheus, a figure from Greek mythology, became a popular subject in Roman art; this mosaic from Vienne in southern France shows Orpheus charming the animals.

Interpretations of the past change constantly as new approaches are developed and new discoveries made. Important finds have been made recently beneath Mexico City, in ancient Tenochtitlán. The row of stone statues, *left*, and the great sculpted and painted snake, *below*, were both found in front of the Great Temple in recent excavations which have greatly enhanced our knowledge of the Aztec capital.

11　Reconstruction and Explanation

How are we to study early civilizations? Although we may sometimes be able to do so partly through the written documents they have left behind, we shall also need to examine their material remains. Indeed, if we wish to study the pre-civilized societies from which the early civilizations emerged, we have to look at material remains alone, for these societies had no writing and have therefore left no written records.

Because archaeology deals with material remains, that is with 'things', and because we feel intuitively that things are straightforward and easy to understand, we may be tempted to think that the methods used by archaeologists must be simple, even obvious. This is very far from true. The things that survive from the past are partial, fragmentary and altered by the processes of decay; more important, in themselves they tell us nothing directly about any aspect of the past. Archaeologists reconstruct the past from these remains by a process of inference – often a series of successive inferences leading, like a staircase, from the original objects studied to a level at which we can make broad statements about the past. These inferences – the steps of the staircase – are based not on common sense, but rather on carefully constructed theories.

Archaeological data is the raw material of archaeological study and the starting point for these inferences. What does it consist of? In the first place, there are artefacts: the remains of man's tools, weapons, containers and other equipment. Secondly, there are structures built or excavated by man: buildings, monuments, engineering works – anything from a simple storage or rubbish pit to massive constructions such as the Colosseum in Rome. Burials are a third major category of evidence; they provide, among other things, one of the few relatively direct sources of information about the physical nature of ancient man himself.

Opposite: One of the most spectacular types of evidence available to archaeologists is the material placed in royal tombs. The first emperor of China, Qin Shi Huangdi, who died in 210 BC, was buried with an entire army of life-size terracotta figures. Here archaeologists are cleaning and recording a group of terracotta horses and bronze chariots.

Below: Some of the grave goods as they were found in the burial of Philip II of Macedon (who died in 336 BC) at Vergina in northern Greece. They include a bronze shield, greaves and leg guard, several bronze vessels, a gold diadem and a sponge.

Archaeologists also study plant and animal remains: some of these represent food debris and can throw light on ancient diet and subsistence, while others help us to reconstruct the general environment of past communities.

It is important to appreciate that archaeologists do not normally study any of these things in isolation. A most important part of their work involves the analysis of relationships in time or in space or between different categories of evidence. For example, archaeologists studying a settlement site will wish to examine the layout of buildings within that settlement, since this may lead to inferences about the size of the community that lived there and its economic and social organization. They will also wish to know about the distribution of different kinds of artefacts within the settlement, which may throw light on a whole range of matters, such as craft specialization, ritual practices, the existence of people with special status, etc. If they are lucky enough to find an associated cemetery, there will be a whole series of possible relationships between the settlement and the cemetery to investigate. The relationship between the site and others in the area, and between the site and its natural environment are important. Chronological relationships too are significant (for example differences in settlement layout or artefact types from one phase of occupation of the site to another), since they allow us to study change in the prehistoric past. Ways of documenting these different types of relationship and of interpreting them are discussed on pp. 192–3.

To illustrate how the interpretation of the past from material remains depends on a series of inferences, we need look only at very simple levels of interpretation, of the type that may seem superficially self-evident. Let us look, for instance, at the *functions* of various artefacts. Archaeology books

Above: Generally archaeologists do not expect to find artefacts made of organic materials such as wood or cloth, since they decay rapidly, but in waterlogged or very dry conditions these materials may survive. Dry conditions prevailed in Tutankamun's tomb and organic objects survived well, many of them in the room labelled 'The Treasury'. The chest in the centre of the picture, with its carrying poles, is made of wood. It is surmounted by a statue of the jackal-god Anubis, also of wood, with a linen shroud around his neck.

Right: One major source of archaeological evidence is provided by artefacts. Different types of tools and weapons were used at different times and places. The illustration shows three different types of bronze axe-heads: *Left*, a crescentic form from mid third millennium BC Egypt. *Centre*, a fenestrated type from later third millennium BC Syria. *Right*, a duck-billed form from early second millennium BC Levant.

are full of illustrations of stone and metal objects, all labelled, usually without qualification, as 'scrapers' or 'arrowheads' or 'axes', to take just three examples. So natural does this seem that we may forget that this labelling is in fact an act of interpretation: the objects do not present themselves to the archaeologist conveniently labelled!

The archaeologist's interpretation is based on the similarity of these objects to others – either in our own toolkit or in those of other well-documented societies – that we know are used as scrapers, arrowheads or axes. And yet, clearly, other interpretations are possible. A stone or metal point (labelled as an arrowhead) could as easily be attached to a stabbing weapon (a dagger) or a throwing weapon (a spear) as to an arrow shaft. And how do we know that our axe-like object was not used as a weapon, rather than a tool? Indeed it may have had no practical use at all, serving rather as an item of currency, or as a symbol of status, or as a religious symbol. All these interpretations of axe-like objects have in fact been argued, and plausibly too, for different prehistoric examples.

In order to arrive at a firmly-based interpretation of the function of a particular object, we can use a number of different approaches. These include analogy, which is the basis of our intuitive interpretation: the comparison of the object with like-looking objects whose function we know.

Buildings provide many types of information, in terms of techniques of construction, building materials, size, plan, internal fittings, decoration and other features. The plan of a large imperial Roman villa can be seen in great detail in this aerial photograph of the Centocelle airfield near Rome.

Another approach might be to examine the object under the microscope for wear marks, since different types of use produce different and characteristic wear patterns. Yet another approach might be experimental archaeology: we can make a replica of the artefact and experiment with various types of use, to see how effectively it fulfils different functions. To these approaches we should add contextual studies, for the contexts in which artefacts are found are clearly related to their functions for the people who made and used them. For instance, if our axe-like objects occurred regularly in graves, but were rarely found in any other context, we might infer that they were not primarily utilitarian tools but rather symbols of some kind, perhaps of status or authority.

Thus a whole range of approaches may need to be used simply to establish the function of an artefact type. If this is true of such basic levels of interpretation, we can see that the reconstruction of other aspects of past societies is likely to be both complex and laborious.

183

Chronology

Sequences through time

Apart from interpreting the nature of the material evidence left behind by past societies, one of the most important things an archaeologist does is to document changes through time, whether the aim is to reconstruct the history of an individual site or that of a whole region.

In the case of an individual site, known through excavation, the key to understanding its history is provided by stratigraphy, a method of interpretation based on an extremely simple principle. The successive phases of use of a site produce a series of layers, or strata, one on top of the other: the earliest layer is at the bottom, the latest at the top. This process is called *stratification* and its study is stratigraphy. However, despite the simplicity of the principle, stratigraphic interpretation is often difficult. This is because the processes behind the formation of archaeological layers are both variable and complex. Some layers are formed entirely by natural processes, for example wind-blown or water-laid deposits (alluviation), or roof-falls in caves. Other layers are entirely man-made; these include construction deposits created by the processes of building, occupation deposits associated with living areas, and rubbish deposits resulting from the disposal of waste. There are also layers created by natural processes working on man-made structures or materials, for example layers of stone rubble or decayed mudbrick resulting from the collapse of abandoned buildings, or layers of silt that have accumulated in neglected ditches or pits.

Because the processes involved are so complex, there is no direct relationship between age and absolute depth on an archaeological site. Although the principle states that the lowest layer will be the earliest and the highest the latest, this is counteracted by man's tendency to dig down and to build up. Pits, wells, ditches, foundation trenches and post-holes are all dug down, often cutting through several earlier layers. The pits, wells and ditches may all contain a number of layers themselves; these will have their own internal sequence, with the earliest at the bottom, but *all* the layers will be later than those that the pit or other feature has cut through. Conversely, buildings are sometimes constructed on artificial platforms, so that a building at a high level on top of the platform will be earlier than the layers that accumulate against the platform later on, although these will be at a lower level. However, although stratigraphic interpretation is complex, it is not impossible: the examples just described and many others can be recognized in the archaeological record, and the archaeologist is therefore able to disentangle the sequence, usually aiming to remove the layers in reverse chronological order, the latest first.

Stratigraphy is very important in enabling archaeologists to reconstruct the sequence of events on an individual site, but it cannot help them to relate one site to another, since these are not normally linked by connected strata (though there are exceptional cases, where, for instance, a number of sites have been buried by a single volcanic eruption, as at Pompeii and Herculaneum). In order to establish the chronological relationships between different sites, archaeologists normally depend on methods of absolute or relative dating, some of which are described on pp. 186–7.

Moments in time

As well as examining the development of a site through time, archaeologists are also interested in studying what was happening at any one time. Strangely enough, this type of information is rather harder to extract from the archaeological record. Archaeologists tend to write as though a site that was occupied in one period only, or, alternatively, a phase of occupation of a multi-period site, did in fact represent a moment in time – a moment being defined as a period so short that its length is insignificant. Archaeologists describe 'Troy IIb' or 'Early Dynastic III Uruk' as an urban geographer might describe existing towns today, as actual functioning communities. In reality, of course, these phases represent considerable periods of time, maybe centuries long, during which changes must have occurred in the structure and use of the

Simplified section through part of the mound of ancient Jericho, showing successive structures and deposits, ranging in time from the Neolithic period (Pre-Pottery phase) through to the Iron Age.

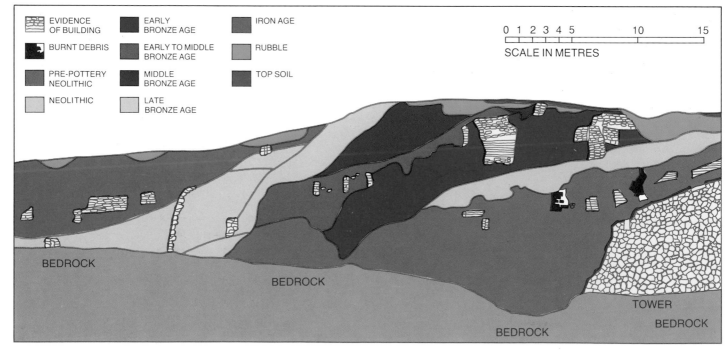

EVIDENCE OF BUILDING	EARLY BRONZE AGE	IRON AGE
BURNT DEBRIS	EARLY TO MIDDLE BRONZE AGE	RUBBLE
PRE-POTTERY NEOLITHIC	MIDDLE BRONZE AGE	TOP SOIL
NEOLITHIC	LATE BRONZE AGE	

0 1 2 3 4 5   10   15

SCALE IN METRES

BEDROCK

BEDROCK

BEDROCK

TOWER

BEDROCK

settlement. The length of the period varies, depending both on the history of the particular site and on the ability of the archaeologists to refine their chronologies for the area and period in question.

There are some archaeological contexts, however, which do genuinely represent specific moments in time. The most important of these are grave groups and hoards. A grave group – the grave itself, the body and any goods buried with it – represent what is sometimes known as a 'closed association'. This means that the objects are found together by the archaeologist because they were deposited together originally. This can be contrasted with an 'open association', where objects found together in, for example, a construction deposit or an occupation layer may not have been associated originally, since disturbance and redeposition may have led to the inclusion of residual material from earlier deposits. In the case of burials, this is unlikely. Provided that the tomb has not been re-opened, either to put in more bodies, or by robbers, we may assume that everything in the tomb was placed there at the time of burial; therefore the goods included may be taken as representing objects in contemporary use.

We can make similar assumptions for many hoards. Hoards are collections of objects deliberately buried, either as offerings for some purpose, in which case the deposition would have been permanent, or for safety in times of threat, when the intention would have been to recover them later. Hoards can contain artefacts of any material and any number of different materials, but hoards of metal objects are particularly common.

Other deposits which can produce closed associations of this sort are foundation deposits (goods deliberately buried to commemorate the foundation of a building) and some destruction layers, particularly where the destruction was both violent and sudden, as at Pompeii and Herculaneum.

Thus, providing they are reasonably fortunate in their discoveries, archaeologists have the analytical techniques both to record change through time and, sometimes at least, to document situations at particular moments in time. Both are important in the reconstruction of the past from material remains.

Below: Moments in time are rarely captured as dramatically as at Pompeii, which was overwhelmed by an eruption of Vesuvius on 24 August, AD 79. During the eruption many people were trapped and became encased by the deposit. Liquid plaster forced into the hollows left by their bodies produces startlingly detailed casts of the victims.

Dating

The dating of sites and finds has always been a prime concern of the archaeologist. In order to reconstruct the history of an area, it is necessary to establish at least the *order* in which the sites and objects were occupied or used, i.e. their *relative dates*. If we wish to study the processes involved in the development of an area, we also need to know the actual lengths of time involved, and for this we need to establish *absolute dates*.

Archaeologists can call upon a great range of dating techniques; for convenience these are here divided into three categories. The first group can be labelled 'documentary' or 'historical'; this includes the study of written documents and reference to recorded calendrical systems. In theory, these documentary techniques provide absolute dates in calendar years, although their accuracy varies considerably. The second group of dating methods can be called 'laboratory' or 'scientific' techniques; they employ a variety of natural ageing processes (sometimes referred to as 'natural clocks'). These provide absolute dates of sorts, though they too vary greatly in both precision and accuracy. The final method can be labelled 'typological' or simply 'archaeological'; it involves the comparison of sites and objects with others, either in sequences or in other areas. In itself this technique supplies only relative dates, but these can be converted to absolute dates by reference to other dating methods.

The long-living Bristlecone Pine (*Pinus aristata*) of California has provided a dendrochronological sequence extending back beyond 6000 BC. This has made it possible to correct radiocarbon dates younger than *c*.6000 BC (*c*. 5000 bc); older dates cannot as yet be corrected.

Documentary methods

Two different classes of document are used for dating purposes. The first consists of written material (incorporating dates) found in an archaeological context. This material may take the form of a dedicatory inscription incorporated in a building, but it more commonly involves an object with a date – perhaps a clay tablet or a coin – found in an archaeological layer. In the former case the inscription provides a direct date for the construction of the building (an ideal situation, but one that occurs only rarely). In the more common case, the date of the object cannot be taken to date the layer, because there might have been a long history between its manufacture and its final deposition. What we can say, however, is that the layer must be later than the date of the object, which therefore provides what is known as a *terminus post quem*.

The second class of document consists of written sources, not necessarily found on an archaeological site, but which make reference to structures or events that may be recognisable in the archaeological record. We know the dates of construction of many Greek and Roman monuments from documents of this sort.

The usefulness of dates derived from written documents is dependent on the accuracy of the calendrical system originally used. Fortunately a great deal of work has been done on the calendrical systems of the ancient civilizations, and most can now be correlated with our own system with some confidence. Needless to say, documentary dates have no application in the prehistoric period, before writing was invented.

Laboratory methods

Over the past thirty years a great number of laboratory dating techniques have become available. These have had a profound effect on archaeology: for prehistory they provide the only means of obtaining absolute dates. We will describe three of the most important of these methods here: radiocarbon dating, dendrochronology and thermoluminescence dating.

Radiocarbon dating

Radiometric dating methods rely on the decay of radioactive isotopes; this decay takes place at a known rate, providing one of the 'natural clocks' we mentioned earlier. Radiometric techniques include potassium-argon dating (generally used on volcanic rock) and uranium dating (used on bone). However, the most important radiometric method for the period of the early civilizations is radiocarbon dating (sometimes known as carbon-14 dating) which can theoretically be used to date all organic material, though results are better with some substances, such as bone and charcoal, than with others. This method is based on the fact that of the three main isotopes of carbon – ^{12}C, ^{13}C and ^{14}C – ^{14}C is radioactive, while the others are stable. Like all radioactive isotopes, ^{14}C decays at a steady rate, but because new ^{14}C is being produced continuously in the upper atmosphere, the proportion of ^{14}C in the atmosphere, and consequently in all living things, remains the same. When a living organism dies, however, the ^{14}C continues to decay but is no longer replaced by new ^{14}C. Since the rate at which the decay occurs is known (measured in terms of the half-life, which in the case of ^{14}C is 5730 years), it is possible to calculate how long ago the plant or animal died by measuring the amount of ^{14}C remaining relative to the non-radioactive ^{12}C. Most laboratories performing radiocarbon analysis require samples of between 10 and 200 grams, depending on the material being tested.

In theory this method ought to produce dates in calendar years, but unfortunately there are complications. Apparently the amount of ^{14}C in the atmosphere has varied at different times in the past, and consequently plants and animals have absorbed different concentrations at different times. As a result, radiocarbon analysis has produced dates that are too recent by varying amounts. Fortunately dates back to *c*. 6000 BC can be corrected by reference to calibration tables provided by the tree-ring dating method – dendrochronology – which we will describe next. It is usual today to write uncorrected radiocarbon dates with the lower-case letters ad, bc, and bp (before present), while the more familiar capitals AD, BC and BP are reserved for corrected radiocarbon dates, as well as all other dates that are thought to represent true calendar years.

Dendrochronology

The most accurate laboratory dating method, dendrochronology, involves the construction of chronologies from the sequences of annual growth-rings formed by trees. Samples for analysis should preferably include a complete cross-section of trunk, but less accurate dates can be set from incomplete samples. Dendrochronology can provide extremely precise dates – theoretically accurate to the actual year, in practice to within a few years – but its use is dependent both on the recovery of wood from excavations and on the existence of a tree-ring sequence for that type of wood in that area (for each dendrochronological sequence applies to only one species of tree in one particular area) and therefore its direct use as a dating method is limited. However, dendrochronology of the very long-lived Bristlecone Pine tree of California has proved invaluable in calibrating radiocarbon dates.

Thermoluminescence dating

A second important non-radiometric method is thermoluminescence dating, which is mainly used to date pottery and other fired clay objects. It can be used on small potsherds or even burnt stones, and is extremely useful because it can be applied to one of the most common of all archaeological finds – pottery. Thermoluminescence is based upon the principle that the minerals present in the clay, when bombarded by radiation (derived from cosmic rays and from the decay of radioactive elements in the environment), build up a store of energy within their crystal lattices. This energy is released in the form of light when the mineral is heated: the greater the energy, the brighter the light. The amount of energy is related to the length of the bombardment and its intensity, so if the rate of bombardment can be established (though this is problematical) the date of original firing of the object can be worked out. Thermoluminescence is not very precise but it is none the less a useful dating method for periods from which pottery has survived but for which no more precise dating methods are available.

Typology

The traditional dating method used by archaeologists long before dating methods were available, and still important today, is based on *typology*. This may involve arranging types of object or site in a sequence which is thought to represent an evolutionary trend and therefore to have chronological significance. In this way objects can be given dates relative to others in the sequence. Another sort of typology involves comparing an object or site in one area with something similar in another region. If the similarities are thought to represent actual connections of some sort, then the two items may be assumed to be of the same or similar date. Both these approaches in themselves supply only relative dates, but these can be converted into absolute dates by applying one of the absolute dating methods to a particular stage in a sequence or to one of the areas being used in a comparison.

Typology is particularly useful when applied to pottery, that most common of archaeological finds. A sequence of pottery groups can be built up on one site and then related to similar types at other sites in order to build up a regional framework. In the 1920s Gordon Childe built up a complete chronological framework for prehistoric Europe based mainly on the evidence provided by pottery.

Left: Inscriptions can provide excellent dating evidence. This Athenian stele, inscribed with a decree against tyranny, is dated to 336 BC, the year after Athens had been forced to join a Greek league organized by Philip of Macedon.

Below: Dateable objects such as this coin (a bronze sestertius of the emperor Titus, who reigned AD 79–81) provide a *terminus post quem* for the archaeological layer in which they are found. This means that the layer cannot be earlier than the date of the coin, but could be later, possibly considerably later.

Understanding past societies

Technology, subsistence economy and demography

One of the main aims of archaeology is to reconstruct past societies. Ideally we would like to learn *everything* about the society we are studying; in practice there are severe limitations to what we learn, and these arise directly from the nature of archaeological evidence.

Some aspects of past life are fairly readily accessible. For instance, it is relatively easy to reconstruct past technology, at least as far as it relates to non-perishable materials: we rarely have the opportunity to study such materials as wood, skin, leather or textiles. However, we can at least study the main materials used for tools and weapons: indeed it was this sort of study that provided the first basis for dividing up prehistory. This was the so-called 'Three Age System', devised in the early nineteenth century by the Danish scholar Christien Thomsen, who envisaged an Age of Stone, when stone was the main material used for making tools, succeeded by an Age of Bronze, and subsequently by an Age of Iron. This scheme, now largely superseded as a way of characterizing prehistoric periods, none the less accurately reflects the broad development of prehistoric technology, at least in Europe and Asia. Modern analytical techniques allow us to learn a great deal about what prehistoric tools were made of, how they were made, and what they were used for.

Another aspect of past life that can be reconstructed from the archaeological evidence is subsistence economy: the way in which man obtains his food. The fundamental distinction here is between hunting and gathering (food collection) and farming (food production) as the basis of life. This distinction can be recognized archaeologically, although interpretation is not always straightforward. In the case of animal remains, domesticated animals show morphological differences (differences in form or shape) from wild ones. These include a reduction in size in all domesticated animals, the loss of horns in female sheep, changes in horn form in sheep, goats and cattle, and the shortening of the jaw in pigs. However, these changes do not take place suddenly on domestication: there is a time lag, perhaps a long one. Therefore, to study the beginnings of farming other criteria must be used, such as the proportions of young animals among those killed (high proportions are thought to indicate a farming economy, or at least some degree of control over herds or flocks, whereas in a hunting economy the proportions of different ages killed should, it is thought, reflect their proportions in the living population). Different types of animal farming can also be distinguished by analyzing animal remains. For example, in cattle, high proportions of mature females and very young males would suggest a dairy herd, rather than one kept mainly for meat.

Morphological changes appear more rapidly after domestication in plants, especially cereals, than in animals. However, plant remains can be difficult to recover and the nature of the samples of plant material can pose problems. Plant remains are far more perishable than animal bones, but the technique of flotation (the agitation of soil samples in water, sometimes with the aid of a frothing agent) allows archaeologists to recover carbonized remains from many apparently unpromising deposits. The representativeness of the sample then has to be assessed; for instance, has a single storage pit or granary been found, or does the sample come from a general rubbish deposit? Such questions must be answered before the significance of the remains, and in particular the proportions of different plants in the sample, can be assessed.

Pollen analysis (the identification of plant species from their pollen grains preserved in anaerobic or acid soil) can reveal something about the general environment in the past – both about the climate and about land use. For example, even where no remains of cereal grains survive, samples of pollen of domesticated cereals or even of the common weeds of cultivation can point to human exploitation of the land by agriculture.

There are particular difficulties involved in assessing the relative importance of plant and animal remains in the diet of any past community, hunter or farmer. This is mainly because the remains are of different kinds. Animal remains are essentially rubbish (as food, that is; they may be used for other purposes such as making tools); they are not eaten and are destined to be discarded. Very few plant remains are of this type, only nut shells and fruit stones or pips. Most plant remains found are *seeds*, meant to be either eaten or sown; the fact that they are found at all means that something went wrong. This data cannot be compared directly with animal

Most archaeological data on diet and subsistence economy come from plant and animal remains, but pictorial representations can provide additional information. This late Maya effigy jar is in the form of a turkey; turkeys and dogs were the only creatures domesticated in Mesoamerica.

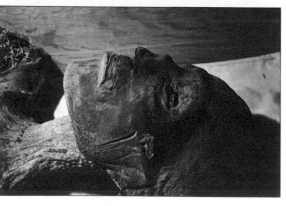

Skeletal and other human physical remains can provide evidence of disease in ancient societies. The face of the mummy of Ramesses V (1160–1156 BC) shows the characteristic eruptions of smallpox.

Population figures for ancient settlements can be assessed by calculating either the number of houses present or the overall living space available. This view shows part of the Inca city of Machu Picchu.

remains, so assessment of the relative importance of plant and animal foods in the diet has to be impressionistic. Despite this, it is usually possible to reconstruct the subsistence economy of past communities reasonably well in modern excavations. In the case of old excavations the situation is much more difficult: there may be no plant remains, and even animal bones may not have been collected consistently, if at all. Such very partial data has to be interpreted cautiously, in the light of evidence from similar sites excavated more recently.

Other aspects of past societies that can be reconstructed to some extent by archaeologists are population and demography: actual population numbers and features of population statistics such as the birth and death rates and life expectancy. We may also learn something about the *health* of past communities: the types of disease, the incidence of different diseases, occupational conditions and injuries, and information about diet and nutrition.

Calculating population numbers is notoriously difficult, though many methods have been tried. One is based on the number of dwellings in a settlement; this is multiplied by an estimated number of people per house to arrive at a figure for the total population. Such estimates are usually derived from ethnographic analogy, although there are pitfalls in this practice. Other uncertainties arise from the difficulty of establishing how many houses were in use at any one time. Another method is based on the overall amount of living space available. Man, like all other animals, needs a certain area of space to live in, and anthropologists have attempted to calculate this figure. One suggestion is $10 \, m^2$ per person, while a more complicated analysis suggests $12 \, m^2$ for the first six people taken together and $10 \, m^2$ for every additional person. Archaeologists

can apply these figures to the living space on their sites, whether the floor area of an occupied cave or the combined floor areas of separate houses.

Cemetery evidence can also provide a basis for calculating prehistoric population figures. If one can be certain that a *whole* cemetery has been found and that it was the *only* cemetery of the community, and if one can establish how long the cemetery was in use, one has the basis for estimating the size of the community. One takes an estimated mortality rate: 40 people per thousand dying annually is about average for a pre-industrial community. One can then calculate the population size: for example, a cemetery of 200 burials in use for 50 years would indicate a community of about 100.

We are dependent on the study of skeletal material for demographic information. In fortunate circumstances this can provide information on the sex of the individual (easily established in adult skeletons which are reasonably complete), the age at death (fairly precisely in the case of infants and juveniles, less precisely in adults), and often on injuries, disease and general health. Injuries and diseases of the skeleton itself are easily recognisable (e.g. arthritis, bone tumours, leprosy), as are some diseases which have secondary effects on the skeleton (e.g. thickening of the skull bones, which occurs in sickle-cell anaemia and thalassaemia). Some aspects of diet and the environment are directly reflected in the skeleton, e.g. rickets, which results from vitamin D deficiency, or the incidence of dental caries, which is related to the amount of carbohydrates, especially sugars, in the diet. High proportions of marine foods in the diet show up in high levels of strontium in the bone chemistry. Such studies give us a fascinating insight into the health and diet of past communities.

Social organization

Archaeologists are particularly interested in reconstructing the social organization of past communities. They have devoted much time and effort to developing hypotheses which enable them to build up a picture of social organization from surviving material remains. These hypotheses draw heavily both on ethnographic analogy and on anthropological theory, and include such diverse subjects as the nature of post-marriage residence, the organization of production and of exchange or trade, the nature of inheritance and the role of ritual. We do not have space here to do more than look at a few

Right: The well-known statues of Easter Island were erected between AD 700 and 1700 by a characteristic hierarchically organized chiefdom society.

Below: It has been argued that monumental structures like Stonehenge could only have been built by a hierarchically organized society, since the organization of both the planning and the construction would have required a powerful central authority.

examples of these approaches to the past. Since many archaeologists have paid particular attention to the recognition of hierarchical structure in society (i.e. the distinction between egalitarian societies on the one hand and societies characterized by salient ranking on the other), and since the emergence of elites and hierarchical structure is of particular relevance to the development of civilization, we shall concentrate on this subject here.

To begin with, we can make a useful distinction between the *institutions* of society and the *individuals* who make up that society. As far as institutions are concerned, we can recognize societies that are centrally organized, having 'higher order' sites where centralized administrative, economic or ritual activities take place. Concentrating on individuals, we can distinguish societies where some individuals have special statuses, not available to everyone. Some may contend, as Colin Renfrew has done, that the existence of central *places*, where centralized activities take place, argues the existence of central *people*, who lived in the places and organized the activities. This may often be the case, but it is possible for central places to exist that are not permanently occupied, being exploited only on special occasions for special activities, which could be organized by some *ad hoc* group (today it would be a committee!). Equally, the existence of special statuses for individuals may coincide with a centrally organized society where the people with high status are also the people with authority. It may also be the case, however, that high status is associated only with prestige and influence, not authority, and that it has to be earned (e.g. by prowess as a warrior, or by generosity in giving gifts). This kind of status can be found in essentially egalitarian societies: in the anthropological literature such societies are often described as 'big-man societies', whereas those societies in which status is associated with hereditary authority are called 'chiefdoms'.

Archaeologists have applied three main approaches to recognizing hierarchical structure in

the archaeological record. Two of these relate to institutional ranking, the third to individual status. The first is the study of the arrangement of sites in space. It has been argued on theoretical grounds – and this is supported by anthropological evidence – that egalitarian societies, which are segmentary in structure, display a settlement pattern characterized by sites of approximately equal size, each carrying out the same functions, fairly evenly spread out on the ground (making allowance for environmental factors that may affect this spacing). This type of settlement pattern is described as modular and cellular. The arrangement of sites in centrally organized societies shows a strikingly different pattern, however, demonstrating a hierarchical ordering. In such societies some sites are noticeably larger that the rest; they are usually characterized by special features, such as monumental buildings, defences, noticeable wealth, evidence of craft production, or indications of ritual activities. These 'higher order' sites are usually centrally placed and surrounded by 'lower order' sites. There may be only a single category of lower order sites, or there may be several categories; in some early civilizations we find a range of towns, villages, hamlets and individual farms surrounding the higher order sites – the cities themselves.

A second way in which we can recognize hierarchical structure in society is through the study of monuments. The labour and organization that must have been needed to construct them can tell us a good deal about the communities involved. Some prehistoric societies which have left no impressive remains in terms of tools or other artefacts, or in settlement traces, have nevertheless erected monumental structures which *are* very impressive. A well-known example is Stonehenge, and there are other large or elaborate monuments in Europe, such as the alignments of standing stones in Brittany or the stone temples of Malta. Examples occur in other parts of the world too, sometimes in the context of technologically undeveloped societies, such as that which erected the huge statues on Easter Island. It is clear from the man-power that must have been required to build these monuments, and from the elaboration of their planning, construction and in some cases their decoration, that a central authority must have been responsible for their organization. Of course, major monumental structures are also characteristic of civilizations, which we know from many sources of evidence were hierarchically organized societies. In the case of the prehistoric societies just discussed, however, the monuments are the only indication of hierarchical structure left to us.

Archaeologists usually base their analysis of ranking of *individuals* on the study of burials, for it is in burials that the individual can be most readily recognized in the archaeological record. It is assumed that people of high status are often provided with special conditions and equipment in death. The tombs of such people may be different in style from normal graves: perhaps monumental, or elaborate in some other way. They may be placed in special positions, perhaps centrally in the cemetery or away from the cemetery altogether. The dead body may be treated in a special way and may be accompanied by special grave goods, indicating unusual wealth. It may be possible to distinguish between achieved

status, of big-man type, and ascribed (inherited) status, of chiefdom type, from the grave goods. For instance, the inclusion of specific symbols of authority among grave goods would indicate ascribed status; examples include special headgear such as head-dresses or crowns, seats such as stools or thrones, and display weapons such as maces or axes. Another occurrence usually taken to indicate hereditary status is the inclusion of rich grave goods in children's burials, since it is unlikely that children would be thus distinguished in societies where status had to be achieved by social actions.

As students of the past, we would also dearly like to discover the ideas, beliefs and feelings of past societies. This type of information is particularly difficult to reconstruct from the material evidence; fortunately, in the case of the early civilizations, we frequently have documentary evidence to assist us. However, Colin Renfrew has argued that it should be possible to develop an 'archaeology of mind'; for instance, he has suggested that systems of weights and measures, which can sometimes be reconstructed from archaeological evidence, may give us an insight into past patterns of thought. This field of archaeology is still largely undeveloped, but it offers exciting prospects for the future.

Top: Chiefdoms and early state societies have a pyramidal social structure, with the central, highest figure – the chief or king – operating as the focus of a redistributive economy. This painted limestone relief from the Eleventh Dynasty Tomb of Emsaf at Thebes shows Emsaf and Hetep receiving offerings.

Bottom: Differences in the status of individuals may be reflected in the manner of their burial. Burials at the Peruvian site of Ancón show a great variety of burial types.

Documenting cultural change

We have looked at some of the techniques on which archaeologists can call in reconstructing the past. However, all we can get from them is a picture of a society at a particular point in time. How can we document change through time? In other words, how can we put the 'history' into 'prehistory'?

First, perhaps we should admit what we cannot do. We cannot observe change as it occurs, as a scientist can who studies phenomena in the present. Indeed, a scientist may be able to observe the same changes many times over simply by repeating an experiment. Students of the past, whether historians or prehistorians, cannot do this, they need to study changes that happened just once and are over, perhaps a long time ago. Although similar changes may have occurred at different times and in different places, there are so many variables involved, which we may be unable even to identify, let alone control, that we can never suggest that we are recording essentially the *same* change on two occasions. If we cannot observe these changes, how *do* we document them? The answer is, through a series of 'before and after' studies. This process can be likened to taking a set of still photographs and putting them together in sequence to produce moving film. If the stills are close enough together in time, we can produce an acceptable simulation of actual movement. If the gaps are too long we end up with a series of records of separate moments; it is clear that changes have occurred, but we do not have even the illusion of seeing them happen. In prehistory the gaps are often *very* long, and it is correspondingly difficult to document how the changes happened. The far greater problem of explaining *why* they occurred has been discussed in Chapter 2.

The process of comparing patterns at different moments in the past can be done at various levels, from individual site at one end of the range, through the local area, to the wider region. At the level of the site, the process involves piecing together the information from structures, finds and stratigraphy in order to work out, for example, which buildings were in use at the same time, the order in which they came into and went out of use, and their possibly changing functions. In the case of a cemetery, we may be able to follow its geographical spread as it

As time passed, buildings were sometimes re-used or adapted for different purposes. In the Middle Ages houses were constructed on top of the ruined theatre of Maxentius in Rome, originally built in the early fourth century AD.

expanded; if this is established, it provides the basis for tracing changes in tomb type, treatment of the body, grave goods, etc. On individual sites, if we are fortunate with the evidence, we may be able to document fairly short-term changes, perhaps not quite comparable with the separate frames that make up a moving film, but acceptably close nevertheless.

The problems are much more daunting when we come to document change on a regional scale. The processes are simple enough in theory, however. The archaeologist must find and plot all the sites in the region, recording as fully as possible all the features that can be established and assessing which were in use in which periods. Aspects of the natural environment like topography, soils, vegetation and mineral sources are also recorded, since man's changing relationship with his environment is an important subject of study. From all this it should be possible to extract a series of 'period maps', equivalent to the successive still photographs we described above.

Problems abound, however. In the first place, it is difficult to define the periods. In any region studied it is likely that only a few sites will have been excavated; the others will be known only from surface survey, and it is rarely possible to pin down a site to a short period of time on the basis of material collected from the surface alone. Therefore the period maps will represent rather long periods of time, usually several centuries at least. This immediately raises problems of disentangling chronological patterns from the data, since it is impossible to establish with any certainty whether different sites occupied within the same broad period were actually in use at the same time. Other problems include 'lost' sites (washed off hills, buried under valley silts, destroyed by modern buildings or simply not yet found by archaeologists) and changes in the natural environment, such as alterations in river courses, erosion and alluviation. All these factors make it very difficult to interpret the evidence.

In spite of all the problems, it is possible cautiously to build up a picture of changing patterns of human settlement. We can only give a few examples here. One may in some cases be able to document changing exploitation of the landscape. For instance, it may be that settlements of one period show a preference for locations on downland or hillsides, avoiding valley bottoms, while in a subsequent phase settlements are situated close to the valley floor. One possible explanation would be that new technology, perhaps a more efficient plough, had allowed cultivation of the heavier valley soils, which had been unworkable before.

We can also study changes in social organization, using the kind of approaches discussed in this chapter. It may be possible, for instance, to document the change from a pattern of sites of approximately equal size, spaced fairly evenly across the landscape, to one in which there are larger sites – possible central places – surrounded by smaller ones. This could be interpreted as a sign of the emergence of hierarchical ordering in society, perhaps marking the emergence of chiefdoms out of an egalitarian tribal background. In some cases the process may develop further in the direction of full urbanization, which is marked in the archaeological record by the appearance of very large population centres, often with defences and monumental buildings of such size that they are apparent even in surface survey. The appearance of these centres is sometimes, but not always, accompanied by rural depopulation, which is characterized archaeologically by the abandonment of many smaller sites around the new cities.

Another type of change which may prove very informative is change in the burial record: not just change within a single cemetery, as mentioned above, but from one cemetery to another. One may be able to document the change from collective to individual burial or vice versa, from simple earth graves to monumental tombs, from cemeteries showing little differentiation in grave goods to those where there are clearly distinguished rich and poor burials.

Thus, although archaeologists have as their raw material only the equivalent of photographic 'stills', the information they contain can, when interpreted with due care, enable them to reconstruct the complex development of prehistoric society.

Left and below: Burial rites frequently changed with the passing of time. In Etruria the Villanovans of the ninth and eighth centuries BC cremated their dead and buried the remains in pottery urns, such as this house-shaped example. Their Etruscan successors practised inhumation in elaborate rock-cut chamber tombs. The late Etruscan Tomb of the Reliefs at Cerveteri (Roman Caere) has sculpted decoration, imitating architectural features such as beams, and painted stucco reliefs of portable objects such as weapons and domestic equipment.

Reconstructing the past

This book is full of statements about the past. How do we put together such statements? How do we test their validity, and why do we prefer one statement to another?

Evidence and data

Surely we start from the evidence? Evidence is often called *data* (Latin: 'things that are given') – items that are fixed, as it were, before discussion begins. Provided that we are logical, surely certain conclusions will follow from the evidence, and the process by which we arrive at our statement will be neutral and objective? Many people would like to believe this.

Unfortunately, however, it is just not so, and it is important to understand why. Evidence does not come ready labelled for us to use in particular problems. What we may use *as evidence* is widely available – remains of earlier buildings, collections of artefacts, inscriptions, literature, etc. – but it is we ourselves, the enquirers, who search out such material, judge what is and what is not relevant, and decide to use our final selection as evidence. As enquirers, we make a large number of choices (from an infinite set of possibilities) as to how to delimit and classify our selected data. We also bring with us a number of preconceived attitudes, values and prejudices. We may not always be aware either of the choices we make, or of the prejudices we import. This may be regrettable, but it is normal and unavoidable.

The process therefore is never so simple as:

evidence
suggests
conclusion

It is rather:

person selects evidence
person classifies evidence
person reaches conclusion

In other words, material only becomes evidence by human selection and processing. Evidence cannot of itself suggest, predict or answer anything. Only people attempt this task.

Problem and hypothesis

But if reconstructing the past is not simply a matter of finding and putting together pieces of evidence, where *do* we start? Let us look at a specific question, remembering that questions, like evidence and answers, are selected and organized by people, and cannot be chosen from some pre-existing world. Let us look at the question: 'What led to the final collapse of Roman civilization?' This is the *problem*.

Since evidence does not lie around ready labelled, our next stage has to be to assemble some ideas about what relevant evidence might look like, and where we might find it. We might call this the *hypothesis* (Greek: 'provisional suggestion') stage. These ideas about how we might tackle the problem are always provisional. It is a misleading over-simplification to speak of a hypothesis as being confirmed or 'proved'. Any hypothesis is also purely an invention of the creative imagination. It is a caprice. It does not grow organically out of the problem, nor is there any way in which it may be deduced from it. In this important way, it is entirely arbitrary.

To proceed to our immediate problem, let us take the rough-and-ready hypothesis that economic decline often leads to the final collapse of a state.

Solution

Hypotheses anticipate a *solution*. In a loose sense, they are 'hunches' about possible answers. In a strict sense, they lead logically to a solution. They predict a solution. *If* the hypothesis holds, *then* certain solutions follow. For our example problem, our solution would now be:

'Economic decline led to the final collapse of Roman civilization.'

Testing and validity

All solutions, however, must be *tested* for *validity*. Two checks in particular are obviously necessary:

1. That the solution proceeds logically from the hypothesis.
2. That the solution conforms with any available evidence.

Neither of these tests is simple or transparent. For our example, we might try to establish what are the indicators, material and otherwise, of economic decline, and then check for their presence in the available evidence.

Theory

We could describe this whole process as *theoretical*. It is a *cycle*. Each stage of the cycle affects or is influenced by some other stage. We may start at any stage. *Testing* a *solution* that has previously been regarded as satisfactory, for instance, will probably lead to a *new* definition of the *problem*, which will permit different *hypotheses*, which will predict varying *solutions* . . . and so the cycle continues. In fact, we can then think of the cycle rather as a *spiral*. This would illustrate the *development* of a theoretical position.

Looked at in this way, *theory* need not cause the usual groans. Theory (Greek: *theoria*, 'a way of looking') is a set of viewpoints and arguments that are *explicitly* justified. We can forget the usual paraphernalia we associate with a 'theoretical' approach, such as charts, tables, graphs, formulae, and miles of computer print-out. In fact, there is nothing inherently theoretical about a graph or a chart, or a collection of formulae. These are all devices which we may choose to use or not. What *is* important about *theory* is that we try to uncover the processes by which we select problems and arrive at conclusions and, by understanding more explicitly what we are doing, gain better control over those processes.

In fact our processes of thought, including analytical thought, conceal many hidden features. These may be overall attitudes, or connections between sections of argument, or a vulnerability to influences we prefer not to acknowledge. These elements are present at an *implicit* level and, even if acknowledged, will tend to be ill-defined and poorly justified. The theoretical approach is a *discipline*. When properly applied, it forces us to try to identify, define and justify *every* connection by which we proceed from *problem* to *solution*. We may then realize with greater clarity why we framed the original problem in the way we did, and perhaps in due course arrive at a more efficient re-formulation.

Model

Closely linked with the theoretical approach in this sense, is the idea of *model*. A conceptual model attempts to build a complete overall picture of the particular 'world' in which the problems we are trying to solve, and the answers we are trying to assemble, are thought to lie. It sketches in and attempts to justify all the background assumptions – the basic 'geography' of the 'world' which is under consideration. It then relates them to the particular problems under review. Since it has much to do with basic ideas and assumptions, *model* has a strong influence not only upon the delineation of the original problem, but also upon the invention and choice of hypotheses.

If we return now to our example problem: 'What led to the final collapse of Roman civilization', we might start by endeavouring to construct a *model* of Roman civilization, perhaps with special reference to the third, fourth and fifth centuries AD. If our *hypothesis* is to name 'economic decline' as the cause of collapse, our model would need to study what kind of an economy we can assume for Rome in that period, and how it related to the political state. Our model would also need to include justification for *generalized* basic assumptions, such as the assumption that the political state and its economic vicissitudes are inextricably interwoven in this way. When investigated, this might turn out to be a simplistic assumption that we should prefer *not* to make.

Fragments of statuary, such as these from Medma in southern Italy, can be regarded as archaeological evidence. But without the intervention of the archaeologist, who interprets them in the light of hypothesis and model, they convey no information at all.

Can we explain the past?

Some of the questions we commonly ask about the past go further than the ambition of reconstructing events. They seek to *understand* the past. Of these questions, the two most troublesome types are:

1. 'What is . . . ?' questions, e.g. 'What is the nature of man?' or 'What is religion?' These questions seek a *definition* as an answer.
2. 'Why . . . ?' questions, e.g. 'Why did civilization develop first in the Near East?' or 'Why did writing not develop earlier?' These questions seek an *explanation*.

Questions such as these look for answers that we intuitively feel will be satisfying. They give the impression of dealing with matters of importance, with issues of universal significance over and beyond the triviality of mere events. They are troublesome, however, because there are good reasons why, in a real sense, they cannot finally be answered.

A question such as 'What is religion?' is looking for a *definition*. We should like to have this or that concept, institution, or even an unfamiliar object, interpreted for us, by translating it into words that we feel we understand better, or by comparing it with some concept or object with which we are now more familiar. One trouble is that every time we replace the original word or phrase by new words or phrases, the new phraseology is bound to raise yet further 'What is . . . ?' questions, which lead to yet further ones, and so on *ad infinitum*. For example, to the question 'What is religion?' we might initially reply, 'Religion is made up of belief in supernatural deities, and of the ritual acts associated with the worship of such deities.' But someone will immediately ask, 'But what are supernatural deities, what are ritual acts, and what is worship?' The interminable character of the succession of definitions is already becoming apparent.

A second difficulty is that every analogy and every comparison introduces some intrusive element – something that is true of the comparison, but not of the original. Consider the question, 'What was religion like in ancient Sumer?' We might innocently reply, 'Religion in ancient Sumer centred around the temple.' But with what latter-day temple can we legitimately compare the Sumerian temple?

Worse still are 'What is . . . ?' questions which embody a would-be powerful generalization. Most common in this context is the concept of 'nature' or a natural attribute: for example, 'What is the nature of man?'; 'Is man naturally aggressive?'; 'Is it natural for men to live together in cities?'. Here part of the trouble is that the word 'nature' is a *language trap*. Questions that use 'nature' and 'naturally', if they are not simply periphrases for definitional questions such as 'What kind of thing is man?', are inviting us to suppose that people, things or concepts necessarily have characteristics, some of which are natural, basic and irremovable, and others of which are only accidental, acquired or environmentally conditioned. This is something which we may choose to believe or not. It is a language trap because these preconceptions arrive as an inseparable component of words such as 'nature'. The conceptual furniture of language is commonly out of step with the more considered viewpoints of its users.

Another reason for the frequency of 'nature'-type questions is the impression they give that, if only they could be answered, we could then *predict* actions, character and development on the basis of that nature. Giving man an aggressive nature, for instance, may seem to explain all the wars of history, but does it really? Generally, 'nature'-type questions are not constructive. Even if we wish to select a philosophy that appears to support such an analysis of the world, none of us is in any position to stand outside existence (which would be necessary) and pontificate upon that is natural and what is not.

All in all, it is usually more practical to use *definitions* the 'other way round', as in 'Religion is the name that we give to ritual practice.' This involves us in assigning only a *provisional* label to phenomena that we are temporarily classifying together for the purpose of discussion; it does not involve us in metaphysical generalizations.

Causation

The case with 'Why . . . ?' questions is as bad, if not worse. These enquiries look for an *explanation*, and here again there are *language traps*. Language invites us to see the world in terms of *cause* and *effect*. One practical difficulty lies in what should be the simple business of identifying the causative *agent* and the *effected action* or *object*. This is particularly the case with the large global issues which tend to be the subject of historical 'Why . . . ?' questions. In 'Why did writing not occur earlier?', we have first to put back into the picture all the actual human people who might have been writing, but were not. This of course we cannot literally do. But even supposing we could, when we consider the very wide range of circumstances and roles in which individuals and groups found themselves over the very long period before the introduction of writing, what conceivable valid generalizations could we make? The question is not in itself nonsensical. Two things are unhelpful. One is the degree of global abstraction. We need to break the issue down into specific contexts where perhaps we might have expected to find writing but did not. The other has to do with the idea of *causation* itself, and particularly its extension from concrete local agents to large-scale global agent-concepts.

It is important to realize that cause-and-effect is a view of the world that man has himself developed. It might well be man's least celebrated but most powerful invention. Our minds are so conditioned by human language and institutional beliefs that we tend to assume that causation exists 'out there' in reality. What we actually observe may be just one event following another; the causal link between them is always a matter of interpretation. In our practical everyday lives, however, the viewpoint of causation is a useful mental strategy. Transferred to a 'world stage', with giant spectral agents and actions that can encompass hundreds or thousands of years, it has to be much more dubious.

Proof

One final but damaging criticism of the 'Why . . . ?' question lies with the difficulty of validation and *proof*. In general, in the study of history, much less can be done in the way of proven demonstration than is normally supposed. A positive statement, e.g.

'Caesar was killed by Brutus', can never be finally demonstrated, simply because in an eternity of time we could never be categorically certain that we had assembled every piece of evidence, that no more would ever come to light, and that our interpretation and weighing of that evidence was without possible error or criticism. By contrast, a negative statement, such as 'The Pharaoh passed no laws', only needs one Pharaonic law to *disprove* it.

The case with would-be causative *explanations* is worse. Neither positive nor negative causative links are capable of being proved. If we assert a cause or deny a cause between what we believe to be the events of history, that is an interpretation, and can never be anything more.

Explanation in archaeology, and in historical studies in general, is fraught with difficulty, Nevertheless, a careful theoretical approach can help us choose between hypotheses. The mysterious 'Nazca lines' — huge pictures drawn in the desert sands of southern Peru – provide a case in point. The recognition that prehistoric man could have drawn a small plan and enlarged it to scale on the ground does not provide a total explanation, but it does allow us to reject fanciful interpretations involving visitors from outer space.

These are just some of the many hazards that are inevitably involved in trying to reconstruct and explain the past. The conclusion to be drawn, however, does need to be negative. Faced with the prospect of crossing a minefield, one is wise to study any map which is offered.

Bibliography

CHAPTER 1

General

Cotterell, A. (ed). *The Encyclopaedia of Ancient Civilizations*. Windward, Leicester, 1980.

Sherratt, A. (ed). *The Cambridge Encyclopaedia of Archaeology*. Cambridge University Press, Cambridge, 1980.

Whitehouse, R.D. (ed) *The Macmillan Dictionary of Archaeology*. Macmillan, London, 1983.

Mesopotamia

Hallo, W.W. & W.K. Simpson. *The Ancient Near East*. Harcourt Brace Jovanovich, London and New York, 1971.

Kramer, S.N. *The Sumerians*. University of Chicago Press, Chicago, 1963.

Lloyd, S. *The Archaeology of Mesopotamia*. Thames and Hudson, London, 1978.

Oates, J. *Babylon*. Thames and Hudson, London, 1979.

Oppenheim, A.L. *Ancient Mesopotamia*. University of Chicago Press, Chicago, 2nd ed. 1977.

Postgate, J.N. *The First Empires*. Elsevier-Phaidon, Oxford, 1977.

Redman, C. *The Rise of Civilization*. Freeman, San Francisco, 1978.

Whitehouse, R. *The First Cities*. Phaidon, Oxford, 1977.

Egypt

Aldred, C. *The Egyptians*. Thames and Hudson, London, 1961.

Aldred, C. *Egypt to the End of the Old Kingdom*. Thames and Hudson, London, 1965.

Baines, J. & J. Malek *Atlas of Ancient Egypt*, Phaidon, Oxford, 1980.

Edwards, I.E.S. *The Pyramids of Egypt*, Penguin, Harmondsworth, revised ed. 1985.

Gardiner, A.H., *Egypt of the Pharaohs*. Oxford University Press, Oxford, 1961.

James, T.G.H. *The Archaeology of Ancient Egypt*. Bodley Head, London, 1972.

James, T.G.H. *An Introduction to Ancient Egypt*. British Museum Publications, London, 1979.

Jordan, P. *Egypt. The Black Land*. Phaidon, Oxford, 1976.

The Indus

Allchin, B. and R. *The Rise of Civilization in India and Pakistan*. Cambridge University Press, Cambridge 1982.

Fairservis, W.A. Jnr. *The Roots of Ancient India*. Chicago University Press, Chicago, 1971.

Piggott, S. *Prehistoric India*. Penguin, Harmondsworth, 1950.

Possehl, G.L. *Ancient Cities of the Indus*. Carolina Academic Press, Durham, 1979.

Possehl, G.L. *Harappan Civilization: a Contemporary Perspective*. Aris and Phillips, Warminster, 1982.

Wheeler, Sir M. *Early India and Pakistan to Ashoka*. Thames and Hudson, London, 1959.

Wheel, Sir M. *The Indus Civilization*. Cambridge University Press, Cambridge, 1968.

China

Chang, K.C. *The Archaeology of Ancient China*. Yale University Press, Yale, 1977.

Hay, J. *Ancient China*. The Bodley Head, London, 1973.

Metropolitan Museum of Art *Treasures from the Bronze Age of China*. New York, 1980.

Needham, J. *Science and Civilization in China*, Vols I-V. Cambridge University Press, Cambridge, 1956–65.

Rawson, J. *Ancient China. Art and Archaeology*. British Museum Publications, London, 1980.

Watson, W. *China before the Han Dynasty*. Thames and Hudson, London, 1961.

Wheatley, P. *The Pivot of the Four Quarters*. Edinburgh University Press, Edinburgh, 1971.

Minoans and Mycenaeans

Chadwick, J. *Documents in Mycenaean Greek*. Cambridge University Press, Cambridge, 2nd ed. 1973.

Chadwick, J. *The Mycenaean World*. Cambridge University Press, Cambridge, 1976.

Dickinson, O.T.P.K. *The Origins of Mycenaean Civilization*. Gothenburg, 1977.

Hood, S. *The Minoans*. Thames and Hudson, London, 1971.

Renfrew, C. *The Emergence of Civilization. The Cyclades and the Aegean in the Third Millennium BC*. Methuen, London, 1972.

Taylour, Lord W. *The Mycenaeans*. Thames and Hudson, London, revised ed. 1983.

Warren, P. *The Aegean Civilizations*. Elsevier-Phaidon, Oxford, 1975.

Greeks

Boardman, J. *The Greeks Overseas*. Penguin, Harmondsworth, 2nd ed. 1973.

Desborough, V.R.d'A. *The Greek Dark Ages*. London, 1972.

Levy, P. *Atlas of the Greek World*. Phaidon, Oxford, 1980.

Ling, R. *The Greek World*. Elsevier-Phaidon, Oxford, 1976.

Snodgrass, A.M. *The Dark Age of Greece: an Archaeological Survey of the Eleventh to the Eighth Centuries BC*. Edinburgh University Press, Edinburgh, 1971.

Greeks and Romans

Boardman, J., J. Griffin & O. Murray (eds). *The Oxford History of the Classical World*. Oxford University Press, Oxford, 1986.

Finley, M.I. *Atlas of Classical Archaeology*. London, 1976.

Stillwell, R., W.L. MacDonald & M.A. McAllister *The Princeton Encyclopaedia of Classical Sites*. Princeton, 1976.

Etruscans and Romans

Banti, L. *The Etruscan Cities and their Culture*. London, 1974.

Cornell, T. *Atlas of the Roman World*. Phaidon, Oxford,

Crawford, M.H. *The Roman Republic*. Cambridge University Press, Cambridge, 1978.

Pallottino, M. *The Etruscans*. Penguin, Harmondsworth, 1955.

Scullard, H.H. *The Etruscan Cities and Rome*. London, 1967.

Vickers, M. *The Roman World*. Phaidon, Oxford, 1977.

Mesoamerica

Bernal, I. *The Olmec World*. University of California Press, Berkeley, Los Angeles and London, 1969.

Bernal, I. *A History of Mexican Archaeology*. Thames and Hudson, London, 1980.

Blanton, R.E., S.A. Kowalewski, C. Feinman & J. Appel *Ancient Mesoamerica. A Comparison of Change in Three Regions*. Cambridge University Press, Cambridge, 1981.

Coe, M.D. *Mexico*. Thames and Hudson, London, 1962.

Coe, M.D. *The Maya*. Thames and Hudson, London, 1966.

Sabloff, J.A. & G.R. Willey *A History of American Archaeology*. Thames and Hudson, London, 2nd. ed 1980.

Weaver, M.P. *The Aztecs, Maya and their Predecessors*. Thames and Hudson, London, 1972.

Willey, G.R. *An Introduction to American Archaeology*. Prentice Hall, Englewood Cliffs, 2 vols. 1966 and 1971.

Peru

Bankes, G. *Peru before Pizarro*. Phaidon, Oxford, 1974.

Bushnell, G.H. *Peru*. Thames and Hudson, London, 1963.

Lanning, E.P. *Peru before the Incas*, Prentice Hall, Englewood Cliffs, 1967.

Lumbreras, L.G. *The Peoples and Cultures of Ancient Peru*, trs B.J. Meggers, Washington, 1974.

Willey, G.R. *An Introduction to American Archaeology. Vol.2: South America*. Prentice Hall, Englewood Cliffs, 1971.

CHAPTER 2

Adams, R. McC. *The Evolution of Urban Society: Early Mesopotamia and Prehispanic Mexico*. Aldine, Chicago, 1960.

Braidwood, R.J. & G.R. Willey (eds) *Courses towards Urban Life*. Aldine, Chicago, 1962.

Carneiro, R.L. 'A Theory of the Origin of the State', *Science*, 169 (3947), 1970, 733–8.

Childe, V.G. *What Happened in History*. Penguin, Harmondsworth, 1942.

Childe, V.G. 'The Urban Revolution', *Town Planning Review*, 21 (1), 1950, 3–17.

Fried, M. *The Evolution of Political Society*. Random House, New York, 1967.

Jones, G.D. and R.R. Kantz. *The Transition to Statehood in the New World*. Cambridge University Press, Cambridge, 1981.

Lee, R.B. & I. De Vore (eds) *Man the Hunter*. Aldine, Chicago, 1968.

Marx, K. *Pre-capitalist Economic Formations*. Trs. Jack Cohen and introd. by E.J. Hobshawm, International Publishers, New York, 1965 (original ms 1857–8).

Moorey, P.R.S. (ed) *The Origin of Civilization*.

Clarendon, Oxford, 1979.

Oates, D. and J. *The Rise of Civilization*. Elsevier-Phaidon, Oxford, 1976.

Redman, C.L. *The Rise of Civilization*. Freeman, San Francisco, 1978.

Renfrew, C. *The Emergence of Civilization. The Cyclades and the Aegean in the Third Millennium BC*. Methuen, London, 1972.

Sahlins, M.D. *Tribesmen*. Prentice Hall, Englewood Cliffs, 1968.

Service, E.R. *The Hunters*. Prentice Hall, Englewood Cliffs, 1966.

Service, E.R. *Primitive Social Organization: An Evolutionary Perspective*. Ramdom House, New York, 2nd ed. 1971.

Service, E.R. *Origins of the State and Civilization*. Norton, New York and London, 1975.

Wittfogel, K.A. *Oriental Despotism: a Comparative Study of Total Power*. Yale University Press, New Haven, 1957.

CHAPTER 3

Adams, R. McC. 'The Origin of Cities', *Scientific American*, 203 (3), 1960.

Childe, V.G. 'The Urban Revolution', *Town Planning Review*, 21 (1), 1950, 3–17.

Davis, K. (ed) *Cities. Their Origin, Growth and Human Impact*. Readings from Scientific American. Freeman, San Francisco, 1973.

Fairman, H.W. 'Town Planning in Pharaonic Egypt', *Town Planning Review*, 20, 1949.

Kraeling, C.H. & R. McC. Adams (eds) *City Invincible. A Symposium on Urbanization and Cultural Development in the Ancient Near East*. University of Chicago Press, Chicago, 1960.

Lampl, P. *Cities and Planning in the Ancient Near East*. Braziller, New York, 1968.

Millon, R. 'Teotihuacan', *Scientific American*, 1967.

Moseley, M.E. 'Chan Chan: Andean Alternative of the Preindustrial City', *Science*, 187 (4173), 1975, 219–25.

Mumford, L. *The City in History*. Harcourt, Brace and World, New York, 1961.

Ward-Perkins, J.B. *Cities of Ancient Greece and Italy. Planning in Classical Antiquity*. Braziller, New York, 1974.

Wheatley, P. *The Pivot of the Four Quarters*. Edinburgh University Press, Edinburgh, 1971.

CHAPTER 4

Brown, J.A. (ed) *Approaches to the Social Dimensions of Mortuary Practices. Memoirs of the Society for American Antiquity*, no. 24, 1971.

Chapman, R., I. Kinnes & K. Randsborg (eds) *The Archaeology of Death*, Cambridge University Press, Cambridge, 1981.

Clark, G. *Symbols of Excellence*. Cambridge University Press, Cambridge, 1986

Fried, M.H. *The Evolution of Political Society*. Random House, New York, 1967.

Moore, C.B. (ed) *Reconstructing Complex Societies: and Archaeological Colloquium. Supplement to Bulletin of American School of Oriental Research*, no.20, Massachusetts, 1974.

Service, E.R. *Primitive Social Organization: an Evolutionary Perspective*. Random House, New York, 2nd ed. 1971.

Service, E.R. *Origins of the State and Civilization.* Norton, New York and London, 1975.

Tainter, J.A. 'Social Inference and Mortuary Practices: an Experiment in Numerical Classification', *World Archaeology*, 7, 1975, 1–15.

Weber, M. *The Theory of Social and Economic Organization.* Trs A.M. Henderson and Talcott Parsons, Free Press, Glencoe, 2nd ed. 1947.

CHAPTER 5

Dalton, G. 'Economic Theory and Primitive Society', *American Anthropologist*, 63, 1961, 1–25.

Earle, T.K. & J.E. Ericson (eds) *Exchange Systems in Prehistory.* Academic Press, London and New York, 1977.

Earle, T.K. & J.E. Ericson (eds) *Contexts for Prehistoric Exchange.* Academic Press, London and New York, 1982.

Finley, M.I. *The Ancient Economy.* Hogarth, London, 2nd ed. 1985.

Garnsey, P. & C.R. Whittaker (eds) *Trade in the Ancient Economy*, Chatto and Windus, London, 1984.

Polanyi, K., C. Arensberg & H. Pearson (eds) *Trade and Market in the Early Empires.* The Free Press, Glencoe, 1957.

Renfrew, C. & S.J. Shennan (eds) *Ranking, Resource and Exchange.* Cambridge University Press, Cambridge, 1982.

Sabloff, J.A. & C.C. Lamberg-Karlovsky (eds) *Ancient Civilization and Trade.* University of New Mexico Press, Albuquerque.

Sahlins, M. *Stone Age Economics.* Tavistock, London, 1974.

CHAPTER 6

Burkert, W. *Greek Religion in the Archaic and Classical Periods.* Trs. J. Raffan, Blackwell, Oxford, 1985.

Cornford, F.M. *From Religion to Philosophy. A Study in the Origins of Western Speculation.* Harvester, Sussex, reprint 1980 (orig. 1912).

Durkheim, E. *The Elementary Forms of the Religious Life.* Trs. J.W. Swain, Allen and Unwin, London, 1915.

Frankfort, H. *Ancient Egyptian Religion.* New York, 1948.

Grimal, P. *The Dictionary of Classical Mythology.* Blackwell, Oxford, 1985.

Jacobsen, T. *The Treasures of Darkness. A History of Mesopotamian Religion.* Yale University Press, New Haven and London, 1976.

Lévi-Strauss, C. *Totemism.* Trs. R. Needham, Merlin, London, 1962.

Lyttelton, M. & W. Forman *The Romans, their Gods and their Beliefs.* Orbis, London, 1984.

Parker, R. *Miasma: Pollution and Purification in Early Greek Religion.* Clarendon, Oxford, 1983.

Skorupski, J. *Symbol and Theory.* Cambridge University Press, Cambridge, 1976.

Sperber, D. *Rethinking Symbolism.* Cambridge University Press, Cambridge, 1975.

Turner, V. *The Forest of Symbols.* Cornell University Press, New York, 1967.

Turner, V. *The Ritual Process.* Routledge and Kegan Paul, London, 1969.

CHAPTER 7

Chadwick, J. *The Decipherment of Linear B.* Cambridge University Press, Cambridge, 2nd ed 1967.

Diringer, D. *The Alphabet.* Hutchinson, London, 2 vols 1968.

Diringer, D. *Writing.* Thames and Huson, London, 1969.

Frankfort, H. et.al. *The Intellectual Adventure of Ancient Man.* University of Chicago Press, Chicago, 1946.

Gelb, T.J. *A Study of Writing.* University of Chicago Press, Chicago, revised ed. 1963.

Goody, J. *Domestication of the Savage Mind.* Cambridge University Press, Cambridge, 1977.

Harris, R. *The Origins of Writing.* Duckworth, London, 1986.

World Archaeology, 17 (3), February 1986; issue devoted to the subject of *Early Writing Systems.*

CHAPTER 8

Boëthius, A. *Etruscan and Early Roman Architecture (Pelican History of Art).* Penguin, Harmondsworth, 2nd ed 1978.

Coulton, J.J. *Greek Architects at Work. Problems of Structure and Design.* Elek, London, 1977.

Hodges, H. *Technology in the Ancient World.* Penguin, Harmondsworth, 1971.

Johnstone, P. *The Sea-craft of Prehistory.* Routledge and Kegan Paul, London, 1980.

Lawrence, A.W. *Greek Architecture (Pelican History of Art).* Penguin, Harmondsworth, 3rd ed 1973.

MacDonald, W.L. *The Architecture of the Roman Empire. An Introductory Study.* Yale University Press, New Haven and London, 1982.

Needham, J. *Science and Civilization in China*, Vols. 1–V, Cambridge University Press, Cambridge, 1956–65.

Singer, C., E. Holmyard & A.R. Hall (eds) *A History of Technology*, Vols I–II, Oxford University Press, Oxford, 1956–7.

Ward-Perkins, J.B. *Roman Imperial Architecture (Pelican History of Art).* Penguin, Harmondsworth, 2nd ed 1981.

CHAPTER 9

Baldson, J.P.V.D. *Roman Women: their History and Habits.* Bodley Head, London, 1962.

Berger, A. *Encyclopedic Dictionary of Roman Law.* American Philosophical Society, Philadelphia, 1952.

Dalley, S. *Mari and Karana. Two Old Babylonian Cities.* Longman, London and New York, 1984.

Finley, M.I. *Slavery in Classical Antiquity.* Heffner, Cambridge, 1969.

Harrison, A.R.W. *The Law of Athens: the Family and Property.* Clarendon, Oxford, 1968.

Kaser, M. *Roman Private Law.* Butterworth, London, 2nd ed 1968.

Kluckhohn, C. 'The moral order in the expanding society'. In C.H. Kraeling & R.McC. Adams (eds) *City Invincible. A Symposium on Urbanization and Cultural Development in the Ancient Near East.* University of Chicago Press, Chicago, 1960.

Oppenheim, A.L. *Ancient Mesopotamia.* University of Chicago Press, Chicago, 2nd ed 1977.

Pomeroy, S.B. *Goddesses, Whores, Wives and Slaves. Women in Classical Antiquity*. Robert Hale, London, 1975.

Sahlins, M. *Stone Age Economics*. Tavistock, London, 1974.

CHAPTER 10

Carpenter, R. *Discontinuity in Greek Civilization*. Cambridge University Press, Cambridge, 1966.

Flannery, K.V. 'The cultural evolution of civilizations', *Annual Review of Ecology and Systematics*, 3, 1972, 399–426.

Friedman, J. & M. Rowlands (eds) *The Evolution of Social Systems*. Duckworth, London, 1978.

Hammond, N. (ed) *Social Process in Maya Prehistory*. London and New York, 1977.

Raikes, R.L. 'The end of the ancient cities of the Indus', *American Anthropologist*, 66, 1964, 284–99.

Renfrew, C. *The Emergence of Civilization. The Cyclades and the Aegean in the Third Millenniumm BC*. Methuen, London, 1972.

Renfrew, C. *Before Civilization*. Penguin, Harmondsworth, 1973.

Renfrew, C. & K.L. Cooke (eds) *Transformations: Mathematical Approaches to Culture Change*. Academic Press, London and New York, 1979.

Sabloff, J.A. & C.C. Lamberg-Karlovsky (eds) *The Rise and Fall of Civilization*. San Francisco, 1974.

CHAPTER 11

Aitken, M.J. *Physics and Archaeology*. Oxford University Press, Oxford, 2nd ed 1974.

Barker, P. *Techniques of Archaeological Excavation*. Batsford, London, 1977.

Bender, B. *Farming in Prehistory*. John Baker, London, 1975.

Binford, L. *An Archaeological Perspective*. New York and London, 1972.

Butzer, K. *Environment and Archaeology*. , 1972.

Chaplin, R.E. *The Study of Animal Bones from Archaeological Sites*. Seminar Press, London, 1971. Doran, J.E. & F.R. Hodson *Mathematics and Computers in Archaeology*. Edinburgh University Press, Edinburgh, 1975.

Fleming, S. *Dating in Archaeology*. Dent, London, 1976.

Greene, K. *Archaeology. An Introduction*. Batsford, London, 1983.

Harris, E.C. *Principles of Archaeological Stratigraphy*. Academic Press, London and New York, 1978.

Hodder, I. & C. Orton *Spatial Analysis in Archaeology*. Cambridge University Press, Cambridge, 1976.

Limbrey, S. *Soil Science and Archaeology*. Academic Press, London and New York, 1975.

Popper, K.R. *The Logic of Scientific Discovery*. Hutchinson, London, 9th impression 1977.

Popper, K.R. *Objective Knowledge. An Evolutionary Approach*. Clarendon, Oxford, revised ed 1979.

Renfre, J.M. *Paleoethnobotany*. Methuen, London, 1973.

Acknowledgements

Illustrator: Jeff Edwards

Front Cover
T   Susan Griggs Agency
BL   Robert Harding Picture Library
BC   Michael Holford
BR   Zefa Picture Library

Back Cover
Michael Holford

Page
Title By courtesy of the Trustees of the British Museum
Copyright Hirmer Verlag
8   The MacQuitty International Photographic Collection
10   Michael Holford
11   Elsevier Books, Amsterdam
12   Hirmer Verlag
13   Photographed by Victor J. Boswell, Jr., National Geographic Society: Courtesy of the Oriental Institute of the University of Chicago.
14   Robert Harding Picture Library Ltd.
15T Zefa Picture Library
15B Madame Jean Vertut
17T Zefa Picture Library
17BL Robert Harding Picture Library
17BR The MacQuitty International Photographic Collection
18   Sotheby's
19T Colin Thomas
19C Robert Harding Picture Library
19B The Institute of History and Philology, Academia Sinica, Taipei, Taiwan, Republic of China
20L Ekdotike Athenon, Athens
20R Dimitrios Harrissiadis, Athens
21T Zefa Picture Library
21B By courtesy of the Trustees of the British Museum
23L Museo Archeologico, Reggio Calabria (photo: Scala)
23R Zefa Picture Library
24   Sonia Halliday Photographs
25   Michael Holford
26   Zefa Picture Library
27   Zefa Picture Library
28T Zefa Picture Library
28B Werner Forman Archive
29T Zefa Picture Library
29B Susan Griggs Agency
30T Ferdinand Anton, Munich
30B Jean Bottin, Paris
31   Michael Holford
32   Zefa Picture Library
33T Jean Bottin, Paris
33B Ferdinand Anton, Munich
34   Ferdinand Anton, Munich
35   Zefa Picture Library
36   John Hillelson Agency Ltd.

         The Louvre (photo: Giraudon)
38   Ekdotike Athenon, Athens
39   Ferdinand Anton, Munich
42   Michael Holford
43   Werner Forman Archive
44T Document Henri Lhote's expedition
44B Bryan & Cherry Alexander Photography
45   Sonia Halliday Photographs
46B Ekdotike Athenon, Athens
47T Robert Harding Picture Library Ltd.
47B Marion & Tony Morrison, South American Pictures
48   From: W. Reiss & A. Stübel: *The Necropolis of Ancon in Peru*: 1880–1887
49   From: *Prehistoric Investigations in Iraqui Kurdistan*, by Robert J. Braidwood and Bruce Howe, with contributions by Hans Helbaek, Frederick R. Matson, Charles A. Reed, and Herbert E. Wright, Jr., The Oriental Institute of the University of Chicago, *Studies in Ancient Oriental Civilisation, No. 31*, The University of Chicago Press, (Chicago, Illinois, c 1960).
50T The University Museum of Archaeology/Anthropology, Pennsylvania.
50B Michael Holford
51   Museo Egizio, Turin/Scala, Florence
52   Kent V. Flannery, Museum of Anthropology, University of Michigan.
53   The University Museum of Archaeology/Anthropology, Pennsylvania.
54   Zefa Picture Library
56   Ekdotike Athenon, Athens
58   Michael Holford
59   Susan Griggs Agency
60   The MacQuitty International Photographic Collection
61   Scala, Florence
62T Michael Holford
62B Susan Griggs Agency
63T Zefa Picture Library
63B Michael Holford
64T From: H. R. Hall & C. L. Woolley: *Ur Excavations*, volume I, plate painting done by F. G. Newton.
64BL Hirmer Verlag
64BR Baghdad Museum/Scala, Florence
65T Hirmer Verlag
65B Zefa Picture Library
66   Peter Clayton
67TL Christie's Colour Library
67TR From: *The Mural Painting of El'Armaneh*: by F. G. Newton, plate V.
67BR Peter Clayton

68–9 Zefa Picture Library
68T Josephine Powell, Rome
68B Robert Harding Picture Library
69B The MacQuitty International Photographic Collection
         Asian Art Museum of San Francisco, The Avery Brundage Collection.
71   Robert Harding Picture Library
72L Zefa Picture Library
72TR Sonia Halliday Photographs
72BR Ancient Art & Architecture Collection
73TL Metropolitan Museum of Art, New York
73TR Sonia Halliday Photographs
73BR Ekdotike Athenon, Athens
74   Michael Holford
75T Zefa Picture Library
75B Michael Holford
76–7 Werner Forman Archive
78T Zefa Picture Library
78B Ferdinand Anton, Munich
79T Werner Forman Archive
79B Ferdinand Anton, Munich
80T Michael Holford
80B Amplicaiones y Reproducciones Mas, Barcelona
81   Werner Forman Archive
82   Michael Holford
83T Susan Griggs Agency
83B Ferdinand Anton, Munich
84   Michael Holford
85T Peter Chèze-Brown
85B Hirmer Verlag
86   Ferdinand Anton, Munich
87   Ekdotike Athenon, Athens
88–9 Dr. J. C. Woodburn
90   Ferdinand Anton, Munich
91T Birmingham Museum & Art Gallery
91B Michael Holford
92T Michael Holford
92B Uni-dia Verlag, Munich
93   Ferdinand Anton, Munich
94T Michael Holford
94B Susan Griggs Agency
95T Zefa Picture Library
95B Susan Griggs Agency
96T Bildarchiv Foto Marburg
96B Giraudon
97   Ferdinand Anton, Munich
98T Zefa Picture Library
98B Ferdinand Anton, Munich
99   Zefa Picture Library
100T Robert Harding Picture Library
100B By courtesy of the Trustees of the British Museum
101 Ferdinand Anton, Munich
102 Zefa Picture Library
103 Roger Wood
104–5 Michael Holford
104B Ruth Whitehouse
105 Robert Harding Picture Library
106T Christie's Colour Library
106B Ferdinand Anton, Munich

Index

All numbers in *italics* refer to illustrations.